MARKETING THE MUSEUM

The history of the museum is one of shifting purposes and changing ideals. Taking a necessarily close look at the specific needs of this sector, this volume asks if it is possible to define the 'product' which the modern museum can offer. Are the theories of marketing developed for manufactured goods in any way relevant to the experience of visiting a museum? Or, as anti-marketing lobbies believe, should marketing play only the smallest of roles, if any at all?

In this volume, the marketing of a museum is not seen in terms of 'product', but rather as the process by which one can build a relationship between the museum and the public. This study is the ideal guide to the ways in which museums can overcome the numerous hurdles on the route to truly achieving a marketing orientation. It gives practical guidelines to the specific ways in which marketing can be tailored to the needs of museums and become a useful as well as an acceptable part of today's museums in fulfilling their ultimate purpose in serving the community.

In covering one of the most highly disputed issues in the field, this book is essential reading for museum professionals, students and anyone who has dealings in the many branches of the heritage industry around the world.

Fiona McLean is a Lecturer in Marketing at the University of Stirling. She has been widely published in journals on her special research interest: the application of marketing to the museum and heritage industry.

The Heritage: Care–Preservation–Management programme has been designed to serve the needs of the museum and heritage community worldwide. It publishes books and information services for professional museum and heritage workers, and for all the organisations that service the museum community.

Editor-in-chief: Andrew Wheatcroft

Marketing the Museum

Fiona McLean

London and New York

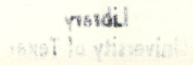

First published 1997
by Routledge
11 New Fetter Lane, London EC4P 4EE

Simultaneously published in the USA and Canada
by Routledge
29 West 35th Street, New York, NY 10001

© 1997 Fiona McLean

Typeset in Sabon by Florencetype Ltd, Stoodleigh, Devon

Printed and bound in Great Britain by
TJ Press (Padstow) Ltd, Padstow, Cornwall

British Library Cataloguing in Publication Data
A catalogue record for this book is available from the
British Library

Library of Congress Cataloguing in Publication Data
McLean, Fiona, 1961–
    Marketing the Museum / Fiona McLean.
        p. cm.
    Includes index.
    ISBN 0–415–10392–4 (alk. paper). –
    ISBN 0–415–15293–3 (pbk.: alk. paper)
    1. Museums–Marketing. 2. Museums–Management. I. title
AM121.M4 1996
069'.5–dc20   96–22435
                                                                CIP

                ISBN 0-415-10392-4
                    0-415-15293-3 (pbk)

To Alan
and in memory of
my Mum and Dad

Contents

List of figures

Acknowledgements

With thanks to everyone in Newcastle-upon-Tyne, where I worked on my PhD, investigating policy and marketing strategies in museums. I would especially like to thank my supervisors Professor Kenneth McConkey of the University of Northumbria and Simon Roodhouse. Thanks also to all the museum curators who helped me and from whom I learned so much, in particular Hilary Wade, Sue Mills, Tony Tynan, and Peter Davis. I am also indebted to the Museums and Galleries Commission and the North of England Museums Service who funded and supported the study.

My thinking on museum marketing has developed quite considerably since those days, and I would like to thank the Marketing Department at the University of Stirling for giving me the chance to pursue my interest in museums. Special thanks must go to my friends at Stirling who have given me moral support and encouragement: Addy Broadbridge, Ian Spencer, Jimmy Young, Jacquie L'Etang, and Sue Horne.

Thanks are also due to Peter Mudie, Timothy Ambrose, and William Tayleur, who reviewed the book, and to Andrew Wheatcroft, my editor.

Last, but definitely not least, thanks to my family and friends, particularly Alan, who not only created the figures for the book, but was there throughout. This book is dedicated to him, and in memory of my Mum and Dad, who gave me the best start in life.

Introduction

The museum is a complex phenomenon. Its history is one of shifting purposes, juxtaposed with changing ideals. It comes in various styles and types, and is governed by innumerable organisations and people. Its intentions are not precise, and its meaning to the public is undefined. A museum is full of contradictions; no two museums are the same. It has been compartmentalised into subject types and organisational structures, but no labels can make an entity out of disparate parts. There is no common understanding of a museum. Definitions are mooted, but debates on the principles of museums continue unabated. The roles assumed by museums are as uncertain and unqualified as the definition of a museum. All that is agreed to constitute a museum is a collection, although even this assumption has recently been called into question.[1] Beyond the collection lies uncertainty. A museum is any number of permutations of collection. It can be an art gallery, a science museum, or in some cases, a railway.[2] What do all these collections have in common that endows them with the title 'museum'? Are these agglomerations of artefacts and relics the detritus of a bygone age? What constitutes a museum?

The organisational and staffing structure is equally diverse. A small, volunteer-run museum is as entitled to call itself a 'museum' as a large, civil service-staffed national museum. A museum that is open by appointment is comparable to a museum that actively encourages access. A museum that maintains an education service has the same generic title as that which operates train rides. The public attracted may vary from specialists and academics to tourists and children. How are these anomalies reconciled in the generic term 'museum'? Can the category be defined if it is composed of disparate and often conflicting meanings and functions?

Marketing is equally uncertain of its credentials. There is no one definition of marketing: its concepts being slotted in to comply with the requirements of differing situations. One concept that does reconcile the various definitions is the notion of the customer. Without people, there would be no rationale for marketing. Marketing is a process that brings together an organisation and people, whether it be for profit, to satisfy their needs or wants, to increase visitor figures, etc. Working on that basis then, marketing at its lowest common denominator is about building up a relationship between the museum and the

1

public. There is no specific reason why the museum should in any way relate to the public. In fact, some museums choose not to do so, by closing their doors to them, such as museums that are open only by appointment, or at certain times of the year. Strictly, restricted access is more common in some major American collections than in the UK. The recent legal wrangles over the Barnes Foundation in Philadelphia is a case in point.[3] The question of why museums want or ought to communicate with a public in some way is a legitimate one. Part, at least, of the museum's *raison d'être* would be 'for the public benefit' (Museums Association 1984). The central questions here are to do with identifying the 'public', establishing the 'benefit' contained, and in governmental terms, the cost of the 'benefit'. Marketing has been in the centre of this dispute. Its business-orientated approach to 'turnover' in visitor figures and 'profit', whilst alienating many museum professionals, has generated an instructive debate about the role, purpose, and self-presentation of museums.

In order to establish a consciousness of the public in the museum, the marketing agent requires a more than superficial understanding of the museum. The fundamental problem to be clarified before any attempt can be made to comprehend marketing in museums is the complicated interests involved in the notion of 'museum'. It is apparent that an investigation of marketing reveals the conflicts within the museum community. Deeply polarised debates rage on in the museums profession on these fundamental concerns. Museology cannot be a straightforward concept. The operations of marketing would be simpler if this were the case. Issues relevant to the museum debate need to be extrapolated. Ambient changes in the wider patterns of economic, political, social, and cultural life will inevitably continue to determine the dispute.

Rather than being set apart from that which is being marketed, a public consciousness is intrinsic to the process. In effect, communication with the public can only be enhanced if it is integral to the whole museum framework. This is paralleled in recent discussions on museums in the postmodern condition, of a 'new museology', where society is considered to be intrinsic to the interpretation of museums. This contextual understanding is the benchmark in the generic museum context. It is equally applicable in the individual museum situation.

A museum is neither a large conglomerate, nor a McDonald's hamburger restaurant, nor a hospital or educational institution, nor a theatre. A museum is different things to different people; it is not one entity, but enshrines a multiplicity of values, images, and attitudes. It cannot be compartmentalised as a service or a non-profit organisation. It has these characteristics, but it is more complex than such definitions would suggest. It does not have a defined 'product', a consistent 'customer' profile, or a defined communication system between a 'product' and a 'customer' (Kotler and Levy 1969). It is not necessarily communicating with a 'customer' in order to make a 'profit' or 'the best financial outcome' (Diggle 1984). It may have various motives for 'identifying, anticipating, and satisfying the needs of its users' (Lewis 1991: 26), which may have little to do with 'public benefit' (Museums Association 1984).

Since museums exist for the public benefit and, by implication, their goals are social, their marketing needs to reflect these social goals. In this regard, some of the more recent marketing theories developed in Europe are considered, theories which do not subscribe to the cut and thrust tradition of marketing espoused in the US, but which appear to be more sympathetic to the way museums actually operate.

This book attempts to reconcile museums and marketing. Marketing has been regarded as a response to funding crises, a means of survival in museums. By appointing a member of staff, usually at a low level in the museum's hierarchy, to deal with publicity and advertising, it is envisaged that the museum's problems will be solved. It is assumed that what the museum has to offer is inherently interesting, and that the public only needs to be persuaded and cajoled to visit. The myths about marketing need to be dispelled.

Fundamental to this book is the belief that marketing is a process that seeks to achieve the museum's purpose in relation to its public. It is not a commercial tool, meted out to serve the politicians of the free market economies. Marketing has been around a lot longer than the free market. It is not marketing that commercialises or compromises the integrity of the museum and its objects. Marketing in museums has been misunderstood. What is required is an understanding of marketing developed specifically for the museum context, one which reflects the purpose of the museum. This book does this by introducing the context of museums and marketing in Part I, by addressing the various issues that impact on marketing in museums, and by challenging contemporary interpretations. It thereby attempts to create a 'philosophy' for marketing which is specific to the museum context. Part II outlines the practice of marketing in museums, acting as a guide to best practice. At the same time it is recognised that in reality, museums face significant hurdles in achieving a marketing orientation, while the practice itself may have limitations. Part II concludes by considering the future for museum marketing, and indicating some areas that require further research if the limitations of current practice are to be overcome.

Chapter 1 attempts to interpret the purpose of the museum, by assessing its continual redefinitions within the context of new technical resources and new social demands (Hudson 1977). The historical dimension is examined, followed by a discussion on the contemporary situation, looking at the museum in the postmodern condition. The various issues that occupy the minds of the museums profession, and which reflect the development of the museum, are debated. The museum is then located in its wider environment and within the public dimension.

Chapter 2 considers the rise of marketing to its seemingly unassailable position in capitalist countries. Recognising that marketing can be harnessed for the unethical and corrupt, a discussion ensues which defends marketing against its detractors, in the form of 'marketing baiters'. A number of arguments have been developed, notably in the diatribes against heritage, placing the blame firmly at the door of marketing. This is disputed. The second half of the chapter assesses the various theories of marketing, suggesting that although museums can benefit from an understanding of the services and non-profit marketing theories, marketing needs to be translated into the context of museums.

Chapter 3 reflects on the various factors in the museum's external environment that can impact on a museum's marketing. Chapter 4 ends the discussion on the issues and challenges for museums in adopting a marketing orientation by focusing on the public, and addressing the changing role of the public's relationship with the museum. Consideration is given to access and an appreciation of why people visit or are deterred from visiting museums.

The second part of the book takes a more practical focus, and continuing the discussion of Chapter 4, Chapter 5 outlines the techniques that a museum can use to understand the public and learn about their needs. A discussion then ensues on the various methods a museum can use to break a public down into homogeneous groups.

Chapter 6 returns to the museum to investigate what constitutes the museum's 'product'. The various aspects of that product are commented on, while the management of the product, so that it meets the needs of the public, is discussed. Some specific techniques developed in the services sectors are introduced and translated for museum use.

Communication or promotion is traditionally viewed as the domain of marketing. Chapter 7 outlines the various activities that can inform the public about the museum and improve its accessibility. Chapter 8 then considers the other traditionally held view of the role of marketing, that of resource attraction, both in terms of income generation and development activities.

The techniques used to implement the marketing effort are outlined in Chapter 9, which takes the reader step by step through the process of marketing planning. Chapter 10, though, argues that for marketing to succeed, marketing planning is not enough. The museum needs to do more than just initiate the activities of marketing; it needs to adopt marketing as a process. This may require some fundamental restructuring and a cultural revolution in the museum. The second half of the chapter anticipates the future for museum marketing if marketing is truly to achieve the purpose of the museum. Finally, some suggestions are posited for future investigation into museum marketing, an area which to date has seen a relative dearth of research.

***

This book is intended to be used by professionals and students alike, to enable them to appreciate marketing that is tailored to the museum situation. Although many of the examples used to illustrate the practice of marketing in museums are predominantly of UK origin, and to a lesser extent derived from the US, this book is intended to be universal, of relevance and applicable in any national context.

It is hoped that this book will shed new light on the discussion of marketing in museums. The main contention is that criticisms of marketing in museums are legitimate, but only in so far as they reflect an approach to marketing that is inappropriate to museums. Adapting marketing techniques developed for manufactured goods is by implication irrelevant to the museum situation. By drawing on the various marketing theories, and by selecting and locating those most appropriate to the museum context, the intention is to posit a marketing approach tailored to the museum. The underlying premise of this book is that museum marketing is the appropriation of the museum's ultimate purpose, that of serving the public.

Part I
Issues and challenges

1

The museum context

> Museums are wonderful, frustrating, stimulating, irritating, hideous things, patronizing, serendipitous, dull as dishwater, and curiously exciting, tunnel-visioned yet potentially visionary. The real magic is that any of them can be all of these simultaneously ... What is a museum and what is it not?
>
> (Bonniface and Fowler 1993: 118)

An examination of the history of museums would suggest that museums are all of these things because of the combination of their inertia to change in the first half of the twentieth century and their more recent transformation in the 1980s and 1990s. The sleepy, balmy days which have existed since their infancy are long gone. Museums have dusted down their glass cases, and have opened them up to ever-accelerating change. The 1980s and 1990s have witnessed a rapid makeover in museums, unprecedented in their history; twenty years of progress to parallel the past two hundred years of quiescence. No longer merely the guardians of the detritus of bygone ages, museums have assumed new roles as the demands and expectations of them have developed. An accumulation of factors, both internal and external, positive and negative, controlled and untrammelled, proactive and reactive, chosen and imposed, have brought museums, sometimes kicking and screaming, into the twentieth century. Instead of gazing at their navels, museums are opening their doors wide and responding to a world beyond the inner confines of their 'cabinets of curiosities'. A revolution is sweeping through museums, a revolution which has seen museums move 'from twilight to spotlight' (Cossons 1991: 186).

The purpose, or *raison d'être*, of museums has expanded in recent years in response to the changes in their environment. In 1904, Murray posited this definition of a museum: 'A museum, as now understood, is a collection of the monuments of antiquity, or of other objects interesting to the scholar and the man of science, arranged and displayed in accordance with scientific method' (Murray 1904: Introduction). A more recent interpretation has been adopted by the UK's Museums Association: 'A museum is an institution which collects, documents, preserves and interprets material evidence and associated information for the public benefit' (Museums Association 1984). These definitions are not dissimilar, although the definition from the turn of the century implies rather than states the functions addressed in modern museums. Whereas in 1904 museums were collections of objects which were arranged and displayed, now they also document and preserve. As scientific methods have improved, so equally have the methods of preservation and conservation. Whereas these objects were displayed 'in accordance with scientific method', now they are interpreted; and significantly, where museums were 'interesting to the scholar and the man of science', now they operate 'for the public benefit'.

The Museums and Galleries Commission (1988) described the Museums Association definition as follows. By 'institution' is meant an establishment that has a formal governing instrument and a long-term purpose. It should 'collect', that is possess or intend to acquire, substantial permanent collections in relation to its overall objectives. 'Documents' obliges the museum to maintain records, while 'preserves' includes not only all aspects of conservation, but also security. Through 'exhibits', at least some of the collection should be on show to the public, while it also implies that the museum will be open to the public at appropriate times and periods. 'Interprets' is all-encompassing, referring to display, education, research, and publication. 'Material' means something tangible, while 'evidence' suggests something authentic. 'Associated information' is the knowledge associated with the object, including all records of its past history, acquisition, and subsequent usage. Finally, 'for the public benefit' means that museums should be non-profit, and indicates that 'museums are the servants of society' (Museums and Galleries Commission 1988: 5).

The international museum community has developed a definition with a wider vision for the scope and parameters of museums. Thus the museum is, 'a not-for-profitmaking, permanent institution, in the service of society and of its development, and open to the public, which acquires, conserves, researches, communicates, and exhibits, for purposes of study, education and enjoyment, material evidence of man [*sic*] and his environment' (ICOM 1974; 1987). A mixed bag of functions, then, which often conflict, leading to tensions in priorities for decision-making. A historical analysis would discern how these functions and conflicts emerged, for as Mergolis commented, 'we cannot really consider the function of a museum without considering something of its history and historical purpose' (Mergolis 1988: 175).

THE HISTORICAL DIMENSION

Museums have existed in some form since the time of Ancient Greece, where a *museon* was a place dedicated to contemplation and learning (Murray 1904). By the eighteenth century a museum had come to mean, according to Dr Samuel Johnson's *Dictionary* (1755), 'a Repository of learned curiosities'. Prompted by the bourgeoisie's new-found wealth and their desire for social prestige, collecting was seen as one way of climbing the social ladder. The opening up of new trade routes and the fashion for archaeological excavations made objects more easily obtainable (Bazin 1967). These collections were private, being collected for their own sake, and not for public view. This was compounded by the social stratification of this period, where class, speech, and manners marked one class off from another, and would have precluded the lower classes and uneducated from mingling in the same rooms as the middle and upper classes and the educated (Hudson 1975). This exclusivity has left a legacy of social exclusion which still exists today.

The adoption of the word 'museum' to signify collections has been attributed to the evolution of a sense of public or social agency in the modern period. Even in the early so-called 'public museums', the advent of which coincided with the eighteenth-century spirit of enlightenment for equality of opportunity of learning, the public did not have automatic right of entry (Hudson 1975). The purpose of the 'public museum' was to share the collections that had previously been the preserve of the private collectors with everyone. However, the practice varied, perhaps inevitably, from the theory (Wittlin 1949). The first 'public museum' was the British Museum, which was created in 1759 from a gift to the British nation of the collection of Sir Hans Sloane. Here a number of rules and statutes disqualified the poor and uneducated from passing through its portals. These included restricted opening times, letters of application, and a refereeing process, where the potential visitor would undergo scrutiny, 'after which the librarian or his understudy decided whether the applicant was "proper" for admission' (Key 1973: 36–7). This only served to perpetuate the tradition of admittance to a museum being a privilege and a favour.

With the establishment throughout the nineteenth century of public museums that housed scientific specimens, a professional staff emerged who cared for and interpreted these collections. The scientific work of the keepers of these collections took precedence over public access. Nothing had changed from the days of the private museums, one owner of which placed a notice in a London newspaper stating:

> This is to inform the public that being tired out with the insolence of the common people who I have hitherto indulged with a sight of my museum, I am now come to the resolution of refusing admittance to the lower class except they come provided with a ticket from some gentleman or lady of my acquaintance.
>
> (quoted in Bogaart 1978: 43)

The whole environment of the museum provoked awe and intimidation rather than learning. The predilection for housing museums in grand buildings, reminiscent of a gentleman's private residence, did nothing to encourage public participation. Nor did the curtailing of access in many of the early museums. Museums were not universally regarded as catering 'for the public benefit' (Museums Association 1984) – there was no immediate right of entry. It perpetuated, according to Hudson,

> an old-established belief, the product of an aristocratic and hierarchical society – that art and scholarship are for a closed circle. The public may

admire in a general way, but it should realise its permanent and unchangeable inferiority and keep its distance.

(Hudson 1975: 3)

The turning point for accessibility of museums was heralded by the succession of world fairs, marked by the Great Exhibition in London in 1851. These exhibitions attracted vast numbers of people, who were able to visit them with the advent of the railway age. These trade fairs persuaded governments that museums could be used as a means of social utility and social control; the population could utilise their spare time constructively by visiting museums and educating themselves, becoming more civilised in the process. These world fairs also persuaded governments that museums had the power to imbue a sense of national pride in the population. The 1851 Great Exhibition unashamedly portrayed its wares with pride in the nation that produced them. Throughout the nineteenth century, monarchs and governments recognised the value of museums in influencing public opinion, almost to the point of brainwashing, regarding museums as a foyer for nationalism, which at that time was the dominating political form in Europe (Bazin 1967).

In the nineteenth century, education was a mission that had a religious fervour. Museums were temples of self-improvement and exacerbated that role by being cold and unwelcoming, with little or no facilities for the visitor. Formal learning had been recognised as a social need, but it was not conceived of as an enjoyable experience. The museum legitimated and affirmed the beliefs and values of the educated classes, the classes to whom it was reaching out. The collection was no longer private, the property of some wealthy individual; now it belonged to the public, and therefore would be meaningful for that public and should become responsible for reflecting their social reality (Cameron 1971). This attitude to education was perpetuated throughout the twentieth century. While education has become more sophisticated in the last hundred years, museums on the whole have remained steeped in nineteenth-century educational values.

By the mid-nineteenth century, museum development had burgeoned with such organisations as mechanics' institutes, philosophical and literary societies, and universities, creating museums from collections often purchased or bequeathed to them from one or more individual collectors and by members of the group. There were now a number of different museum types: private cabinets; semi-public collections; public institutions; society museums; mechanics' institutes; exhibitions; and popular museums. Commensurate with the variety of different types of museum, there was also a variety of opinions on the purpose of museums: classical learning; scientific discovery; mechanical utility; moral uplift; national, cultural, economic, or political well-being; entertaining recreation; or social control. As Teather commented, these opinions, 'were absorbed into the vague museum metaphor ready to be reformulated into the language of succeeding eras' (Teather 1983: 133).

Generally, governments did not directly involve themselves in museum creation. The attitude was one of ambivalence, where the value of museums was recognised but was not translated into legislation. The government's role was uncertain and contradictory (Teather 1983). In the UK, for example, the Royal Commission on National Museums and Galleries commented:

> In general it is true to say that the State has not initiated. The Collections, whether artistic, literary or scientific, once formed by the zeal of individuals, and thereafter bestowed on or acquired by the State, have been maintained out of the public purse at the lowest possible cost. The attitude of the State to the National Museums and Galleries has for the most part been a passive and mainly receptive attitude. Development has been spasmodic.
> (Royal Commission on National Museums and Galleries 1929: 10)[1]

It was not until the twentieth century that any significant number of museums were established by municipal authorities. During this period, museums became an issue of regional pride, instilling a sense of social responsibility. The municipal museum has evolved as the local community has taken on a responsibility for its past.

Throughout the twentieth century, and especially after the Second World War, with its changing balance of politics and publics, the role of museums was subject to reforming ideas. But this was not a golden age for museums, even although attitudes to them were changing. Poor funding, neglect, and changing fashions meant that many museums, especially society museums and private collections, were dissipated if governments would not agree to take responsibility for them. With the Depression in the 1920s the reformist ideas were not achieved. The financial constraints and poor museum organisation were not the only factors affecting the stagnation of museums at this time – the confusion of museum ideas also created problems and may have been the cause of the underfunded museum system. Once again, the lack of direction or unified policy for museums was to contribute to not so much a decline in museums, as a stagnation. This was especially unfortunate in an age where reformist social legislation was rife, which if transferred to museums, would have transformed them. Instead, they remained locked in their history, waiting until well after the Second World War when there was enough ideological, political, and economic momentum to attempt to reform them to any extent (Teather 1983).

Since the Second World War the institutional nature of the museum has developed quite considerably. A national framework for government intervention in museums has emerged and a new managerial ethos has been imposed on museums. The collection has met bureaucracy. Museum sectors may vary across nations, although on the whole they are either government-run (central or municipal), university-run, or independent (a significant number of these, particularly in the US, being created by wealthy benefactors). Today, in the UK for example, the museum sector is divided into three parts: national museums (75 per cent funded by central government); municipal museums (about 85 per cent funded by local taxation); and independent museums, which are dependent on self-generated income for operating costs but which rely heavily on local government grants (Davies, S. 1993). The UK has an abundance of independent museums which have sprung up in recent years. As museums have grown in number, though having slowed from the initial impetus of one museum a fortnight in the 1970s and 1980s (Hewison 1987), they have assumed new roles in the societies which they serve. As Lumley remarked:

> Museums are an international growth industry. Not only are they increasing in numbers, but they are acquiring new functions in the organization of cultural activities. It is through museums that societies represent their relationship to their own history and to that of other cultures and peoples. Today, there are great differences and conflicts both inside and outside museums about how this should best be done, leading those concerned with running them to question the traditional concepts of what a museum is, what it can offer its public, and how history is conceived and presented.
>
> (Lumley 1988: 2)

MUSEUMS AND HERITAGE

History is no longer the preserve of museums. The soul-searching referred to by Lumley has been exacerbated by the popularity of heritage, a term that seems to have no definition, but 'means everything and it means nothing' (Hewison 1987: 32). Hewison in his landmark book *The Heritage Industry: Britain in a climate of decline*, identifies the boom in the heritage industry with a need to retain a comforting sense of continuity with the past in a period of economic decline. As in the US and many other European nations, in the 1960s and 1970s traditional manufacturing industries were closing down throughout Britain, causing dislocation in the communities that depended on them for employment. The simple notion that by reinventing the past, people were better prepared to cope with the present and future, apparently led to this growth of what has been dubbed 'the heritage industry' in the 1980s. Much of the nostalgia has been for the industrial past. Nevertheless, 'The protection of the past conceals the destruction of the present. There is an absolute distinction between authentic history (continuing and therefore dangerous) and heritage (past, dead and safe) . . . Heritage is bogus history' (Urry 1990: 110). Museums are part of this heritage industry; they give meaning to our present lives by interpreting the past. Thus, 'In the twentieth century museums have taken over the function once exercised by church and ruler, they provide the symbols through which the nation and a culture understands itself' (Hewison 1987: 84).

It is debatable whether museums actually subscribe to the almost religious function suggested by Hewison. Can all museums transcend the functional; are they imbued with a sense of the past? The public experience of the museum is actually determined by its contents and the scope of its collections. Where a national art gallery could prove to be an enlightening experience for one visitor, it might only instil a sense of inadequacy in another. Equally, a visitor to a small local museum may identify and reminisce with the collection, while to another it may appear as a jumble of meaningless objects. Is Hewison pushing the notion of enlightenment just a little too far?

Kevin Walsh in *The Representation of the Past* (1992) agrees with Hewison that heritage is a consequence of a climate of decline in Britain. While industry disintegrates, heritage replaces it by literally developing within its ruins, as on Tyneside in the north east of England and the Rhondda Valley in Wales. Walsh, though, believes that heritage should be seen as part of the service culture which expanded during the 1980s throughout Western nations. It is inextricably linked not only with the economic climate, but also the political climate, where the New Right, led by Margaret Thatcher in the UK and Ronald Reagan in the US, emphasised the radical individual, operating freely in the marketplace. Heritage is an element of this condition, where as a leisure service it has been 'concerned to market ephemeral images of the past' (Walsh, Kevin 1992: 4). Walsh further accuses heritage of 'neutering' the past, by promoting a past that is complete and entirely removed from the present.

On the contrary though, as Lowenthal (1985) describes, the past is indelibly stamped with today's predilections. By interacting with heritage, the nature and context of the past are continually being altered, whether by choice, through preservation, or merely by chance. Samuel even suggests that: 'Aesthetically, as well as historically heritage is a hybrid, reflecting, or taking part in, style wars, and registering changes in public taste' (Samuel 1994: 211).

Samuel in his discussion on those who criticise heritage, or 'heritage-baiting' as he refers to it, alludes particularly to Hewison's polemic and to Wright's attack on heritage, where, in *Living in an Old Country* (1985), Wright refers to heritage as part of the self-fulfilling culture of national decline. Samuel remarks that 'The charge of vulgarity could be said to be a leitmotiv of heritage criticism, and may account for the frequency with which heritage is bracketed with theme parks, toytowns and Disneyland' (Samuel 1994: 265). Heritage is scorned and denigrated, with museum curators such as Julian Spalding of Glasgow Museums and Art Galleries making such comments as, 'for down-market populism, we have to turn to Disney' (Spalding 1991: 171). Perhaps more fundamentally, heritage is discredited because of its association with consumerism. Heritage is a hybrid, dressed up in simulacra, for the consumption of a gullible public.

But are the public so gullible? Do they not recognise that what they are being offered is not 'real'? For example,

> Concepts of the death of the past and its commodification have both been over-emphasised in the literature because they ignore the different and creative ways in which individuals construct their own past from their previous experience and memories, and from the materials, such as museum presentations, that are given to them by others.
>
> (Merriman 1991: 18)

Moreover, research has shown that people are more than capable of distinguishing between image and reality (Elliott *et al.* 1993). It could also be argued that there is no appreciation in the heritage baiters' arguments of the complexity of the gaze of different visitors who will read an object in quite different ways (Urry 1990). To develop the argument one stage further, it could also be asked whether the critics perhaps over-emphasise the interest or genuine concern of the public to be educated about an authentic past? The critics themselves are patronising at best, politically manipulative at worst. How many of us are, or want to be, 'critical visitors'?

Heritage is an easy target for baiting. But the critics place too much emphasis on the role and importance of history. Heritage does not 'insult' the consumer as suggested by Kevin Walsh (1992); it is not just heritage which requires that we 'rewrite history'. History is continually being rewritten under postmodern interpretations. As history is 'appreciated for its own sake, the less real or relevant it becomes' (Lowenthal 1985: xvii). It does not need heritage to recreate its reality. History is equally subject to (mis)interpretation. History is equally a commodity. Why would history enfranchise any more than heritage? The reason why there is no satisfactory definition of heritage is that it is too redolent of history to be distinguished from history. Heritage is not a looming spectre of a postmodern world; it is a (re-)interpretation of history which itself is a (re-)interpretation of history *ad infinitum*.

THE POSTMODERN CONDITION

The discussion on heritage needs to be set in context with the contemporary condition of postmodernity. The rise of heritage to some extent parallels the postmodern turn. It may be regarded as a 'postmodern institution' since it reflects or incorporates the most studied and discussed condition of post-modernism, that of hyperreality, where 'Reality has collapsed, and today it is exclusively image, illusion, or stimulation. The model is more real than the reality it supposedly represents' (Rosenau 1992: xii).

Before considering postmodernity, it is necessary to appreciate the modern condition. Modernity entered history during the Enlightenment, 'promising to liberate humankind from ignorance and irrationality' (Rosenau 1992: 5). Modernity championed metanarratives such as capitalism, Marxism, and humanism, which identified eternal truths supported by scientific analyses, which in turn rivalled other metanarratives. Fundamental to modernist thought is the idea of progress, a progress which invested in attributing faith in humankind's dominance over the environment. It signifies a belief in the rational order, where science is the basis of universal knowledge, that there is a scientific universal which imposes order and unity. There is a rational explanation for all phenomena, an explanation formulated within a metanarrative.

By contrast, postmodernity rejects authority, unity, continuity, purpose, and commitment. Instead postmodernity is characterised by complexity, multiplicity, fragmentation, resistance, negation, rupture, and irreverence for any specific goal or point of view (Venkatesh 1989). Postmodernism is confusing precisely because there are probably as many forms of postmodernism as there are postmodernists (Featherstone 1988). There does appear to be a consensus though, that there is no one single way of perceiving reality; that there should be a recognition of difference; that there is a diversity of metanarratives that liberate from all conformity; and that there should be freedom to experience as many ways of being as desired. Thus, there is no one dominant philosophy, ideology, or agenda.

Postmodernism is a relatively new departure for discussion. It has not necessarily superseded the modern period. It is still evolving as a concept, or more accurately concepts, and may even be more in the minds of the commentators than in real life. However, to ignore it because of this would be at our peril. A reading of the (often complex) discussions on the postmodern would nevertheless be recognisable as the contemporary scenario. Much has changed in recent years, and the postmodern discussion clearly reflects these changes.

For many postmodern commentators, the most significant and easily identifiable component of the postmodern condition is a distinctive postwar artistic and cultural movement (Boyne and Rattansi 1990). In postmodern art, for example, where it is considered that there is no more room for innovation, the only way forward is to imitate the old, often in an ironic and parodic form (Crowther 1990). There is also a denial of the elitism of art, in Warhol's soup cans, Judd's use of mass-produced industrial objects, and the growth in popularity of body art and street art, which eschews the institutionalisation of art in museums. The effacement between 'high' art and 'low' art is manifest in all cultural spheres, where Pavarotti tops the hit parade, and classical music is performed by 'punks' (Brown 1995). Museums have also been caught up in this populist impulse to break down elitism.

Nevertheless museums still contribute to the modernist hegemonic project by reinforcing the notion of progress and the ordering of time and place. Thus, 'The basic form of representing the past through the static museum presentation has not really altered in spite of many changes in fashion and style' (Walsh, Kevin 1992: 31). Postmodern commentators are opposed to the modern assumption that history is chronological or linear (Derrida 1981). This linear history has been the conventional wisdom for museum interpretation. Only recently have museums developed beyond the systemised classification redolent of nineteenth-century museums, where a linear, time-restricted context represented the meaning for the object. To break out of this mould has required a reappraisal of the role of museums within their economic, political, social, and cultural contexts. In the postmodern condition their espousal of time, space, and history needs to be re-evaluated. In response to this, Walsh (1992) has suggested that we may need to move away from the use of dates in order to personalise the past. Thus, 'an emphasis should be placed on thinking of time in terms of human generations. Dates could be referred to for example as "when your great-grandparents were alive"' (Walsh, Kevin 1992: 167). He also suggests that it would be worth cross-referencing with that which is likely to be known, such as the Roman Period or the Middle Ages, rather than dates. Shanks and Tilley (1987) propose that artefacts

17

should be broken from their fixed chronological narrative and from their original contexts by reassembling them with contemporary artefacts that have also been decontextualised. In this way alternate meanings can be illustrated, and attention can be drawn to official cultural meanings of artefacts, thereby creating a critique of commodification.

The loss of history is also reflected in a further postmodern condition, that of fragmentation. Firat and Venkatesh (1993), on discussing fragmentation, cite Baudrillard's free-floating signifier, where fragmentation has been created by decontextualisation, where each moment or entity is separate from its original context. The entity or moment is isolated and so becomes manipulable because its connections have all been removed. Firat and Venkatesh give as an example a sand painting from the Native American ceremonies:

> Once the sand painting was removed from its context which is the medicinal ceremony, it became an object of desire, as an art object, to be sold as a commodity. As a commodity it loses its original meaning and function, stands out to be viewed and admired, becomes an object of voyeurism, a spectacle.
>
> (Firat and Venkatesh 1993: 234)

'The ?Exhibition?' at the Ashmolean Museum in Oxford was an attempt to address some of the issues of postmodernism by unravelling what 'meaning' really means. 'The ?Exhibition?',

> was intended as a provocation: not a provocation against the museum (the Ashmolean, any museum), not a critique of boring displays, incomprehensible labels, creeping commercialisation or untouchability; but an attempt to provoke reaction, response, interrogation, engagement . . . within the museum and on the museum's behalf.
>
> (Beard and Henderson 1992: 20)

The purpose of the exhibition was to challenge some of the museum's conventional certainties, using a series of questions to the visitor, such as: Why does a museum make it hard to find the loo? What aren't they showing you? What does this label think you need to know? There were 'piles of shards, shelves of objects and labelling which keep up a barrage of undermining questions about what the organisers, the museum and we the visitor think we are doing' (Phillips 1992: 21). Visitors became the object of the gaze themselves, reflected in wall mirrors and watched by twenty or more lifesize heads. The visitors' response was polarised, from those who felt it to be unworthy of the museum to those who felt it had, 'somehow saved civilisation' (Beard and Henderson 1992: 20). As Phillips commented, 'Trying to turn authority over to the visitor, do we end up with a mystifying display which replaces collections with a preoccupation with ourselves as curators, in the guise of presenting our role in an unprivileged way?' (Phillips 1992: 21). Despite this, 'Unless more of us are brave enough to try we will not know' (ibid. 21). A constructive debate on the role of museums in a postmodern society is required.

AUTHENTICITY OR HYPERREALITY?

Heritage is denigrated for reflecting the hyperreal, 'that which is already reproduced' (Baudrillard 1983: 146). It is a model 'of a real without origin or reality' (ibid. 2), a model which is more real than the reality it supposedly represents. Hyperreal exemplifies a tendency amongst consumers to prefer hype or simulation to the 'real', witnessed by the explosion in popularity of virtual reality, computer games, theme parks, and of course heritage centres, where the simulation becomes 'real'. Museums have an advantage over 'heritage', being object-based and thus ostensibly 'authentic' (MacCannell 1976). According to Costa and Bamossy,

> The desire for authenticity flows in both directions in the museum context. It is not only the consumers, the purchasers of the opportunity to view the museum exhibits...who are concerned with the authentic. Perhaps with a greater depth of concern, as well as with what may be seen as a professional responsibility over a moral obligation, are the museum curators, managers, and staff, who also concern themselves with authenticity.
>
> (Costa and Bamossy 1995: 301)

This quest for reality has occupied the minds of several theorists. Boorstin (1964) holds that we cannot experience reality directly but thrive on 'pseudo-events' – staged events that are remote from reality. Contrary to Boorstin, MacCannell (1976) considers tourists to be seeking not pseudo-events or the inauthentic, but the authentic, the reality of other times and places. Pseudo-events are the consequence of social relations of tourism. Museums contribute to this, by both affirmation and subordination, since

> Modern museums and parks are anti-historical and unnatural . . . not in the sense of their destroying the past or nature because, to the contrary, they preserve them, but as they preserve, they automatically separate modernity from its past and from nature and elevate it above them. Nature and the past are made a part of the present, not in the form of [an] unreflected inner spirit, a mysterious soul, but rather as revealed objects, as tourism attractions.
>
> (MacCannell 1976: 84)

Thus museums control and subordinate history and nature to contemporary definitions of social reality. They embody the past for 'the tourist gaze' (Urry 1990). By putting objects in glass cases, they are controlled by the society that is exhibiting them, defining the social reality, not of the past to which they belong, but of the present in which their past is reinvented. The latest in technology, elaborate dioramas, complex audio-visual aids, lifesize reproductions of actual settings do not alter this, rather they demonstrate and exhibit the superiority of the technology (Halpin 1978).

Traditionally, museums were based on a sense of aura premised on authenticity of the historical artefact, which was supposedly scarce or unique (Horne 1984). The museum functioned as a metaphor for the power of the state, the learning of the scholar, and the genius of the artist. Horne argues that this reverential attitude towards the objects in museums merely because they were authentic created problems for museums. The object may be authentic, or avowedly a replica of the authentic, but the authentic may be distorted by the mere arrangement of the objects and their exposure to the 'tourist gaze' in museum exhibits (Urry 1990). The museum visitor trusts the museum to have superior knowledge about the object and to inform them of its history. Artefacts are mute, they cannot express their own history – that is the responsibility of the 'interpreter', the curator.

Equally, museums display artefacts in a setting divorced from their original context. They impose preservation on art, and non-utility on natural and human-utility objects. They are not reflecting the true nature of their collections. Sir John Pope-Hennessy has expressed this museum dilemma thus:

> the whole museum situation is inherently an artificial one. The works exhibited were intended for a vast variety of purposes . . . the only purpose for which we can be confident they were not designed was to be shown in a museum . . . they have been wrested from their setting and alienated from whatever role they were originally intended to perform.
>
> (Pope-Hennessy, quoted in Hall, M. 1987: 11)

The 'new museology', or the reappraisal of this static portrayal of artefacts, recognises the interaction between the object and its economic and political past and present. The object and its interpretation are value-laden, through the decision for accession, the decision to conserve or to preserve, the decision to interpret it. As Vergo puts it in *The New Museology*:

> Whether we like it or not, every acquisition and indeed disposal, every juxtaposition or arrangement of an object or work of art, together with other objects or works of art, within the context of a temporary exhibition or museum display means placing a certain construction upon history, be it the history of the distant or more recent past, of our own culture or someone else's, or mankind in general or a particular aspect of human endeavour.
>
> (Vergo 1989: 2–3)

By dressing up the object through dioramas, living history, and contextualisation, the model can become more real than the reality it supposedly represents – it becomes hyperreality. The objects are no longer revered for their authenticity, but merely contribute to an imagined re-creation of their reality. As Walsh claims: 'The accelerated overproduction and reproduction of signs is the life-blood of hyperconsumerism' (Walsh, Kevin 1992: 59).

One of the most significant concerns for museums is that these changes, albeit popular with the visitors, are redolent of the hyperreal. The museum is turned into a Disneyland, where the objects are no longer revered for their authenticity, but merely contribute to an imagined re-creation of their reality. In fact, Disneyland is derided for going one step further, for creating simulacra, copies of copies for which there is no original (Baudrillard 1983). According to Hewison,

... we have begun to construct a past that, far from being a defence against the future, is a set of imprisoning walls upon which we project a superficial image of a false past, simultaneously turning our backs on the reality of history, and incapable of moving forward because of the absorbing fantasy before us.

(Hewison 1987: 139)

Disneyland celebrates commercial vulgarity, through kitsch or pastiche, 'an imitation that mocks the original' (Jameson 1985: 113). But, 'many prefer Disneyland's "historic" facsimiles precisely because they are copies, not demanding the solemn awe felt to be due to the originals' (Lowenthal 1985: 306). Moreover the debate on hyperreality gives little credit to the public. The tourist or visitor brings a set of expectations of the experience when interacting with the museum (Ryan 1991). Cohen (1979) suggests that the tourist would be able to view a tourist event as being either staged or real. This though presupposes that the visitor has a high need for authenticity, since Cohen fails to recognise that the tourist may perceive the event to be false, and thus suspend belief and enjoy the spectacle on its own terms (Ryan 1991).

Ryan (1991) further criticises the discussion on 'authenticity' of the tourist experience, since he considers that the quality of experience is not dictated by whether or not the event has an elitist meaning, as these authors imply. On the contrary, quality of experience is embodied in the tourist's own needs and the quality of provision of the service and management of the tourist area itself. As Ryan states:

There would appear to be nothing intrinsically wrong with a desire for relaxation. The tourist can enjoy the experience of the fantasy as portrayed at theme parks ... tourists do not leave behind their critical faculties, and recognize [it as] 'show business'.

(Ryan 1991: 46)

Feifer (1985) refers to these tourists as 'post-tourists' who almost delight in the authenticity of the normal tourist experience.

Although the spectacle offered by museums is not deliberately false, and the viewer would have the faculties to recognise this, they still offer an 'artefactual history' (Urry 1990), where social experiences are necessarily ignored or trivialised. However, contrary to Hewison's (1987) belief that enjoyable experiences cannot also be educational, Urry (1990) criticises him for ignoring the complexity by which different visitors can gaze upon the same set of objects and read them in quite different ways. We assimilate the objects and resurrect them in our own personal reality. Perhaps, then, rather than looking at social reality, we should be considering individual reality, seeing the public not as an amorphous mass, but as individuals with their own interpretations and realities created by their own world view of what is reality.

This authenticity debate further creates a tension for museums, between on the one hand looking at 'real life', while on the other hand seeking quality of material and visuals with diversity in the objects and displays, along with fun and entertainment for the visitors (Porter 1988). Samuel (1994), though, condemns the 'heritage baiters' who talk about the 'tyranny' of the past, where history becomes a commodity created by marketing people who are not actually communicating with the public, but entertain at the expense of education. By contrast, Samuel contends that:

> The perceived opposition between 'education' and 'entertainment' and the unspoken and unargued-for assumption that pleasure is almost by definition mindless, ought not to go unchallenged ... people do not simply 'consume' images in the way in which, say, they buy a bar of chocolate. As in any reading, they assimilate them as best they can to pre-existing images and narratives. The pleasures of the gaze ... are different in kind from those of the written word but not necessarily less taxing on historical reflection.
>
> (Samuel 1994: 271)

By trusting the artefacts and the (re-)interpretation of them to be authentic, museums are then seen as superior to 'heritage'. Museums need to regard authenticity as a marketing niche in a hyperreal world, at the same time recognising that nothing is 'real', not even history, as it is always interpreted and reinterpreted. Thus according to Lowenthal, 'a heritage wholly saved or authentically reproduced is no less transformed than one deliberately manipulated' (Lowenthal 1985: xviii).

Ultimately, though, the museum needs to remember the public in this debate. How can they best be served? Without recommending that museums slavishly imitate the techniques of Disney, it is also worth remembering, in the words of Lowenthal: 'Better a misinformed enjoyment of history than none, a light-hearted dalliance with the past than a wholesale rejection of it' (Lowenthal 1985: 408).

Museums can learn from the popular theme parks, while at the same time retaining the integrity of the objects. Few people have either the taste or the training to appreciate the past merely from gazing on objects from the past. They only become coherent and evocative when reconstituted and 'brought alive' (Lowenthal 1985). The object thus becomes a signifier, communicating meaning from the intellectual framework which placed that object in its interpretative context to the public that perceive that object. The museum is constantly disseminating values, and the issue is, 'how to make these values manifest, how to bring them up to consciousness for both ourselves [the curators] and our visitors' (Weil 1990: 52). Artefacts are social, since they reflect social relations, while at the same time being of social utility. The implication then is that the primary responsibility of museums is not, as many would declare, the care of collections, but that 'the primary and central relationship of museology is between the museum and its visitors and other clients and not between the museum and its collection' (ibid. 56). The museum is socially derived, its artefacts are social creations and manifest social relations. Decisions on its artefacts are socially constructed, and the purpose of the museum is social utility. The museum is a social construct, not merely a display of the authentic. History is no more authentic than its (re-)interpretation. The artefact is further removed from history, in that its muteness is dependent on professional knowledge to create its understanding. Thus,

> authenticity has to include the social relations as well as the artefact, the viewer's culture as well as the culture of the object, and neither should be obscured by museum culture, which must be as invisible but as omnipresent and effective as a simultaneous translator.
>
> (O'Neill 1991: 35)

By definition, then, museums are social constructs, which meet social needs.

THE PUBLIC DIMENSION

But which social needs is the museum meeting? There is no identifiable 'need' for museums as there is for food to eat or for soap to wash (Van der Vliet 1979). However, as Maslow (1970) highlighted in his theory of motivation, when basic human needs are partially satisfied, further needs develop. In the 1990s, the needs of Western European and American publics in terms of their physiological, safety, belongingness, love, and esteem, are capable of being partially gratified. Consequently, self-esteem needs become paramount, where self-fulfilment is an overriding factor. Hewison has suggested that, 'for the individual, nostalgia filters out unpleasant aspects of the past, and of our former selves, creating a self-esteem that helps us to rise above the anxieties of the present' (Hewison 1987: 46). Museums can act as a tool in helping the public to become self-fulfilled. The extent to which a museum enables fulfilment of self-esteem needs is dependent on the individual and is therefore difficult to define in a museum context.

This raises the question of what self-fulfilment means in terms of museums. Museums have the potential to enlighten, to provoke awe, to stimulate, to educate, and to entertain. But often they serve only to intimidate, to overawe, to numb the senses, to give a sense of inferiority, and to bore. Again, this situation is often a legacy of the museum's past, of its exclusion of the public – physically, mentally, and emotionally – and of its conflicting purposes. Preservation is the antithesis of access. Museums were not originally created for the public. Today, though,

> rather than museums existing for the purpose of preserving and studying collections ... museums ... now exist more and more for the purpose of serving the public. This changing emphasis ... has profound implications for the social organization of museums and for the conditions of work within them.
>
> (Ames, M. M. 1986: 11)

Access, though, can diverge in its understanding. At its lowest common denominator, 'access' is perceived as democratisation, as facilitating access by opening the doors of the museum to the public. At the other end of the spectrum, 'access' denotes democracy, the active participation of the public in determining the goals of the museum (Simpson 1976). Nearly all museums, adhere to the first understanding of 'access'. Some have addressed the second interpretation of 'access' by inviting intervention. The most enlightened, such as Springburn Museum near Glasgow, have involved the local public in the affairs of the museum, inviting them not only to participate passively, but also to be active in the running of the museum. For many museums, though, the democratic interpretation of 'access' involves the creation of 'Friends' organisations. Often, this is an elite form of access, whereby a social club evolves, the nature of which excludes the general public.

The accusation of elitism is often levelled at museums, particularly art galleries, since 'ever since their inception, museums have been associated with the elite' (Merriman 1991: 2). Museums are created by the elite for the elite. Even today, surveys still confirm that museums are visited overwhelmingly by the upper and middle classes (Bryant 1988; Touche Ross 1989). But who do museums regard as their public? Jenkinson would have us believe that: 'There are very few other cultural institutions that interpret their potential audience so broadly and attempt to provide for the whole population' (Jenkinson 1989: 142). However, does an art gallery decide that what it offers is so predominantly of interest to the higher social echelons that it cannot penetrate further down the social scales, or does it go to the other extreme?

The Laing Art Gallery in Newcastle-upon-Tyne has been attempting to diversify its visitor profile by offering exhibitions such as 'Art on Tyneside' – a 'popular' exhibition, which was considered to be more palatable to its current non-visitors. The exhibition tells the story of art on Tyneside over some thirty years. It was 'the first art display to use scenic recreations, interactives, sounds, smell and models, not to mention a talking tug-boat' (Millard 1992: 32). The exhibition proved successful, attracting 70 per cent more visits than the same period in the previous year (Millard 1992). But does this alienate the gallery's traditional clientele, and does it eventually serve to inculcate artistic taste in its non-visitors, or even attract them back to a more traditional exhibition?

The argument of elitism and populism, particularly in art galleries, becomes paramount. Pierre Bourdieu (1984) has written about the accessibility of art, developing it in terms of the notion of 'cultural competence'. The knowledge of codes specific to the art forms upon which 'cultural competence' depends, is imbibed through the family background and education. Bourdieu argues that the exclusivity which his concept implies, reinforces class divisions, enabling the cultural elite to dismiss those who have not attained its level of 'cultural competence'. Many questions surround the operation of this model. Is the formation of elites, underscoring class divisions, inherently mistaken? Would the excluded public want to be included, or would they want to be offered an alternative, such as the Laing Art Gallery's 'Art on Tyneside' exhibition? By recognising that a certain public does not have the cultural competence to understand art, the gallery has offered it a substitute. Whose needs or wants are actually being met by this? By negating elitism, is it necessarily populist? Is it patronising the public and satisfying the conscience of the curator? And is elitism, with all of its pejorative connotations in this context, a bad thing? Is the wider public ever to be capable of attaining what are considered to be the required levels of cultural competence?

Bourdieu's work needs to be set in context. As Merriman points out, Bourdieu's critique referred specifically to art galleries, 'where visitors are much more sharply differentiated along lines of education and status than they are in museums' (Merriman 1989: 163). Second, according to Merriman, Bourdieu's critique was written in 1960s France, before the meteoric rise of heritage, and so is not necessarily of contemporary significance. It could also be added that postmodernism heralds a new era where the elitist divisions of culture are being eradicated. Society is increasingly becoming subject to de-differentiation, where established hierarchies such as politics and showbusiness, and high and low culture, are being eroded and effaced (Brown 1995). This erosion of high and low culture can be embraced by museums, whose goal is to enable access for all regardless of their cultural competence.

Lumley (1988) claims that the act of 'consumption' can have a democratising potential denied by those who criticise commercialism. Referring to Bourdieu, who claimed that the department store is 'the poor man's gallery', Lumley suggests that the 'introduction of museum shops, display techniques taken from window-dressing, and the juxtaposition of everyday and "art" objects can make museums more accessible' (Lumley 1988: 11). As O'Neill has suggested, where 'political pressure for increased responsiveness to the public is . . . expressed in terms of market forces, the argument has become blurred, and museums defended against commercialization when what is often at stake is democratization' (O'Neill 1991: 34). As the cultural activity that is currently the most democratic (Davies 1994a), museums are in a strong position to ensure that they are truly serving society.

At the same time as postmodernism has globalising tendencies, it is also anti-foundational. Thus, 'questions of fact, truth, correctness, validity, and clarity can neither be posed nor answered' (Fish 1989: 344). Postmodernism is characterised by a deconstructive urge, particularly towards metanarratives, which represent modernism's search for universal truths and objective knowledge. This has led to the 'seemingly inexorable disintegration and demise of political stability, social organisation, mass market economics, the unified self, the nature and grounds of knowledge, and inevitably, the all-pervasive, disconnected array of visual images generated by the increasingly hydra-headed media' (Brown 1995: 106). The consequence of this is the fragmentation of markets into increasingly smaller segments, or groups of a similar nature to be targeted through publicity. This offers a particular opportunity for museums: first, to fulfil their societal role by segmenting the public into minority groups, such as the disabled, single parents, and ethnic minorities, and second, to target a particular product or aspect of the museum at each of these groups.

This focus on the individual can perhaps best be understood by considering social and economic transformations in the postmodern world. Minority issues such as gender and ethnicity now inspire the foci of our reality. There is an inexorable fragmentation of modern life – traditional family values have collapsed and the nuclear family is the exception rather than the rule. Narcissistic self-absorption, dysfunctionalism and delinquency have become the norm (Brown 1995). This has been paralleled by the economic transformations, from a Fordist 'mass market', to post-Fordism 'flexible specialisation', where markets are fragmented, with the diversity of consumer demands, and the creation of niche markets and one-on-one marketing (that is marketing to the individual). Thus the reality of the postmodern world is in fact hyperreal (Baudrillard 1983). So much so that Disneyland has been created as imaginary in order to make us believe that the rest is real, to disguise the fact that it is in fact a simulation. As Brown comments, though:

> Ironically, however, this demise of the real spawns a nostalgic search for authenticity, though as nostalgia and authenticity are easily reproduced or created, this tendency is also sucked inexorably into Baudrillard's black hole of hyperreality, as are any attempts at subversion or critique.
>
> (Brown 1995: 81)

Interest in the vernacular and quotidian has been a typical response, with Urry pointing out that: 'There has been a quite stunning fascination with the popular and a tendency to treat all kinds of object, whether it is the Mona Lisa or the old cake tin of a Lancashire cloth worker, as almost equally interesting' (Urry 1990: 130). The growth of museums of the vernacular and the rise of heritage centres that portray what is meant to be authentic, but is in fact perfect simulacra, has been the result. As the vernacular replaces aura, the relevance of MacCannell's observation of museums, as affirming the subordination of other values and images, is increasingly becoming tenuous. Urry (1990) argues that the gaze in museums has changed in three fundamental respects. First, there is the broadening of objects deemed worthy of being preserved: the shift 'from aura to nostalgia', where the ordinary has joined the reverential. Museums themselves have changed, placing an emphasis on visitors participating in the exhibits themselves, not just in handling them, but in creating museum displays. Finally, the relationship between other institutions and museums has changed, with other institutions, such as shops, factories, and pubs, becoming more like museums; either becoming museums themselves, or being 'museumified'.

It is relevant at this point to assess the museum's purpose in terms of a public. Clearly, the notion of access is fundamental to this discussion. But so too is the underlying premise of the museum role for the public, where

> the absence of consensus about learning in museums stems also from a paradox of significant proportions, a tension of values that is inherent in the very mission of museums. Stated quite simply, the concerns of preservation and the demands of public access are a contradiction lived out in every situation.
>
> (American Association of Museums 1984: 57–8)

Here it is still not clear what that role is. Implicit, but not explicit, is education.

There is no consensus on how a museum can and should educate a public. At the same time as the focus on public education has intensified, albeit slowly, tensions have emerged between the educative and research functions of a museum. During the twentieth century the curatorial function has become more specialised in subject orientation, and has developed in the field of academic research. This specialisation and learning have often been reflected in the attempts to interpret objects for the public, where they reflect scholarly concerns, rather than an attempt to induce or stimulate learning.

More recently, though, the long-standing debate between research and education has been further opened up by the latest issue to concern museums: the dichotomy between education and enjoyment. Is the museum about 'spiritual enrichment' or fun? 'Disneyfication' has led to the fun aspect dominating, where the education is relegated to a sideshow for attracting visitors from competing leisure attractions. Enjoyment relegates education to second-class status, with museums positioning themselves as emporia of pleasure, an alternative to the theme parks. The discussion has tended to neglect the possibility of education and entertainment being bedfellows. Rather than detracting from education, entertainment can reinforce it. Are we not more likely to learn if we are enjoying a museum? Moreover, as Hooper-Greenhill claims, 'in recent years, education itself has become closer to leisure. Progressive educational theory has always maintained that we learn while we are involved, committed and enjoying ourselves' (Hooper-Greenhill 1994: 114).

This inevitably leads to the consideration of how museums can best communicate with their public. A museum communicates with the visitor through presentation; the juxtaposition of objects with other objects; through interpretation; use of media; and creation of atmosphere. As Walsh comments,

> in a museum display, the object itself is without meaning. Its meaning is conferred by the 'writer', that is, the curator, the archaeologist, the historian, or the visitor, who possesses the 'cultural competence' to recognize the conferred meaning given by the 'expert'.
>
> (Walsh, Kevin 1992: 37)

But there are gaps in this interpretation (Jenkinson 1989). Recent museum ideology has been populist, attempting to open museums up to everyone, regardless of class or interest group. In fact, museums were seen as a way of compensating the deprived and minority groups, such as women and disabled people, for the deficiencies of society (Smith 1991). But, in the past, in this they have failed. As Jenkinson states: 'Ironically, our aim of a populist museum practice, informed by notions of cultural enfranchisement for "ordinary" people, is confounded by our very position within the process of cultural production' (Jenkinson 1989: 143). By trying to be neutral, by attempting to avoid controversy and debate, museums have merely reinforced the dominant contemporary political perspective, since 'putting one's faith in artefacts and technical processes is a political act, because it ignores the social relations of production and consumption which are never self-evident' (West 1988: 53).

Instead of being bias-free and objective, museums must always reflect a reality or ideology which is contemporaneous.

At the same time, 'The curatorial approach is centred on the object, from which curators extrapolate a more general historical statement. They rarely reverse the process, to look at the whole material culture and to choose representative artefacts from it, relying instead on social process and material degradation to make selections' (Porter 1988: 104). Exhibitions reinforce the norm and do not attempt to take a critical stance. Instead the approach is object-centred, portraying the past as inhuman, separate from the social context (Morton 1988). Museums create an 'artefactual' history, where a whole variety of social experiences, such as war, famine, or disease, are either ignored or trivialised (Jordanova 1989). Museums have also ignored or neglected the role of women, the working class, and different ethnic groups, in our society (Porter 1988); and have denigrated aboriginal lifestyles (Durrans 1988). Equally, global social issues – such as environmentalism, globalisation, and the rise and demise of Marxist doctrines – are rarely addressed. Instead, museums remain inherently conservative in their approach, preferring to adopt well-trodden paths of interpretation, uncertain of how to deal with controversial or 'difficult' issues (Jones 1992). All that is sometimes changed are the media through which these interpretations are made. The situation has evolved, and is evolving, with genuine attempts to redress the balance, but too often the efforts are token, and merely scratch the surface. Museums do not want to be politically motivated, they want to be neutral; but by doing so they neuter the history they portray. It is seen from their own world view, the view of their own society and ideology. In the 1990s that ideology is of the New Right.

Recently, though, some museums have started to tackle contentious issues, such as AIDS, homosexuality, death, and war. For example, 'What About AIDS?' is a new American travelling exhibition about HIV (human immuno-deficiency virus). The exhibition tackles issues such as illness, sex, substance abuse, and death. The style is clear and factual, drawing on various techniques, such as puzzles, interactives, risk games with dice, personal stories, needles, and condoms (Goldshlag Cooks 1994). Devised by the National Aids Exhibit Consortium (a partnership between a national health organisation, a national medical organisation, and a group of science museums) the exhibition has been enthusiastically received by communities all over the United States.

In 1993, Glasgow Museums and Art Galleries created a touring exhibition, 'From Here to Maternity': an exhibition on pregnancy and childbirth. Using interviews with more than twenty women (among them doctors and midwives), photographs of the birth of a baby, and around 120 objects, the exhibition explored the act of birth from a historical perspective. The exhibition was not afraid to tackle some of the more harrowing issues related to childbirth, such as cot deaths. It attempted to take the mystery out of childbirth by celebrating motherhood. As the exhibition planner commented, 'the subject may be difficult, but tackled with sensitivities it can be rewarding' (Carnegie 1994: 33).

Moore and Tucker (1994: 22) have criticised the newly popular, people-oriented approach to museum display, claiming that it leads to 'book-on-the-wall' exhibitions. By focusing on people, objects may become redundant, while curators are unlikely to have the expertise to address people-oriented issues. Instead Moore and Tucker demand a return to an object-led exhibition. Davies has responded by arguing that, on the contrary, 'it is time to adopt a wider social purpose and define more explicitly what contribution museums and art galleries make to society' (Davies 1994b: 22). Not only are social history curators increasingly interested in developing a people-oriented approach, so too are stakeholders and even the public. The philosophy of the museum, with its commitment to educate, suggests that the museum's role must go beyond that of guardianship. Decisions need to be made on where the museum stands in relation to society. Often stakeholders may make these decisions, with local politicians, for example, making demands on museums to respond to issues such as environmental education or to address ethnic minority communities. Equally, visitors may be more interested in people than in the objects, or in the social purpose of the objects.

It is worth considering the collection in relation to the public. Museums have often inherited collections with no particular policy for their acquisition. In many instances the nature of this agglomeration appears unplanned. It may contain objects of great value, such as works of art. It may simply be the lumber room of the past, of interest primarily to the social historian. Decisions about restoration, preservation, display, or de-accessioning have to be made. De-accessioning has become a live issue, particularly in the early 1990s, with museum directors such as David Fleming of the Tyne and Wear Museums Service, joining in the debate, by claiming that if circumstances permitted, he would sell off particular items in the Service's collection (Fleming 1991). A consensus is required: a consensus built on the value of the collection, not only to the museum, but also to the museum public. Questions need to be asked in this respect. Why conserve a collection? Who is the collection being preserved for? Could the collection be justified for its own sake, for research, or for education? Do the artefacts have significance for society? What are the needs of society for which the artefact is useful?

MUSEUMS, HERITAGE, AND POLITICS

The foregoing discussion suggests that museums, by definition, are political. By representing artefacts of the human condition and environment, museums are inextricably linked with politics. Since their inception, political motives have been a driving force for their establishment. To consider the museum condition is to recognise that the political past and present are omnipresent. A political dimension can be traced to the political ideologies prevalent at the time, which created and formed the museum, and in particular the governmental activities, which led to its creation or continued existence in a particular form. According to Ames, 'Museums are products of the establishment and authenticate the established or official values and image of a society in several ways, directly, by promoting and affirming the dominant values, and indirectly, by subordinating or rejecting alternate values' (Ames, M. M. 1986: 8). Ames gives as an example of subordination of values a painting that is kept in a storeroom which is likely to be forgotten.

Since the Second World War a national framework for government intervention in museums has emerged in many countries. For example, the government has assumed a greater role in UK museum provision with the creation of the Museums and Galleries Commission and the Area Museum Councils. These are advisory bodies to the museum community, which also have grant-in-aid status.[2] The role of municipal museums has also altered since the Second World War. Regional pride induced a number of additional museums to be created. Many municipal museums, though, have been subject to political influences. With dominating political parties, the nature of the museum has in certain circumstances been manipulated to reflect the political stance of the party, although the influence has tended to be more covert than openly interventionist. It should also be noted that the local government environment can be difficult for museum professionals, where 'they cannot interest council members and senior officers in the problems which must be addressed if local authority museums are to respond adequately to the new pressures they face' (Audit Commission 1991: 6).

Since the 1980s though, support for museums, from both government and private benefactors has been increasingly subject to the free market economy. Under the leadership of the New Right, this market-led economy has been hailed as a new commercial era in museums. The political debate in museums now tends to centre around issues of funding. The New Right emphasised plural funding, with governments exhorting museums to access financial resources beyond the public system, through sponsorship, charitable grants, and benefactors. Museums have been encouraged to consider money-making schemes, such as introducing shops, cafés, publishing ventures, societies of Friends, and business clubs. De-accessioning is also being considered as an alternative money generator.

The New Right principles can be discerned in independent museums, by virtue of the nature of their constitution. Although operating on a non-profit basis, they nevertheless need to generate enough income to ensure their survival. Many are only semi-independent, receiving substantial grants from external sources. However, the rest of their income needs to be obtained through the market economy, since

> The independent museums first of all depend on visitors; they are consumer oriented; they are user-friendly, so they have an instinct and a need to reach out and serve their public. They have a dialogue with their clients; we cannot possibly forget that we are there to serve.
>
> (Sekers 1984: 37)

Thus, museums are exhorted to concentrate on 'the three Es': Economy, Efficiency, and Effectiveness (Audit Commission 1991). Performance indicators and quality standards are the new language of the museum professional.

The funding debate has further considered what is also regarded as a fundamental shift in museums; the accountability factor. It is argued that in a climate of financial stringency, the use of money is being scrutinised. There is competition between the services for undetermined and scarce resources, the emphasis of municipal authorities being on empowering rather than solely providing. Funding bodies want value for money, where the political situation becomes a politics of justification (Smith 1991). However, this accountability is often seen in terms of increased visitor figures, rather than in terms of who is visiting and why. Accountability, it could be argued, is not impinging to a great extent on the operation of museums. They are perhaps not so much accountable as subject to the vagaries of specific funding bodies, and their whims for spending cuts. It may not matter how well the museum is performing when the ultimate decision is made on where to make cuts in expenditure. Did Derbyshire County Council, when it sold off part of its museums' collections in 1991, take into account the Museum Service's improved performance at cost-cutting, as claimed by its former deputy county museums officer Mick Stanley (Murdin 1991)? Perhaps the question to be asked here is why local authorities and other funding agencies actually fund museums?

Here we are not simply dealing with fifteen years of New Right hostility to what was perceived as profligate spending; we are also reacting to a new and heightened sense of social responsibility within museums themselves. In the UK, for example, many museums are subject directly to the demands of the centrally funded Museums and Galleries Commission and to the central and locally funded Area Museum Councils, not only for additional funding but also for their acceptance in the museum community. These bodies dictate policy, and individual museums react accordingly in order to obtain grants and to obtain status as a museum. The Museums and Galleries Commission's registration scheme is the manifestation of this policy.

At the end of the 1980s the Museums and Galleries Commission introduced a system whereby museums had to meet certain standards in order to be registered as a 'museum'.[3] Failure to achieve registration, for whatever reason, means ineligibility for grant aid and no recognition in the museum community. The full impact of this piecemeal policy-making on individual museums will only be clear from a historical perspective. By dictating museum standards, which are upgraded as and when required, the Commission is making demands on museums from which they have been relatively immune in the past. Registration lays the foundation of newly professionalised museum operations, incorporating new techniques of management.

External imperatives for change in museums are a crude reflection of pressures within the sector. The museum profession has developed in the twentieth century to a situation where the curators have been joined by conservators, educationalists, and designers. Museums have become public property, arousing the interest of the public at large. The question of who should run museums, and how, has moved 'from the professional domain to the public stage' (Cossons 1991: 186). Curiosity surrounds the appointment of key curators, with the national media generating comment on the appointment of such controversial figures as Elizabeth Esteve-Coll as director of the Victoria and Albert Museum and of Julian Spalding as director of the Glasgow Museums and Art Gallery Service. This interest often percolates down to the lower-tier appointments, where controversial directors are imposing their policies through choice of appointees. The appointment of Mark O'Neill as social history curator at Glasgow Museums and Art Gallery Service over Elspeth King (the front-runner, who had, with critical acclaim, developed Glasgow's show-piece museum, the People's Palace), prompted heated debate in the editorials and letters pages of the Scottish press.

Commenting on the New Right forces for change, Walsh remarks that

> in many areas, including museums, there has been an attack on profes-sionalism. This is not because of a desire to see the quality of the service improve, but rather due to a craving for economic 'efficiency', the imperative to survive in the marketplace.
>
> (Walsh, Kevin 1992: 45)

The emphasis has changed from academic thinkers to doers: those who can create wealth. At the same time, according to J. Russell, the ideal museum director 'is expected to be a combination of a lobbyist, an escort, a public relations executive, a talk show host, an investment counselor, a tour guide, an unpaid psychoanalyst, a marriage counselor and a probation officer' (Russell, quoted in Phillips 1983: 11).

The professionals, though, are not blameless: the attack on professionalism having to some extent been brought upon themselves by their distancing within ivory towers. Thus, 'museum directors are high priests in the religion of culture, and often behave like them' (Hewison 1987: 85), and 'curators . . . are all in some ways representative of a new secular priesthood' (Sorensen 1989: 66). Some have even suggested that museum collections, their acquisition, and choice for display, have tended to reflect the preference of the social background of the museum professionals, who are usually well-educated, middle-class members of the white majority (O'Neill 1991). According to Shanks and Tilley:

> The language of cultural resource management might be termed the language of cultural capitalism . . . a practice in which a series of individuals assert a hegemonic claim to the past and organize the temporal passage of this cultural capital from its historical context to the present of spectacular preservation, display, study and interpretation. The profes-sional body decides on the basis of its claimed knowledge what is worth either preserving or excavating. After subsequent interpretation or conser-vation the public, or non-professionals, are informed that it is their past, and that it should be meaningful to them.
>
> (Shanks and Tilley 1987: 24)

This has been manifested in the recent extension of the National Gallery, where the design of the new Sainsbury Wing has been dictated very much by the tastes of the curators involved.[4] They have expected the public to share their tastes and preferences, and to reflect their cultural competences. However, O'Neill (1991) claims that younger specialists, with a new social and cultural agenda, have entered the profession.

It is not just the question of who runs museums that has taken centre stage. The museum building itself is coming under public scrutiny. Controversy surrounds the construction of museum buildings – should they reflect the past or assume the designs of their time? The Prince of Wales, with his suggestion that the proposed modern design for the extension to the National Gallery in London was like a 'monstrous carbuncle', has brought this question to the forefront of public debate. The design for the new Museum of Scotland in Edinburgh has also been surrounded by controversy, with the Prince of Wales again precipitating it, by resigning as chairman of the Museum's Trustees, in protest at what he considered to be a lack of public participation in the choice of design.

These various 'public' influences on the museum have meant that 'the museum's . . . image is inseparable from those of the people who have built it, who use it, or who feel alienated from it' (Sherman 1989: 1).

TOURISM AND THE ECONOMIC DIMENSION

Museums are also located in the wider spheres of the arts, tourism, and leisure. Consequently, 'Now a foreign country with a booming tourist trade, the past has undergone the usual consequences of popularity' (Lowenthal 1985: xvii). This is manifested in both the sense of competition and degree of co-operation between these organisations. Samuel, describing the UK situation, remarks that: 'The association of heritage and the arts – institutionalised and formalised in the amalgamation of the two government ministries devoted to them – is quite recent' (Samuel 1994: 214). New initiatives in Scotland are interesting in this regard. Here museums and the arts are encouraged to build stronger links and develop consortia, this aim being a key point in the recent *Charter for the Arts in Scotland* (1993). Tourism, the arts, and museums are also co-operating, with a strategy enshrined in a report on *Tourism and the Arts in Scotland* (Scottish Tourism Co-ordinating Group 1991), for the arts and museums to attract and strengthen tourism in Scotland. This is also seen as contributing to the role played by the arts and museums in economic generation and regeneration; a role recognised since the publication of Myerscough's report on *The Economic Importance of the Arts in Britain* (Myerscough 1988). As Cossons comments,

> Museums . . . have political as well as cultural significance. They are perceived to have values more far-reaching and perhaps less altruistic than they once did. They provide economic benefits; their presence impacts upon leisure and tourism as well as education and enlightenment.
> (Cossons 1991: 186)

Myerscough (1988) indicated that around £230 million is spent each year directly on attendance at museums and art galleries in the UK. Some museums have considered the economic impact of temporary exhibitions in their own area. In 1988 Edinburgh District Council secured the 'Gold of the Pharaohs' exhibition for the City of Edinburgh Art Centre. In just over three months 447,560 people were attracted to the exhibition, making it one of the most significant events to be staged in Scotland since the Second World War (Coutts 1989). With a policy of low admission charges, the exhibition nevertheless yielded a net profit of £151,536 – what was saved on admission was spent in the exhibition shops, which had a turnover of £454,673.

A survey mounted during the exhibition, with a sample of 2,207 visitors, proved that three sections of the Scottish economy benefited quite substantially from spending associated with the exhibition. Visits to the exhibition stimulated spending on travel, food and drink, and consumer goods. It is estimated that the exhibition stimulated around £9.9 million worth of economic activity within Scotland. Admittedly, not all of this would have been 'new' or extra expenditure, and so revised estimates suggest that around £5.3 million extra expenditure occurred as a direct consequence of the exhibition. Thus, although the purpose of the exhibition was to broaden the audience for the visual arts, the economic spin-offs were extremely important.

Museums can also make a significant contribution to transforming the image of a city, from one of terminal decline to a vibrant centre. This has been the case in cities like Liverpool and Glasgow. The restoration of the Albert Dock in Liverpool has been essential for the renewal of the surrounding area and the turnaround of the city's image (Lorente 1995). The Albert Dock attracts up to 3.5 million visitors annually and includes the Beatles Museum, the Merseyside Maritime Museum, and the Tate Gallery. They have contributed not only to a renewal in the cultural life of the city, but have also acted as a catalyst for further urban regeneration.

Museums and heritage centres have become major developments; for example, £127.2 million was invested in heritage and museums in Britain in the period January–June 1988 (Urry 1990). The initiatives included a chemicals museum in Widnes and a Museum of Nursing in Lambeth. Such developments are not confined to the United Kingdom: similar developments are taking place throughout many industrial countries (Lumley 1988). A number of municipal authorities have regarded tourism as an opportunity for generating employment in a period of rapid de-industrialisation. The demise of the manufacturing industry also left a legacy of empty buildings, such as the Albert Dock in Liverpool. There is little alternative but to convert such derelict sites into tourist attractions (Urry 1990). A tourist image can be successfully constructed from cultural tourism. Museums have an essential role to play in economic intervention.

CONCLUSION

The dilemma of the modern museum was foreshadowed in the complicated roots of the museum both as a word and as a phenomenon. A number of factors have contributed to this dilemma: between the image of a museum as a temple and as a public forum; between the museum as a pedagogic pursuit and as a place for enjoyment; between the museum as a process of collecting and research, and the outreach of education and exhibition; between the scholar and the layman; between objects as unique items and objects as specimens; and between museums as private and public.

If the artefacts are wrested from their original role, then the dilemma is compounded by the creation of a role for the public. The museum collection was not originally created for the public, nor is it in its natural setting. The result is that the museum may not even be relevant to the public. Balancing the role of the collection with the role of the public is the key to the current purpose of museums. This can only be achieved through an understanding of the public in relation to the collection, which requires therefore an understanding of the collection and the museum in which it is housed. As Weil commented: 'The question we must ultimately ask ourselves is this: do our museums make a real difference in, and do they have a positive impact on, the lives of other people?' (Weil 1990: 56).

2

The marketing context

Marketing. Three syllables that conjure up images of used-car salesmen, seedy advertising ploys, and continued inducements to encourage conspicuous consumption.

(Fronville 1985: 169)

There is no denying that marketing can be corrupt and unethical. It cajoles, manipulates, distorts, and even deceives. Perhaps more sinister to some, though, is that nothing is sacrosanct from the inroads of marketing, not even religion. Take, for example, the packaging of politicians, where the marketability of the personality and the policies is paramount, and the Gulf War campaign, which was more a marketing campaign than a military campaign. The cult of the pop singer Madonna owes much to her recognition that she is a marketable commodity that constantly needs to create new spectacles. The trial of O. J. Simpson underlined the importance of image, where he wore a grey suit and crisp white shirt throughout the trial, rather than a dark suit which was deemed to evoke a 'threatening' personality to the jury. Each of these suggests an era where marketing is omnipresent, the perpetrator of a consumer culture which has engulfed if not the globe, then at least Western cultures.

Why would the hallowed halls of museums want to have anything to do with this corrupt and corrupting concept? What has marketing got to do with conservation, preservation, research, and education? The concept of marketing in the museum context is a recent one. An examination of the available literature shows that one of the earliest references to museum marketing is contained in 'Broadening the Concept of Marketing' (Kotler and Levy 1969). Kotler and Levy comment that, 'for many people museums are cold marble mausoleums that house miles of relics that soon give way to yawns and tired feet'; and that, 'a large number of citizens are uninterested in museums' (ibid.: 11). They then go on to pose the question: 'Is this indifference due to failure in the manner of presenting what museums have to offer?' (ibid.: 11). At the time Kotler and Levy were writing, though, museums were relatively immune to marketing forces.

Perhaps it would be fair to say that even now, many museums would not be adopting marketing techniques if they had not been persuaded (forced) to do so, by various stakeholders. Equally, as Bryant astutely observed, 'the goods on offer in the first public museums effectively sold themselves . . . Today the circumstances are somewhat different' (1988: 1). In the UK, for example, while overall the number of visits to museums rose during the 1980s, attendance per museum in the UK fell, from an average per museum of 72,000 visitors in 1978, to 48,000 in 1988 (Middleton 1990). Competition was becoming more acute as the growth in number of new museums resulted in a reduction in attendance per museum. The public have also become increasingly demanding, expecting quality of service, as alternative leisure offerings recognise customer service as a competitive weapon.

Governments have taken the lead in encouraging the adoption of marketing, emphasising quality of service and the development of performance indicators. Municipal authorities have also made demands on museums which have required them to develop marketing. In a climate of financial stringency, where, in many countries, municipal authorities' budgets are decreasing in real terms, the use of money is being scrutinised. Funding bodies want value for money. Too often, though, this accountability equates with increased visitor figures. Museums have come to regard marketing in terms of the benefits that can accrue from the hope that marketing will increase visitor figures, and thereby directly or indirectly generate further income for the museum.

The language of management is relatively new to museums, only still reluctantly being adopted, several decades behind most other institutions. The museum profession, trained in conservation and preservation techniques, has little comprehension of management. It has had to learn a whole new way of thinking, a whole new language. As in the health service and higher education, the debate between 'professionals' and 'managers' is a live one.

The new orientation towards the public where, as in the health service and higher education the patient/student brings money to the service, has challenged the *raison d'être* of the museum. In the UK, in particular, where free admission has been a tradition of many museums, charging for admission has become a contentious issue. The proposition that the movement of the turnstile should trigger funding has led to heated debate. Generally, for laudable social reasons, the British museum profession are against the introduction of compulsory charges (Davies 1990: 2). Anxieties are most acutely felt in the museums' other core functions of conservation, the preservation and management of collections, and research.[1] In many cases, 'curators often . . . perceive the commercial function as an embarrassing second-rate enterprise that compromises the museum's standards' (Duchesne *et al.* 1988: 1).

Museums, though, are becoming much more receptive to marketing. In the UK, for example, in 1988 there were merely five full-time marketing posts in museums, while by 1992 this had increased to forty (Museums and Galleries Commission 1992). In the annals of museum professionals' journals, marketing is no longer a dirty word; it is now accepted as a fundamental aspect of a museum's organisation. However, interestingly, there are still a lot of misconceptions about the role and practice of marketing within the profession itself, while there has been an academic backlash against the marketing concept in museums. To appreciate the issues involved, it is worth considering where museum marketing lies in the overall history of marketing.

THE HISTORICAL DIMENSION

Although marketing has probably existed since the days of Ancient Greece (Nevett and Nevett 1987), and was being studied in American and German universities in the early 1900s (Jones and Monieson 1990), the marketing era came into its own in 1950s America. Historically, marketing is principally concerned with the exchange of goods in trade. As a surplus of goods is produced, they are traded for other goods that satisfy a need or want of both parties in the exchange. In modern exchange transactions, money is the usual medium of exchange, but the concept remains the same.

With the onset of industrialisation, the production of goods became more geographically concentrated, in factories in towns which were springing up to serve these industries. Their production was also carried out on a much larger scale for distribution not just locally, but often nationally, and even internationally. The producer no longer had immediate contact with the market.

A number of eras can be discerned in the development of what is now understood as the marketing era. The philosophy of the marketing concept emerged in the third of these eras, the marketing era, preceded by the production and sales eras. Surprisingly, though, forty years after the marketing era was acknowledged, a considerable number of businesses have still not adopted the marketing concept.

During the second half of the nineteenth century, the fruits of the Industrial Revolution brought about the production era. There was strong demand for manufactured goods, which poured into the marketplace. New technology and working practices enabled the mass production of goods. Little or no account was taken of the customer in the production of the goods; the goods effectively sold themselves. The production orientation continued until the beginning of the twentieth century.

In the 1920s, during the Depression, consumer demand for manufactured goods subsided. The world production of goods began to exceed demand. Producers were competing for a finite market. Goods, which were now being made quite efficiently, needed to be 'sold' to the consumer. The sales era lasted until the mid-1950s, where sales were viewed as the major means of increasing profit. This was the era of personal selling and advertising.

Increasingly, though, business people began to recognise that efficient production and promotion of products did not guarantee that people would buy them. The marketing era, or the era of customer orientation, held that customer needs must be determined before producing goods, rather than manufacture products and then persuade customers to purchase them. Peter Drucker (1954) is traditionally held to have raised marketing to comprise the single most important management function and the key to success in business. He was the first commentator to argue forcefully for a marketing orientation in businesses: that is, to view the business from the customer's standpoint and to place the customer at the very centre of its endeavours.

> The customer is the foundation of a business and keeps it in existence. He [*sic*] alone gives employment. And it is to supply the customer that society entrusts wealth-producing resources to the business enterprise . . . Because it is its purpose to create a customer, any business enterprise has two – and only these two – basic functions: marketing and innovation . . . Marketing is the distinguishing, the unique function of the business . . . Actually marketing is so basic that it is not just enough to have a strong sales department and to entrust marketing to it. Marketing is not only much broader than selling, it is not a specialised activity at all. It is the whole business seen from the point of view of its final result, that is, the customer's point of view. Concern and responsibility for marketing must therefore permeate all areas of the enterprise.
> (Drucker 1954: 35–6)

In order to be competitive, products not only had to take into account the needs and wants of customers, they had to start with them. Marketing theories actualised the exchange process where human needs and wants were satisfied. The increasing sophistication of needs and wants create needs for new products, which are satisfied by the producer. At the same time, new needs are created by introducing products for which there had been no previous demand. The consumers are persuaded, through marketing techniques, that they want this new product. Thus, the management process of marketing involves the process of planning and implementing the exchange mechanism to the benefit of both the consumer and, particularly, the producer. It has been suggested that marketing is manipulative and monopoly-seeking, that in many instances customers are unaware of their needs; that marketing shapes needs by determining customers' perceptions and persuading them of the attractiveness of the product to be sold (Dickinson *et al.* 1986).

This process has been interpreted by Marxists through the concept of 'surplus value'.[2] Surplus value represents new value that is greater than the exchange value of a product. Thus, the product has more value for the producer than the consumer; the exchange is unequal. As various producers compete for customers, competition becomes the driving force for growth. Marketing was developed in this climate to create advantages for one competitor over another.

The way in which marketing can be manipulated appears to be almost unethical, and is certainly justification for the bad name that marketing has received in some circles. However, it could equally be argued that it may be possible to persuade consumers that they want a new product, but that this cannot be a long-term strategy. Consumers will soon discover that they have been duped, that the product does not meet any real need on their part. They will withdraw their future custom and will recommend that friends and relatives do so too. The Sinclair C5 electric car is a case in point. No amount of persuasion would force the public to admit that they had a need for a car that looked more like a pedal car, and that travelled little faster than a bicycle. Moreover only one in ten new consumer goods survives in the marketplace. The public are not gullible fools!

However, to suggest that new products are created only when the public expresses a need for them would be to stifle innovation, which Drucker (1954) considered to be as important as marketing. New products need to be tested on the public. Otherwise we would never have known that we admired the work of a Henry Moore or an Eduardo Paolozzi; we would never have known how exciting a visit behind the scenes of a museum could be; we would never have known that we would have enjoyed attending a business function in a museum gallery.

Marketing can manipulate, and in the wrong hands could be unethical. However, marketing is merely an orientation within a museum which sets out to achieve the museum's mission using a variety of practical tools. Marketing is intended to look to the future, to have a long-term strategy. Cheating the public can have only short-term results, and certainly will not achieve the mission of the museum.

It was not until 1969, in Kotler and Levy's seminal article 'Broadening the Concept of Marketing', that marketing was regarded as an all-pervasive activity which applied to services, people, and non-profit organisations as much as to manufactured goods. Kotler and Levy contended that because of the postwar social change in the US and the emergence of professionally managed, non-business organisations, such as museums, the concept of marketing ought to be broadened. Marketing techniques therefore needed to be transferred to non-business organisations, since, 'the choice facing those who manage non-business organisations is not whether to market or not to market, for no organisation can avoid marketing. The choice is whether to do it well or poorly' (Kotler and Levy 1969: 15).

The concept of the profit exchange mechanism has moved from the domain solely of goods to that of services and non-profit organisations. Although some non-business organisations adopted the tenets of marketing more quickly than did others, on the whole many have remained production-oriented or sales-oriented. Addison has accused museums of remaining production-oriented: 'Museums must make a fundamental shift away from being inwardly oriented organizations, production-oriented in marketing terms, to becoming organizations more responsive to external forces and audiences, and more flexible in terms of attracting corporate and individual support' (Addison 1993: 2).

A reading of many articles and anecdotes on marketing in museum journals would suggest that museums are to a degree still production-oriented. The museum is resigned to the stasis of the collection, and somehow the public should be interested in it, and wish to visit. Most museums though, also subscribe to the sales era, believing marketing to be merely promotion, whether it be through personal selling, advertising, or sales promotion. Traditionally, marketing has been seen as a publicity officer's role, rather than as a senior management function. Marketing is too often regarded as a bolt-on feature, which is not integral to the museum's activities. Frequently, it is a separate function managed by a junior member of staff who has responsibility for publicity. Is it any wonder that marketing has had its detractors?

Few museums are anywhere near attaining a marketing orientation. Many curators have undervalued the part that marketing can play in the museum. They have also been deterred by the connotations of the word 'marketing' itself, which smacks of jargon and a commercialism which is alien to the world of museums. Peter Lewis, for example, refers to marketing as 'mumbo jumbo' and declares that 'reference to the seven Cs, the four Ms and the three Ps of marketing do nothing but reinforce our doubts' (Lewis 1988: 147). Marketing somehow is seen as compromising the integrity of the museum – it has become a commercial venture, far removed from serving the public. On the contrary, marketing is an integral part of meeting the purpose of the museum. It is guided by that purpose and creates the space in which that purpose can be realised (Arts Council of Great Britain 1993). Commentators on museum marketing have consequently tended to be polarised towards either accepting or denouncing marketing principles.

A distinction needs to be made between a marketing-led and a market-led approach. A market-led approach finds out what people want and gives it to them. This is perfectly acceptable in an organisation which is profit-led, but entirely inappropriate when the purpose is of a social nature. Instead, a museum needs to be marketing-led, which involves the more imaginative task (and this is where Drucker's 'innovation' comes into its own) of linking the purpose of the museum to the potential users of the museum. Consequently, it has been shown that it is not necessarily appropriate to automatically transfer concepts derived from a for-profit business situation to a non-profit service, such as museums (Bradford 1991; McLean 1993). Thus, 'Marketing has most to contribute when it has been thoroughly translated into the situation and culture of the organisation that it is intended to serve' (Wright 1990: 13).

Possibly the chief difficulty in comprehending marketing is because it has developed over time, and has not remained as a static theory. As circumstances in Western economies and societies have changed, so the tenets of marketing have altered accordingly. For many this only serves to complicate matters. It is also further complicated by marketing's increasing aspirations to dominate over other operations within an organisation. Thus, 'for an organisation to succeed in a complex, competitive, ever-changing world, marketing must not only take precedence over production, human resources, finance and so on, but . . . these functional areas are actually part and parcel of marketing' (Brown 1995: 52). Marketing, it is contended, is facing a crisis (Brady and Davis 1993; Wilson and McDonald 1994): a crisis of identity. The complexity of the contemporary marketing discipline has led to much misunderstanding and criticism. It is worth considering this criticism with regard to museums.

MARKETING BAITING

Marketing baiting has become a popular pastime with academics writing on museums within the heritage context and in the postmodern condition. Thus:

> In a consumer-led society, in which everything has its price, and market values are unchallenged, [heritage] 'traffics' in history and 'commodifies' the past. It turns real-life suffering into tourist spectacle, while at the same time creating simulacra of a past that never was. Museums are particularly suspect. They are 'part of the leisure and tourist business', and thus intimately linked to the Disneylands and theme parks.
>
> (Samuel 1994: 242)

The past offered by museums is a commodity, a marketable product devoid of any traces of meaning. All our yesterdays are today's commodities. The past on offer is simulacra, hyperreality, a past to gaze at, but which is no longer authentic. Museums have sold out to the voracious appetites of the 'marketing men' where commercial success, value for money, and quality and quantity of service are paramount. They manipulate the past until there is nothing but appearance (Walsh, Kevin 1992). This is compounded by the fact that

> Man [*sic*] is limited to what his senses perceive of the world. His approval can be won only by influencing that perception. He can be enticed only by playing skilfully on his sensations and feelings. And the art of enticement requires a knowledge of how to conjure up appearances out of words and to present objects and people in a flattering light.
>
> (Laufer and Paradeise 1990: 3)

'Marketing men' are technicians, doers not thinkers: their role limited to that of winning over the public. Belief in what they are doing is not a precondition of their actions – they are not there to think, but to act. Their ultimate intention is to persuade, using, 'a collection of vulgar processes within the reach of anyone' (Laufer and Paradeise 1990: 5). Moreover, marketing is seen as a symbol of youthful America which is besieging the old order and tradition of a European culture. Marketing though was introduced to American museums at roughly the same period as to UK museums (Robinson 1983; Fronville 1985; Adams and Boatright 1986). American museums have also been beset by the dilemmas of a profit-led marketing discipline and the values of museums (Addison 1986; Ames, P. J. 1989). Nevertheless, American museums have led the field in adopting marketing techniques and innovating with marketing practice. In 1983, for example, Colonial Williamsburg in Virginia spent the incredible sum of a million dollars on advertising (Hooper-Greenhill 1994)!

Marketing and postmodernism also go hand in hand, where 'Consumerism and postmodernism . . . share similar ideological foundations' (Ames, M. M. 1992: 165). One defines the parameters for the other; one creates the existence for the other. Each individual is in control of his or her own needs, since need is subjective. Marketing anticipates these needs by obtaining information about them and meeting them. Marketing acts as the medium of communication between the producer satisfying the need, and the consumer whose need has been expressed (or has been anticipated). Anything that can be marketed is marketed. Even by anticipating need, marketing can allay accusations of orchestrating need, since in every culture there is a need to signify difference. Each individual has distinct needs, since 'Everyone is his or her own authority, just as the consumer is always right' (Ames, M. M. 1992: 165). One argument goes:

> Those museums forced into the market, along with the heritage industry, rarely respond to the needs of the visitor. They merely respond to the perceived needs of an abstract element within a marketing niche, where revenue performance is the prime factor in any equation.
>
> (Walsh, Kevin 1992: 64)

On the other hand, marketing is also accused not only of ignoring the visitor, but of pandering to the visitor: 'To cater successfully to tourists from other cultures, a producer must avoid offending his [*sic*] customers. His product must be "market-led". But how much will his product have to be fashioned in an alien image to suit his audience?' (Bonniface and Fowler 1993: 4).

Marketing is denounced as an economic paradigm that rejects social relations, where 'the marketing concept suppresses our vision of the interaction between individual and objects as a complex social and cultural event. It becomes instead a "purchase", an uncomplicated, underspecified act of getting, having and consuming' (McCracken 1990: 42). The objects and experience are the commodity that is consumed. There is no recognition of the complexity of the object, of the experience, of the historical process. Instead marketing radiates only historical surfaces (Walsh, Kevin 1992).

Marketing is a 'product' of its time, a legitimator of the political processes in power. It legitimates New Right thinking. The products created in the 'culture industry' are a 'mass deception', part of the New Right hegemonic project (Adorno and Horkheimer 1979). Marketing negates any notion of self-fulfilment, the only needs being fulfilled are those of the predominant ideology. Culture is homogenised, the death knell being the influence of North American programmes on television. Individuality is lost under the weight of the over-whelming dominance of Disney.

Despite this, marketing is sold as a social paradigm. As Ames states, 'the marketplace is typically represented as an ideal paradigm for organizing social as well as economic relations' (Ames, M. M. 1992: 166). Yet according to sociologists such as Bourdieu and Baudrillard, this would mean recognising that man's (*sic*) nature is immersed in culture. But 'what [the marketing concept] has been traditionally unprepared to comprehend are the social and cultural contexts in which [consumer choice behaviour] takes place' (McCracken 1990: 41).

Recent postmodern (re-)interpretations of marketing are addressing this paucity of social and cultural contexts in the understanding of the marketing concept

(Firat 1991; Venkatesh *et al.* 1993; Firat and Venkatesh 1993; Firat *et al.* 1995; Brown 1995). These (re-)interpretations, though, are the products of academic thinkers, not of the practical doers, the marketing people themselves, who are still acting as technicians. Practice is still economically motivated, not socially refined. Revenue performance is still the driving force behind marketing initiatives. The New Right emphasis on market forces permeates every part of the marketing concept, belying the cries of marketers in non-profit sectors that marketing sets out to achieve the goals or mission of the organisation. If the marketing concept is not grounded in the social and cultural aspects of society, then how can it expect 'effectively' and 'efficiently' to address social and cultural issues in the goals of a museum? But is it true to say that museums address social and cultural issues? Such arguments are putative where museums are equally guilty of neglecting the social and cultural context. It is only relatively recently that any concerted effort has been made to tackle social and cultural issues in displays, to locate objects in their social context. Many museums still reflect a chronological interpretation of objects. Can marketing be blamed for perpetuating the tradition of museum interpretation? If museums expect marketing to have social relevance, then surely museums must be socially relevant first, and reinforce this in their mission.

The marketing baiters continue by asserting that marketing's master (*sic*) is commercialism, the market forces' profit. Marketers are not social workers. They exist to persuade in order to make 'the best possible financial outcome' (Diggle 1984: 22). Services are created not because they meet customer needs, but because they enable museums to compete, to attract more visitors, to generate additional income. Marketers are not idealist thinkers, they are doers. They may do things for laudable social reasons, for they are human after all, and have hearts and consciences. But at the end of the day, they will not receive their pay cheque unless they have got results. And in marketing terms these results are increased visitor figures (sometimes perhaps increased visitor profile), increased income, and increased prestige. Thus, talking about Tyne and Wear Museums, Runyard applauds the marketing efforts of their newly appointed 'professional marketing office', since, 'In 1992 their attendance figures doubled and they enjoy an increasingly high profile and a greater sense of identity' (Runyard 1994: 5).

A response to these criticisms of marketing might suggest that the critics are referring to 'heritage' which is distinct from 'museums'; that it is the heritage industry that is spurious, and that museums still remain true to the authenticity of their objects. To some extent it would be fair to lay the blame at the door of heritage. But, like it or not, museums are also heritage. They may rely more on artefacts to peddle their wares than heritage centres which use simulacra, hyperreality, and fantasy to create history. Museums also create history – the artefacts may be authentic, but the experience is not authentic. By removing the objects from their past, they immediately represent something inauthentic. Their display and interpretation is a created history. It may not be fantasy or a distorted history, but it is often no more true to the past than is heritage. Recent attempts to locate objects in their past by displaying them, for example, in the context of their use, in dioramas, still imposes a (re-)presentation of that past, even if a genuine attempt is being made to be true to the past. The use of media, such as videos, smells, and sounds, are used just as frequently in many museums nowadays as in heritage centres. They create an artificial past, an aura, a past of 'the tourist gaze'. The object is real, but in a museum setting it is hyperreal. Museums cannot ignore their place in heritage. They may think themselves superior, but in fact they are merely the apotheosis of heritage. Museums are caught up in the shackles of heritage. They contribute to the commodification of the past.

But none of this is new. The objects on display at the great fairs of the nineteenth century were also commodities, (re-)presentations of a nation's pride in the commodities that it had produced. These objects were no more 'authentic' than the objects in museums today. The museum situation has not changed. What has changed, though, is the (re-)interpretation of the purpose of museums. Museums are intended to educate, whereas heritage centres are intended to entertain, although increasingly heritage centres are also offering educational experiences (Mintz 1994). What makes a museum an educative experience as opposed to entertaining, if the experience it offers is of simulacra? If museums were merely to entertain, then why not be heritage centres? In order to enable the function of education – or as the American Association of Museums (1984) prefers to put it, 'learning' – and also, research, a museum needs to transcend the gaze, to (re-)present a past that has an educative value. Of course, this is to presuppose that all visitors to museums want to learn. This, though, is a museum dilemma, not a marketing problem. However, by using the carrot of entertainment to persuade people to visit, marketing is then beating a stick of its own making. Where is the line drawn between education and entertainment?

Marketing is 'commercialisation' only when the goal is to commercialise, or where the goal is not clearly being pursued and marketing becomes distorted. Financial market pressure need not modify the purposes of the museum in response to the need for funds. Instead the museum should carefully balance its goals as reflecting 'the public benefit'. The museum will only attract more visitors and additional funding if it can generate enough interest amongst a sufficient diversity of people who will wish to return again and again. Funding bodies want to see statistics that prove that they are putting money into something worthwhile; in other words, that the public deem it worthwhile to visit. Thus, contrary to Kevin Walsh (1992), rather than put revenue performance before the needs of visitors, in the long term, revenue performance will depend on marketing responding to the needs of visitors. If the goal of the museum is to democratise learning, then marketing should be harnessed to achieve this. Marketing is not merely a commercial function of the museum. On the contrary, the commercial aspect should exist only to ensure that the goal of the museum is achieved.

Is marketing to blame? Or are the manipulators of marketing to blame? Marketing should set out to achieve the goals of the museum. If marketing contributes to the hegemonic project of the New Right, then that is because the museum's own purpose dictates it. Marketing as a philosophy seeks to achieve the purpose of the museum, and is not subject to the will of external forces. The marketing baiters seem to suggest that marketing is the predominant ideology's conspiracy. It is a management tool implanted on organisations in order to confirm the authority of the New Right. Marketing people are the puppets of that authority, manipulating and cajoling in order to legitimate their masters' (*sic*) power.

It may be that the museum has little influence in choosing its own purpose, being dictated to by, for example, its funding bodies. However, to suggest that marketing has any role to play in directing the purpose of the museum would raise marketing above its masters (*sic*). Marketing is not to blame for the mass deception of society. It is merely a management tool, which in enlightened hands can be directed towards achieving all that a public-minded museum could wish.

It seems appropriately ironic that marketing, which was heralded as the answer to all our ills, is blamed for our failings. Marketing has become a scapegoat, a whipping boy which is held up as the emblem of all that is wrong with contemporary society. Marketing may be corrupt and unethical, but only if it is in pursuit of corrupt and unethical goals. Marketing is not the cause of change in society; it is merely a tool that is appropriated by society.

Equally, if museums have got their marketing wrong, they are not to blame. For one thing, we cannot become marketing experts overnight – museums have only been practising marketing for a matter of years. For another, the museum's purpose is evolving, to embrace a social role that was not inherent in its history. Marketing too is still evolving and learning, particularly in the non-profit service sector. Furthermore, as McCracken has pointed out, 'the marketing model . . . may even obscure some of the very things we need most to understand and manipulate' (McCracken 1990: 42). Perhaps that is why marketing lays itself open so easily to baiting.

WHAT IS MARKETING?

It is time to consider what is actually meant by marketing. There are various definitions which could be found from a perusal of the marketing textbooks. For example,

> Marketing is the management process responsible for identifying, anticipating and satisfying consumers' requirements profitably.
> (UK Chartered Institute of Marketing)

> Marketing is the process of planning and executing the conception, pricing, promotion, and distribution of ideas, goods, and services to create exchanges that satisfy individual and organizational goals.
> (American Marketing Association)

Marketing consists of individual and organisational activities that facilitate and expedite exchange relationships in a dynamic environment through the creation, distribution, promotion and pricing of goods, services, and ideas.

(Dibb *et al.* 1991: 5)

Marketing is the management function that most explicitly links an organization to its external environment – not only to its current and prospective customers, but also to its funding sources and other relevant constituencies.

(Lovelock and Weinberg 1988: 10)

This last definition refers to non-profit organisations in particular, although it does integrate Kotler's (1972) generic concept of marketing. This concept widens the notion of customers to include all the relations between an organisation and all of its publics. These publics would include, for example, employee publics, supplier publics, and government publics. This generic concept is the precursor of the relationship marketing formulation which recognises the importance of multiple markets.

More specifically for museums:

Marketing is the management process which confirms the mission of a museum or gallery and is then responsible for the efficient identification, anticipation and satisfaction of its users.

(Lewis 1991: 26)

This is the most useful definition for museums, although 'users' is a limiting concept, since it ignores the various other publics that need to be recognised. Thus, it would be better to add 'stakeholders and other relevant constituencies'. The key task then is to understand the nature of the organisation and the environment in which it operates, and to balance the needs and concerns of its many constituencies.

Lovelock and Weinberg (1988) detail the four fundamental concepts of marketing: exchange, market segmentation, the marketing mix, and competition. Exchange is considered to be the very essence of the marketing condition (Baker 1987; Houston and Gassenheimer 1987; Dwyer *et al.* 1987). The concept of exchange involves the transaction of value between two parties. Thus, what benefits does the consumer seek to obtain and what costs is the consumer prepared to pay? In museums the costs may be financial, manifested in the admission cost, but they are more complicated than that, particularly where no charge is made. An exchange should be satisfying to both the producing organisation and the consumer, otherwise only short-term benefits will be gained by either party. It is also difficult for the consumer to perceive what is being offered, and so defining the product is also more complex.

The concept of exchange is a useful one for museums, particularly because it does not reconcile with the notion of consumer sovereignty (Foxall 1984). Rather than the consumer dominating in the exchange process, the exchange should be of mutual benefit to both parties. One of the fundamental misinterpretations of marketing in museums is that implicit in the marketing model is the belief: 'The customer is king'. On the contrary, though, 'marketing = exchange is very deeply entrenched in the disciplinary psyche' (Brown 1995: 39). By implication, then, the marketing = exchange analogy puts the museum and the user on an equal footing.

Each person is different and requires different benefits, and is prepared to pay through differing costs. Needs, behaviour patterns, and characteristics will vary. In addition a museum will achieve its mission by attracting some members of the public rather than others. Market segmentation groups individuals according to predefined characteristics and focuses attention on these groups or segments. Segmentation, then, requires an understanding of the market.

Segmentation is an invaluable tool for museums, particularly where their goals are social. Although in an ideal world most museums would wish to attract every member of the public, in reality decisions have to be made as to whom to focus attention upon. Dividing the public up into groups with associated characteristics is the most logical solution, to ensure that the museum's energies are focused and are not spread too thinly.

Marketing involves the use of a number of marketing tools to execute a marketing strategy. These tools together facilitate the exchange transaction between the organisation and its customer. Traditionally the tools have fallen into four broad areas: the product that is offered; the price that is charged in the exchange, both the amount and how it is paid; the distribution of the product or when, where, and how the product is delivered to the consumer; and promotion, the nature of the messages communicated to the prospective customers and influencers about the organisation and its products, as well as the means by which these messages are transmitted. Collectively these tools are known as the marketing mix, or 4Ps. Basically the principle of the marketing mix is to break down an offering 'into a number of component parts and to arrange them into manageable subject areas for making strategic decisions. Decisions on one element of the mix can only be made by reference to other elements' (Palmer 1994: 32).

Competition has been a driving force for marketing in businesses. Competitive firms pose a threat to the success and survival of any organisation, and so it is essential to be aware of and anticipate the activities of the competition, in order to counter or deflect the threats. Museums tend to have little sense of competition, either direct competitors (such as other museums) or indirect competitors (other leisure opportunities). Adjusting to competitive realities can often be difficult for museums, particularly where in the past there was no requirement to anticipate and respond to 'competitors'. Originally most museums were established 'to fill gaps in the existing social fabric or to supplement and extend the offerings of existing institutions – not to compete with them' (Lovelock and Weinberg 1988: 14). The political, economic, and market situations have changed in museums, however, necessitating a competitive orientation. Economic realities and demands from funders, exacerbated by the expansion and developments in the leisure industries, have created a competitive environment to which museums must respond.

It is clear then that the environment of marketing consists of many changing forces: political activities, legislative changes, changing economic conditions, societal pressures, and technological innovation. Each of these forces impacts on how effectively an organisation can facilitate and expedite exchanges. An organisation needs to keep abreast of these changes and even anticipate them. In museums these changes have placed increased significance on the discipline of marketing. As change has accelerated in the museum's environment, so the need for marketing to cope with this speed of change has increasingly been recognised.

Marketing then is a set of tools used to achieve a philosophy – a philosophy that sees what museums are doing through the eyes of the people they are doing it for: both the people who use museums and those who support museums. Marketing is an attitude of mind, an attitude that permeates throughout an organisation. These attitudes are then transmitted into actions which are implemented through the marketing tools. According to the marketing concept 'an organisation should try to provide products that satisfy customers' needs through a co-ordinated set of activities that also allows the organisation to achieve its goals' (Dibb *et al.* 1991: 13). It has already been proven that a marketing orientation is the key to long-term profitability and survival in business organisations (Baker and Hart 1989). A marketing orientation in a museum could by implication be the key to achieving the museum's goals and to ensure survival.

It is apparent from such a definition of the marketing concept that marketing affects all types of organisational activities. Consequently management must adopt the marketing concept wholeheartedly. Leadership should come from the top if marketing is to be the basis of the goals and decisions of the organisation, and if everyone concerned with the organisation is to be convinced of the merits of marketing and equally wholeheartedly adopt marketing principles. Museums are particularly guilty of ignoring this, leaving marketing – or more often what is thought to be marketing, that is publicity and selling – to a junior member of staff. However, as Drucker (1954) stressed, marketing is too important to be left to the marketing department. It must permeate throughout the whole organisation, and in order to do so must have the full backing of the leaders. In the museum situation these will be not only the museum director and senior staff, but also the museum's trustees or board.

The separation of the marketing department or function from other departments does not necessarily facilitate good working relations between the different functions. Where marketing assumes a significant role in the museum's staffing structure, with a marketing department and marketing officers, it does not necessarily tally that its influence is more pervasive than in a museum which does not employ marketing officers. On the contrary, these marketing personnel have other, considerably greater, difficulties in overcoming hostile attitudes from some staff members to the extending influence of marketing. In a smaller museum where few people are employed, it may be easier to negotiate the integration of marketing techniques, when opposition is encountered to a lesser degree or on a smaller scale. Thus, although the marketing may be more sophisticated in terms of the types of techniques adopted, a museum with a marketing department or officer may not necessarily reflect more of a marketing orientation. Co-operation needs to be facilitated from the other members of the staff. To overcome the attitude that marketing is a threat to the other functions, a sense of trust and a validation of the other functions need to be forged.

Many museum professionals are still suspicious of marketing, and perhaps rightly so, since in many circumstances what is considered to be marketing is in fact equated to a 'hard sell'. If fears are to be alleviated within the profession itself, then the museum must ensure that the basic conditions for marketing are being met. This may require reorganisation, a restructuring that will enable the co-ordination of all the museum's activities. The member of staff responsible for marketing should be part of the senior management. There must be communication between different departments or functions within the museum. Regular staff meetings are essential. It will take time for a museum even to begin to develop a marketing orientation. It will take time, as well as encouragement and commitment, to inculcate a marketing philosophy in the staff. It is important therefore to think long term.

To some extent it could be argued that the state of marketing is an ideal, a dream statement, an unattainable goal. Success in marketing does not assuage funding bodies that are determined to make budget cuts. As other non-profit organisations have found, goal achievement does not necessarily equal increased funding. Equally, to imply that marketing will succeed so long as the museum's leaders are committed to it, and the staff can also be persuaded of its merits, is also to oversimplify. It is unlikely that marketing will be fully assimilated and appreciated by every figure in authority in a museum, or that every member of staff will be persuaded that it is an essential aspect of a museum's activities. How realistic is it to expect curators, who are professionals in the care of objects, to appreciate the language and norms of management? Moreover, if marketing were so successful, why is it not unequivocally embraced by every organisation? Why are there so many doubters of its efficacy?

Museums have found they need to tread warily when adopting marketing techniques. There are a number of problems associated with creating a marketing orientation, a number of hurdles to overcome. The path of marketing is littered with danger areas, particularly in a context where it is a relatively new departure for discussion. Those charged with developing marketing in a museum need to inject a degree of realism into what can at times seem like a crusade. Marketing is a guiding tool, not a prescription.

NON-PROFIT AND SERVICES MARKETING

It is understandably difficult for a museum professional to relate to the profit-oriented references to exchanges of mutual benefit to both customer and manufacturer in the commercial marketing textbooks. Of more relevance are the services marketing and non-profit marketing literature, although the former tend to refer to organisations such as health services and financial services, while the latter tend to take examples from medical and conservation charities. Museums are service organisations, and are usually non-profit. In order to understand the unique position of museums, it is necessary to consider them in relation to both of these sectors.

Non-profit institutions, according to Lovelock and Weinberg (1988), require a distinctive approach to marketing because of the following characteristics. By definition, non-profit organisations do not seek to make a profit for redistribution to owners or shareholders: if they do generate a surplus, they reinvest it. Thus their goals are non-financial, which creates difficulties in measuring success or failure in strictly financial terms, particularly since they have multiple goals. This is exacerbated if no entrance fee is charged to visitors. When a payment is made, sales revenue goals can be set as well as performance measures in terms of revenue. Related to this, non-profit organisations need to attract revenue from sources other than sales revenue. Sometimes these resources are free, such as volunteers or donated facilities, or are at a reduced rate, for example, tax concessions. Resource attraction in museums, it could be argued, is more complex than is suggested here. Resources are not merely financial or 'in kind'. A museum is also dependent on recognition and on moral and professional support. Thus, trustees may not fund the museum, but their status in society may contribute to the prestige of the museum. Similarly, a municipal authority may not fund a museum, but its encouragement and recognition could be essential to a museum's existence.

Non-profit organisations also tend to be expertise-driven rather than customer-driven. Lovelock and Weinberg (1988), drawing from Andreasen (1982), have highlighted a number of indicators:

1   Managers and board members are so enamoured of their organisation's programmes and services that they believe these must be what the public needs.
2   Marketing activities tend to centre on stimulating awareness through advertising and publicity, and on developing promotions that will give prospective users an incentive to act.
3   When prospective users fail to respond to the organisation's offerings, this disinterest is ascribed to ignorance or inertia, rather than to shortcomings in these offerings and the way they are priced and distributed.
4   Little or no use is made of marketing research, and such research as is conducted fails to assess the needs and concerns of people whom the organisation is trying to serve. Findings that conflict with management beliefs tend to be ignored.
5   Distinction in market segments are ignored or played down in preference to development of 'one best strategy' to suit everyone.
6   Marketing managers and staff members are chosen for their product knowledge or communication skills, rather than for their marketing

expertise and sensitivity to the needs of the people the organisation is trying to reach.

7   Management and board members assume that the only form of competition comes from organisations similar to their own: they ignore the presence of 'generic' competitors which offer alternative solutions to similar consumer needs.

It is easy to allow a love of the objects in the museum's collection to obscure the reality that the public may not be equally enamoured with them. It is also easy to forget that there are a plethora of alternative activities to occupy the minds and time of the public, and that they may feel a museum is not relevant to them, or may not even be aware of its existence. Moreover, the public are making increasing demands for quality of service. As Lovelock and Weinberg warn: 'Numerous nonprofit organizations have discovered to their dismay that consumer expectations are higher than management had anticipated, and that users demand quality service from public and nonprofit organizations just as they do from private firms' (Lovelock and Weinberg 1988: 7).

A market-driven museum, on the other hand, may compromise its integrity by pandering to the current tastes and fashions of society. It needs to take a longer-term view, if it is to encourage learning rather than just to entertain. The profit motive appeals to the lowest common denominator, which is the widest possible audience. But inevitably, some art, for example, is not immediately popular. It needs to be given the chance to be absorbed into the culture. It needs to be recognised that to be populist, all exhibitions will not appeal to all audiences, and may appeal to only a small audience. Picasso and Cézanne exhibitions may command large audiences, but even they had to be given the chance to be accepted.

Non-profit organisations more often depend on a number of groups or publics, whereas business is considered primarily responsible to three groups – shareholders, employees, and customers (Hannagan 1992). The number of constituencies faced by museums can include visitors, users, funding bodies, municipal authorities, central government, government agencies, businesses, tourist boards, employees, the media, in fact any constituency that has a continuing interest in the performance of that museum.

Because non-profit organisations receive public funding, they are more subject to public scrutiny, and are held accountable for the funds they receive (Kotler and Andreasen 1987). Often too, they seek this scrutiny, by attracting publicity from the media for events and fundraising successes. Non-profit organisations may also be subject to non-market pressures. Museums, particularly those controlled by central or local government, may be directed or influenced by their political wishes. Legislation, such as compulsive competitive tendering, where internal markets and devolved budgets are established, acts as a non-market pressure (Walsh, Kieron 1995). Moreover, professional associations, such as the American Association of Museums and the UK Museums Association, can impose ethical restrictions on their members through their Codes of Practice.

Finally, Lovelock and Weinberg (1988) warn of the dangers of management in duplicate or triplicate in non-profit organisations. They highlight the problems encountered by the differing ideologies of 'managers' and 'professionals', and paint the darker picture of a strong political or volunteer board that seeks to organise management control over an organisation composed of both professionals and managers.

The main difference between commercial companies and non-profit museums is the ultimate aim of the marketing itself. Non-profit museums are generating income not for shareholders but in order to recycle it into the museum, to justify or attract funding or sponsorship and to ensure the continuance of the objects in their care. Any marketing initiative must take particular account of these factors and guard against over-commercialisation of the central product, which may result in a loss of integrity.

Museums are also service organisations. As their function in society takes on new dimensions, so their provision of a service takes on increasing significance. Nevertheless, although their underlying philosophy is to offer a service to the public, conflict within the operations often reduces, either intentionally or against their better judgement, the service that is offered to the public. This has been manifested with the almost universal condemnation from the museums' press of the developments at the Natural History Museum in London. Here, the market-orientated approach of placing emphasis on the public has been directly associated with one hundred redundancies in the research and conservation functions (Murdin 1991).

The various interests involved in the service, which is both direct (to the present public), and indirect (to future publics), can cloud the issues involved in providing a service. Where are the museum's limited resources channelled? To active conservation of artefacts for future generations, or to display and provision of support services to the present public? This dilemma is largely being answered by the demands of funding bodies, which, on the whole, require the museums to perform a function for the current public. Future publics tend to take second place in this new thinking. This is not a conflict in other services, and yet sharply illustrates the problems for museums.

Marketing theory distinguishes between consumer goods and services according to a classificatory system with five key dimensions: intangibility, inseparability, heterogeneity, perishability, and lack of ownership. The concept of intangibility is the most frequently discussed element and, it has been argued, is the only characteristic that is common to all services (Klein and Lewis 1985). Unlike goods, services are not physical products; they cannot be touched, although as Flipo demonstrates, they are 'possibly perceptible by one of the four other senses' (Flipo 1988: 287). At first sight a museum professional would consider this incongruous in an institution which is essentially object-based. The artefacts are clearly tangible; it is the emotions they evoke which are intangible. Experience, therefore, is the intangible characteristic of the museum, while support services, such as the café and shop, lie along the product–service continuum which goes from 'pure product' to 'pure service' (Shostack 1977).

This continuum itself demonstrates the loosely defined sense of the intangibility of a service where the service is not uniformly intangible.

Most services marketing researchers advocate that the intangibility of services should be reduced by emphasising their tangibility. Thus, the Victoria and Albert Museum adopted an advertising campaign based on its 'Ace Caff' (Macdonald 1988). However, the intangible 'experience' remains. Flipo (1988) suggests that when intangible elements have great credibility, which he considers to be in most instances, the tangible cues will have little impact. Thus, word of mouth recommendation, which is often a choice factor for services (Young 1981), may persuade an intending museum visitor to visit the old-fashioned, rather intimidating museum over the new welcoming museum, where the tangible factors would appear to carry less risk.

Services by their very nature are physically intangible: they cannot be touched, tasted, smelt, or seen. This contrasts with the physical substance or tangibility of goods. In addition to their physical intangibility, services can also be difficult for the mind to grasp and thus can be mentally intangible. Services cannot be possessed; they can only be experienced, created, or participated in. This creates a number of problems for museums. Use of the service cannot be stored. Thus if the museum is quiet on a Monday morning, it cannot be filled with members of the public who were queuing to get in on Saturday afternoon. It is also difficult to sample the service before use. A visitor may have some idea of what to expect before entering a museum, but will not be cognisant of the ensuing experience prior to admission. It is also difficult to communicate or display exactly what is on offer in a museum. How can a leaflet or poster adequately explain what the museum experience will consist of?

Grönroos (1982) developed the buyer–seller interaction characteristic as described by Rathmell (1974), where the creation or performing of the service occurs at the same time as full or partial consumption. Goods are produced, sold, and consumed whereas services are sold and then produced and consumed. Inseparability is valid in museums where the educational and entertainment aspects are inseparable from the consumption of the museum service by the visitor. Clearly, as Thomas (1978) argues, the staff are an important element in the delivery of the museum service. However, the visitors are in a position to define the inseparability, since what they actually consume, and the quality of its consumption, depends on their attitudes towards, and expectations of, the service. What is actually being consumed? It may be education, entertainment, a visit to the café, or perhaps social acceptance. Unlike some services where the buyer–seller interaction is relatively straightforward (where for example, the customer's hair is cut), the interaction in a museum is more complex and can take a multiplicity of combinations of interaction.

The delivery process of services is therefore complicated by the consumer being involved in the production. The product has to be right first time. As with manufactured goods, it is not possible to stop the assembly line when the machine starts to manufacture faulty products. There can be no quality control of this kind in the production of the museum service. This creates problems, particularly when the user is not sure what to expect from the museum. Other consumers are also involved in the production, and they may spoil the enjoyment of the experience for individual consumers (such as a large tour group visiting the museum).

Each service transaction is unique and therefore difficult to measure. Heterogeneity refers to the difficulty of achieving standardisation of services (Cowell 1984). The vast and various collections of museums would prohibit any standardisation of the museum experience. Standardisation in terms of interpretation of the museum through labels and support services is theoretically feasible, but because of variations in the museum's location and staff, cannot be implemented. Because services are difficult to standardise, there is a potential of high variability in their performance. This gives rise to two problems: the standard is dependent on who provides the service, while quality assurance is difficult. Since service delivery is heavily dependent on people, variability in their performance will inevitably lead to variability in quality.

Unlike goods, services are perishable and cannot be stored; they operate in time, not in perpetuity. This may be accompanied by fluctuating demand leading to under-utilisation. Since the provision of many services involves a high proportion of fixed costs, perishability can be a significant factor. A museum without visitors will still have to sustain the majority of costs associated with a full museum. The museum experience is perishable. It is not necessarily irrevocably perishable, though. It may be possible to return again and again to view a museum object and re-create the same experience.

In direct contrast to the purchase of goods, services lack ownership. The customer can have access to, or use of, a service, but cannot own it. A museum visitor is allowed to visit and view exhibits but is not in a position to acquire an ownership interest in them. Municipal museums may counter that their local public owns the museum, not directly, but through their local taxation. Sponsors could also be regarded as temporary owners.

It should perhaps be noted here that, as non-profit organisations, museums are marketing both to the public and to their funders. Therefore their efforts are not solely geared towards producing a service for visitors. They also perform the function of persuading or reiterating their value to their funders and influencers. This is not a service *per se*. This brings an additional element to the nature of the museum service which is not covered by the service characteristics above.

Because of the characteristics of services, additional factors will need to be taken into account in the implementation of marketing. This requires a reconsideration of the marketing mix, which was originally devised by Borden (1965) and subsequently abbreviated into the now popular 4Ps form (Product, Price, Place, Promotion) by McCarthy (1981). Borden's original list was derived from research in product manufacturing organisations and referred specifically to manufacturing. Recognising that this list was not comprehensive enough for services marketing, Cowell (1984), drawing on the work of Booms and

Bitner (1981), expanded the marketing mix. To the original 4Ps is added 3 new P's: People, Physical evidence and Process, although it is noticeable that by 1994, Cowell had decided to omit 'Physical evidence' (Cowell 1994). Other service commentators such as Christopher and his colleagues (1991), add People, Process, and Customer service as additional elements. It could also be argued that some aspects of the new elements are implicit in the original 4Ps.

Shostack (1977) emphasises the importance of people in influencing consumers' perceptions of a service organisation. Drucker (1990) also underlines the importance of good staff and in particular calls upon service organisations to promote teamwork instead of relying on one or two committed individuals as is often the case. Moreover Wittreich (1966: 127) claims that 'the selling of a service and the rendering of the service can seldom be separated'. In many museums, though, there is little contact with museum personnel. Attendants and café and shop staff are often the only public interface, although the people behind the scenes, the curators and educationalists, create the image of the museum. This clearly has implications for hiring and training front-of-house staff.

Shostack (1977) stresses the management of the physical evidence or environment of the service organisation. The tangible aspects of the service need to be stressed, such as the café or gift shop. Eureka! The Museum for Children, in Halifax, owes its immense popularity to its physical environment: hands-on models, interactive technology, and sound effects all encourage audience participation. An atmosphere can be created, which according to Kotler (1973), can act as a competitive tool.

Zeithaml, Parasuraman, and Berry (1990) regard the delivery of a quality service as being essentially dependent on investment, not only in people but also in processes. In terms of the overall service delivery process, marketing needs to be integrated with the other operations. Marketing professionals working in isolation cannot increase audiences and work the other miracles commonly expected of them. There is a need for a total marketing orientation of the whole organisation – a marketing culture. This requires commitment to the marketing ethos by all service organisation personnel, including top management. Kelly (1991) demonstrates the success of this approach with reference to the Metropolitan Museum of Art in New York, where curators, historians, designers, conservators, and other backstage personnel serve on committees with marketing tasks.

Customer service is 'the total quality of the service as perceived by the customer' (Palmer 1994: 35). Managing the quality of the service is dependent on the organisation's policy on product design and management of the delivery of the service and of personnel. As customers become more demanding about quality of service, customer service can be a competitive tool for service organisations, and is an important element of relationship marketing (Payne 1993).

The debate about the number of Ps or elements that apply to service organisations can appear nonsensical, an esoteric debate, even self-reverential – perpetuating the mystification of marketing through additional layers of marketing jargon. As Payne remarks, 'the definition of the elements of the marketing mix is not scientific – it is largely intuitive and semantic' (Payne 1993: 35). Each of the aspects that are considered in the additional elements is relevant in the museum situation. It is up to the individual who is developing the marketing strategy to decide on where the emphases lie, since 'As museums vary enormously by discipline, collections, scale, facilities, context, location, funding, and history, so too must the mix of benefits they can provide be varied from institution to institution' (Weil 1990: 50).

The following chapters include detail on each of the additional elements. The chapter on the museum product will recognise the importance of both physical evidence and people in product decisions, as well as the importance of quality in customer perceptions and the processes that deliver that quality. The chapter on communications will consider the place element, or how to distribute the service in order to maximise access. Finally, price will be dealt with in the chapter on attracting resources.

MUSEUM MARKETING

To transplant marketing theories from a manufacturing situation to a non-profit service such as a museum would surely be mistaken. Criticisms of marketing theory are made by Bartels (1974), who contends that marketing has an identity crisis comprising three main elements. First, an emphasis on quantitative methodologies rather than the usefulness of findings. Second, developing an increasingly esoteric and abstract marketing literature. Third, a concern for increasingly sophisticated methods of data analysis rather than problem solving. Willmott (1984) also censures managerial researchers for failing to penetrate the ideology of the people or organisations being studied. On researching local authority recreation and leisure departments, Cowell concluded that 'There are basic problems in trying to apply marketing ideas without adaptation in and to institutions which are different in kind from business institutions and which regard their consumers in different ways' (Cowell 1984: 51).

These criticisms are levelled at a body of theory that often fails to regard marketing as an activity, carried out by people. Marketing theories have been deductively derived and based on speculation rather than observation (Bradford 1991). When empirical testing has taken place, it has been conducted in environments with some or all of the following characteristics:

- North American rather than European
- large corporations rather than small businesses
- goods rather than services
- profit-making rather than non-profit
- homogeneous rather than heterogeneous markets
- private rather than public.

An examination of the context of the museum would suggest factors indigenous to the museum that are noticeable by their absence in the marketing literature.

Since the ultimate marketing goal of profit does not exist in the non-profit situation, the ultimate role of marketing in the museum context is to achieve the organisation's mission or overall objectives. As DiMaggio has commented on the arts:

> In order to assess the influence of the marketplace on the arts, economists have had to raise their theories to take account of the goals of arts managers and trustees. If artistic firms do not maximise profit, then what they do maximise needs to be discovered in order to anticipate the effects of market forces on their behaviour.
>
> (DiMaggio 1985: 29)

However, as P. J. Ames (1988) has warned, this does not mean that the museum should be market-driven. On the contrary, the museum should have established a clear goal to be pursued, which would then become an attitude of mind throughout the organisation, which is then transmitted into actions (Lewis 1991). Marketing should ultimately achieve the overall purpose of any museum. Marketing, though, does not dictate the mission, but should follow it (Ames, P. J. 1988).

Costa and Bamossy, commenting on the museum's condition, where it will have multiple goals and multiple publics, suggest that these goals and publics 'may at times . . . seem antithetical, even antagonistic, toward one another' (1995: 309). The varied goals, though, should all contribute to the museum's mission, despite the fact that they appear to conflict. Costa and Bamossy then describe how the conflicting goals will be manifest:

> With respect to the curators, the board of directors, other museums, and any other academic-, scholarship-, or class-based audience, the manager must focus on the sanctity, authenticity, and protection of the object. On the other hand, with respect to the lay public on whom the museum must increasingly rely for economic and political support, the manager must pursue, at least to some extent, a policy of democratization of education, knowledge, and access to the object while still maintaining control over its authenticity.
>
> (Costa and Bamossy 1995: 307)

The collection is perhaps unique to museums, and poses problems of its own. The duality of the role of the professional curator in terms of the collection and the public leads to 'schizophrenia' (Squires 1969), compounded by 'the impossibility of being a full-time administrator, a full-time curator, and a full-time exhibit specialist' (Guédon 1983: 253); and now equally a full-time marketer! The conflict will vary depending on the purpose of the individual museum. However, it will also be an underlying feature of marketing, and will require a fine balancing of the market with the mission.

The extent to which museums have adopted marketing varies quite widely between nations and between museums. Recent research into the leisure industry in the UK, which included museums, found that

The marketing function has grown from a promotions-focused heritage to control all aspects of customer service, and to increasingly be involved in product development. The understanding of the marketing mix, supported by improved customer information, is still a priority, but from a somewhat narrower perspective, with little involvement in organisational objectives and wider marketing strategy issues. The strategic role of marketing – anticipating and pre-empting the future – is missing, compounded by the often narrow definition of competition, vague understanding of customers and misunderstanding of the potential impact from broader environmental issues. Marketing as a function in the leisure facilities area exists primarily to develop tactical marketing programmes, focusing on pricing policies and the communications tools.

(Dibb and Simkin 1993: 123)

Thus although many of the tools of marketing are increasingly being adopted, long-term and comprehensive marketing strategies have not been formulated. In the UK, though, the Museums and Galleries Commission's registration scheme has required museums to start thinking in terms of a corporate plan. From this it is only a short step to develop and adopt a marketing plan. However, there are still a lot of hurdles to be overcome, not least because 'Marketing is still undervalued, or feared; many organisations are still not taking their relationships with their audiences really seriously, long term, and many marketing officers are in truth glorified publicity officers' (Arts Council of Great Britain 1991: 6).

The degree of adoption of marketing in museums can best be summarised by illustrating the British situation, where, although there are over 2,000 museums registered under the Museums and Galleries Commission registration scheme, there are only forty full-time marketing and development officers (Hooper-Greenhill 1994). A recent survey carried out by the Museums and Galleries Commission found that more support staff were required for marketing, and that most marketing officers felt isolated and under-used (Runyard and Anderson 1992). This worrying trend and the statistics alone suggest that the adoption of marketing in museums is not exactly wholehearted. Museums still have a long way to go if they are to become even remotely marketing-orientated. However, as businesses have become more successful as they have become marketing-oriented (Baker and Hart 1989), so may museums. Thus according to the American Association of Museums:

Marketing as a consistent effort builds a foundation of public understanding and appreciation. Over time, the public learns about the values on which museums are founded, the heritage they collect, the knowledge they embody and the services they perform. In turn, with greater understanding, the public will use and support museums more fully.

(American Association of Museums 1984: 100)

A museum needs to focus clearly on its goals. It needs to develop these goals by assessing them in terms of societal values and needs: examining why the collection is being kept, and what the public should be receiving from that collection. Ultimately, though, the museum itself is responsible for marketing. Only the museum can ensure that marketing is pursuing the purpose of the museum, and as Weil commented, 'the worthiness of a museum must ultimately depend on the worthiness of its goals' (Weil 1995: xv).

3

The museum's environment

Marketing is about matching the museum's product with the market, taking into account the museum's resources (Kotler 1991). It also requires an understanding of the environmental issues that may impact on any of these factors; the public, the museum's product, and the museum's resources. The emphasis and nature for each of these variables will differ depending on the individual museum. The museum's product and resources are its own internal affair, and will be unique to each museum. Its own structure and politics will affect the manner in which it responds to changing consumer needs. However, a marketing orientation requires a museum to monitor its external environment and to adjust its own product offerings so that consumer needs are fulfilled, thereby facilitating the museum in meeting its goals. Palmer defines an organisation's marketing environment as 'all of those uncontrollable events outside the organization which impinge on its activities' (Palmer 1994: 35).

The environmental issues to be considered would normally include the following variables: politics, economics, legislation, technology, competition, and the market. To these, museums need to add a further variable: the museum's stakeholders and other publics. This chapter will look at each of these variables in turn. It will assess trends and developments for each, focusing particularly on the UK situation, although many of the issues are universal.

THE MARKET

There are two aspects to be considered here in terms of the market: the social and cultural environment and the demographic environment. In other words, 'the structure and dynamics of individuals and groups and the issues that engage them' (Dibb *et al.* 1991: 39). Attitudes in society change over time and at any one time between different groups. For example, the dominant cultural attitude towards the role of women is changing, presenting obvious challenges to museums. The cultural diversity of ethnic minority groups also poses a challenge. As society becomes more conscious of environmental concerns, which are becoming mainstream cultural values, museums need to ensure that they are responding.

Equally, any changes in the size and structure of the population can be critical both for predicting the demand for museums and even the availability of a workforce. Palmer (1994) has outlined the two key contemporary demographic issues for most countries as: the increase of elderly people and the cyclical nature of the birth rate. Structural shifts in communities can also affect where and how people live. The development of new towns, for example, has increased the need for support services, such as museums (Payne 1993). A further consideration is the changing composition of households, particularly the increase in one-parent families and the growing diversity of ethnic minorities in the population (Palmer 1994).

Demographic trends vary from country to country. These trends will affect not only the potential visitor profile, but also the potential workforce. The age structure of the population is changing. There is a trend towards earlier retirement, while the number of over-65s is steadily increasing as life expectancy increases. In the UK, for example, in 1991 the over-65s accounted for 15.7 per cent of the population, while it is predicted that by 2031 they will account for 22.5 per cent (Davies 1994a: 16). The support for museums from the older age group could be significant because of their comparatively greater affluence (Museums Association 1991a). The potential here is great, although the over-65s are not renowned for their propensity to visit museums (Merriman 1991; Davies 1994a). Often this is owing to structural reasons, such as mobility and transport, but also because the older generation tend not to have been 'socialised' into museum visiting, although this should change as the younger, relatively more socialised generation takes over.

Trends in the under-16s age group could also be significant for museums, particularly since they account for a substantial proportion of many museums' visitors. In the UK, for example, a third of all visits to museum are accounted for by the under-16s (*Sightseeing in the UK* 1992). Museums should be aware of the predicted trends for this age group, since any change could have a severe impact on visitor figures.

Museum visiting tends to be divided equally between men and women, although there are exceptions for particular types of museums, such as science, military, and transport museums (Davies 1994a). Nevertheless, more women are joining the workforce, while the 'nuclear' family is declining as single-parent families increase. Thus, the 'family' group will alter in size and composition. Also, contrary to popular perceptions that leisure time is continuing to increase, leisure time for those in employment is in fact decreasing (Davies 1994a).

A further trend is that of increased awareness of the disadvantaged in society, particularly the elderly, the unemployed, ethnic minorities, and disabled people. Currently the unemployed are under-represented amongst museum visitors (Merriman 1991). Ethnic minorities can form a significant sector of the population in specific regions, such as Greater London, where they account for 20.2 per cent of the population (Davies 1994a). The disabled may account for up to one in ten of the population in Europe, and this offers its own challenge to museums to enable access (Weisen 1991). Each of these population sectors presents significant, often seemingly insurmountable challenges for museums. However, provision of services to the disabled is now an obligation for museums in a number of countries. For example, according to the UK Museums Association Codes of Ethics (1995, rule 5.1): 'Museum professionals must uphold the fundamental principle of museums that the collections are maintained for the public benefit, and the implication of non-discriminatory public access which this carries'.

Public expectations are increasing – a consequence of greater overall affluence and altered values on spending and consumption. Attitudes reflect a wider view of quality of life, of leisure, and entertainment. As people become more mobile with increased car ownership and foreign holidays, their demands become more sophisticated as they visit other attractions that offer high standards of facilities and customer care. Museums therefore need to ensure that the public believes that museums, 'provide worthwhile experiences and contribute to their idea of the quality of life' (Middleton 1990: 29).

Related to this change in attitude is a further factor, that of the public's new-found interest in heritage, reflected in the increase in the number of theme parks. As the Museums Association warns though:

> These are to be welcomed as stimulating further interest, but there is concern that people may fail to distinguish between museums, with their long-term educational role, and heritage attractions, which are geared to the short-term and rely rather on the replication of history and dramatic effects than on original material.
>
> (Museums Association 1991a: 9)

A further change in attitude is to that of environmental issues and the preservation of the countryside with its concomitant interest in the natural world. The potential for museums, particularly natural history museums, is immense but largely untapped.

The creation of a new Europe in 1992 is having an impact on public attitudes towards nationality, patriotism, history, and culture, resulting in a gradual shift in public opinion. Equally, the easing of mobility of individuals within the European Union and the removal of trade barriers is speeding up these developments. There are also implications for mobility of employment within the museum sector.

A further development in the market potential for museums is in education. The population is becoming more educated as more students graduate from higher education. Since the more educated are more highly represented at museums (Merriman 1991; Hooper-Greenhill 1994), this can only benefit museums. As Hooper-Greenhill, referring to Hiemstra (1981), suggests: 'Theories of adult learning indicate at this stage in their lives, people are inclined to enjoy more thoughtful pursuits and to be prepared to make long-term investments in fruitful ventures such as the opportunities offered by museums and galleries' (Hooper-Greenhill 1994: 18).

Although a substantial proportion of all museum visitors are children, only a small proportion of these visits are made as part of an organised school trip, and more significantly their motivation for visiting is rarely 'educational'. As Davies suggests, there is 'a need for museums and art galleries to give at least equal weight to the "experience" that they offer as to their "educational mission" (Davies 1994a: 81).

The final market factor that will significantly affect museums is developments within tourism, with the transformation of the tourism industry during the 1970s and 1980s. As overall leisure time has increased, so the number of holidays taken has increased. Throughout Europe and the US tourism has been one of the growth industries for both domestic and foreign holiday-makers. The trend is towards taking more than one holiday per year, with short-break stays. This change should benefit museums, 'in that short trips are much better spread throughout the year, are higher spending, and appeal to a relatively older and more affluent market' (Middleton 1990: 35). Also, as increased car ownership increases mobility, the day-visitor market is expanding, which is another lucrative market for museums.

As more people travel abroad, they will have access to high-quality presentation and interpretation centres in other countries, and this will raise their expectations of domestic attractions (Museums Association 1991a). Equally, as more overseas visitors are attracted to a country, they will have high expectations of the attractions that are on offer. This could be significant for some museums, especially since they can account for a substantial proportion of museums' visitor numbers (*Sightseeing in the UK* 1992).

The museum provider, then, needs to be aware of the general trends within the population, in terms both of demographics and of changing cultural values. Much of this information is reported in newspapers, but can be found from census data. An appreciation of the trends within the museum sector as a whole is also required, and often the sources of this data will give information on general demographic information.[1]

ECONOMIC

As Dibb and her colleagues postulated:

> The overall state of the economy fluctuates in all countries. These changes in general economic conditions affect (and are affected by) the forces of supply and demand, buying power, willingness to spend, consumer expenditure levels, and the intensity of competitive behaviour.
>
> (Dibb *et al.* 1991: 43)

Organisational development then tends to be related to the rate of economic growth. An organisation needs to be aware of current economic conditions both nationally and locally. From this information it should be possible to assess the strength of the public's buying power, and thus the levels of discretionary income (that is the disposable income available after the basic necessities such as food and fuel have been purchased, which can then be spent on leisure activities, holidays, pets, and of course, museums).

Since the Policy Studies Institute published *The Economic Importance of the Arts in Britain* (Myerscough 1988), museums have increasingly been seen as important contributors to the economic well-being and regeneration of an area. Cultural institutions, which include museums, are increasingly regarded as a significant infrastructural support to economic activity, although the evidence for this is not always easily demonstrable (*Charter for the Arts in Scotland* 1993). Museums are catalysts for attracting day-trippers and tourists to an area and can contribute to the attractions of an area and to new investment (Audit Commission 1991). The Audit Commission cites as an example of success the Wigan Pier Heritage Centre, which received funding from various public and private sources, including the European Community Social Fund, central government, and the English Tourist Board. In its first year of operation it attracted half a million visitors, while its success has contributed to the economic regeneration of Wigan by attracting investment in the area.

The heritage boom owes much of its existence to the two world energy crises in 1973 and 1979. Economic recession as well as the New Right's policy of curbing union power, has led to the demise of heavy manufacturing industries. At the same time as these manufacturing plants closed, the infrastructure used to supply them, such as railways, mines, and docks, fell into disuse. The result was considerable potential for the creation of museums!

As Middleton (1990) suggests, these redundant buildings and infrastructure have been put to good use in the furtherance of economic regeneration, by being converted into tourist attractions. It was seen as a way to ameliorate the harsh effects of the recession, while 'the fact that much of the redundant infrastructure represented the essential architectural character, heart and historic ambience of the towns and cities whose past it represented, added poignancy to the crisis' (ibid. 21). Municipal authorities regarded economic intervention as a natural response to rapid de-industrialisation, and saw the opportunities for creating employment in tourism. Estimates suggest that the cost of creating one new job in tourism in the UK is £4,000, compared to £32,000 in manufacturing, and £700,000 in mechanical engineering (Lumley 1988: 22). Local government has supported tourism initiatives because, 'this has been one area where there are sources of funding to initiate projects which may also benefit local residents' (Urry 1990: 155).

More recent initiatives include the creation of partnerships between tourism and museum agencies. *Tourism and the Arts in Scotland* (Scottish Tourism Co-ordinating Group 1991), a report formulated by a number of relevant organisations, among them the Scottish Tourist Board, the Scottish Arts Council, the Scottish Museums Council, and the economic development agency, Scottish Enterprise, 'marks the beginning of a new phase of co-operation between the arts and tourism structures in Scotland, which could be of great mutual benefit' (*Charter for the Arts in Scotland* 1993: 94). The report found that arts organisations (including museums) allowed tourism a very limited role in their planning and marketing. Its recommendations include facilitating links between arts, tourism, and economic development organisations, and encouraging strategic arts tourism marketing.

The economic situation of a country also obviously impacts on the personal disposable income of the public. As the manufacturing industries declined, so unemployment rose. Because leisure spending is non-essential, it competes with essential purchases and the decision to save for a rainy day (Woods 1994). Discretionary leisure spending is likely to be cut in times of recession, which will impact on spend at museums, although free museums should not feel the full impact (Davies 1994a).

Of immediate importance for museums are the whims of their funding bodies. Future predictions suggest that museums can no longer rely on year-on-year growth in public funding, which was previously regarded as an automatic right (Eckstein 1993). The financial pressures on museums are increasing as municipal authority budgets are squeezed, resulting in discretionary services such as museums coming under intense scrutiny. Because 'public patrons . . . represent the community and are spending public money for the public benefit . . . they are accountable to the public and must justify their actions' (Mennell 1976: 55). As demands are made on museums to generate their own income and rely on plural funding instead of the 'dependency culture', so the harsh economic realities are likely to hit hard. As the Museums Association points out,

> although the benefits of incentive funding and sound financial management are not in question, it must not be forgotten that neither these nor any number of trading activities with which museums are involved, will ever generate sufficient income to eliminate the need for public funding.
> (Museums Association 1991a: 8)

POLITICAL/LEGAL

Politicians are instrumental in shaping the external environment for any organisation, as well as being responsible for introducing legislation that can affect an organisation directly and indirectly. The shift in political emphasis, with the emergence of the New Right in the 1970s and 1980s, has led to a new consensus of opinion. The Museums Association succinctly outlined the most relevant elements of this new consensus:

> a reduction of the centrally directed provision of public services and a growing acceptance of the role of the market-place as a regulatory influence in the public sector; plural funding for a wide range of services, including museums (previously seen as the semi-exclusive responsibility of government); competition between the services for undetermined and scarce resources; changes in the position of local authorities – the emphasis on supporting and empowering rather than solely providing;

and a new stress on public accountability and performance standards in the provision of public services.

(Museums Association 1991a: 8)

Unlike many other service organisations, museums are particularly subject to the influence of politics; in many countries their funding largely being provided from a political benefactor. As Pearson remarked: 'there is a politics to decision making, a politics in the exercise of power, and a politics to the notion of cultural or aesthetic criteria' (Pearson 1982: 2).

It would be fair to say that in the past museums were usually left to their own devices. They collected their subsidy and acted as they saw fit. The rise of independent museums in the UK showed that museums could and had to survive in the marketplace, although most of them were still dependent on funds received from political donors. The new economic planning of the New Right and what Walsh has described as a 'sustained attack on local government' (Walsh, Kevin 1992: 44) was played out in the UK and in the US, while many other Western and First World nations, including those with socialist governments, followed suit.

In the UK, for example, the Audit Commission, which oversees the auditing of local government in England and Wales, is a quango (government appointed body) funded almost entirely by professional fees paid by the authorities being audited. Its remit covers value-for-money reviews, one of which was undertaken in 1991 into local authority support for museums and art galleries. In this report it made government policy quite explicit, stating that, 'activities which contribute to meeting the [local] authority's objectives and feedback on achievement should be a prerequisite for support' (Audit Commission 1991: 6). Consequently, it recommends that performance indicators be introduced to compare achievement with objectives, to assess the efficiency and effectiveness not only of the local authority's own museums but also independent museums receiving grant aid. Museums, therefore, 'need to demonstrate that they are meeting genuine public needs, that they are well managed, and that they require, and make good use of, the subsidy they receive from their authority' (Audit Commission 1991: 19).

The immediate implication of such a stipulation is whether municipal authorities expect museums to pursue their objectives to the letter. Political control over policy can be the subject of concern. Kirby cites the case of Edinburgh District Council, which 'views the museum as a tool for the pursuance of its wider policy objectives' (Kirby 1988: 98). Two exhibitions were mounted in order to examine one side of contentious contemporary issues, with material being excluded by council members, against the judgement of museum staff that it be included. 'Not Just Tea and Sandwiches' explored the role of women's support groups during the 1984 Miner's Strike, while 'No Easy Way to Freedom' was included as part of the council's anti-apartheid campaign, depicting the struggle in South Africa.

Censorship can also be enforced by government in response to public demand. A controversial exhibition, 'The Last Act: The Atomic Bomb and the End of

World War Two', scheduled to open at the Smithsonian's Air and Space Museum in 1995, was toned down before its opening. Veterans' groups and law-makers complained that the 'Enola Gay' aspect of the exhibition, which featured the B-29 bomber, 'portrayed the US as aggressor and Japan as victim of racist American politics' (Noble 1995: 75). Members of the American House of Representatives demanded the dismissal of the museum's director, and replacement of the exhibition. Moreover it has been suggested by Mayo (1992) that funding can become a not-so-subtle form of censorship, where demands for 'politically correct' content from both liberals and conservatives with a political agenda require the content of interpretive labels to be altered, or they will refuse to fund the exhibition.

Through both finance and legislation, politics can have an impact on both the attractiveness of museums to potential users and on the general population's perception of their value (Davies 1994a). As public subsidy is reduced, financial self-sufficiency encouraged, and performance indicators allocated, central and local government are moving away from the role of provider to that of enabler. Museums are encouraged to develop partnerships both with industry through sponsorship and with the voluntary sector.

Legislation in the 1980s has had little direct impact on museums, although social and economic developments in other spheres have been immense. These inevitably impact on museums, particularly the education legislation. The tenor of the new economic policies is to reduce the influence of the public sector and encourage private sector control of public services. Thus, 'legislation often puts increased pressure on local authority services and managers, making the discretionary services (such as museums and art galleries) even more vulnerable' (Davies 1994a: 26).

MUSEUM STAKEHOLDERS

The museum has various publics. Davies (1994a) suggests that a museum has four sources of demand: visitors, users, stakeholders, and society. 'Visitors' and 'users' are interchangeable, since there are various ways of using the services of a museum, other than merely visiting it, such as undertaking research; enquiring about objects; obtaining materials, for example, for school group use. Stakeholders are 'individuals, groups or organisations which have a legitimate interest in the sector, at the national, regional or local level' (Davies 1994a: 11), which can include central and local government, business, the media, tourist boards, economic development agencies, museum organisations such as the UK Museums and Galleries Commission, museums associations, governing bodies, the staff, members, and volunteers. Finally, museums exist for the benefit of society, or of whoever in society wishes to take up their services.

Stakeholders can be extremely influential in museums, with Davies commenting that:

In some instances the strength of their views and influence, often expressed either through participation in the governance of a museum or art gallery or as a significant source of funding, will be greater in determining the museum or art gallery's future than that of the normal market demand forces of the consumer.

(Davies 1994a: 11–12)

It is useful to break down the notion of 'stakeholders' into individuals/groups that impact directly or indirectly on a museum and its policies. Direct influence comes from the museum's funding bodies, governing bodies, and staff: in other words those bodies that impact on the day-to-day operations of the museum. Indirect influence comes from individuals/groups that may impact on a museum's policies and activities, but do not directly influence the day-to-day running of the museum.

Let us look first at the direct influences. Funding bodies often expect museums to reflect their overall objectives, and clearly have the power to withdraw funding as a coercive mechanism. The only curb on the policy-setting of these funding bodies is if that nation has a museums association which has developed Codes of Practice, as in the UK and US, or if the museum's governing body differs in composition from the funding agencies.

A museum's governing body is, 'the principal body of individuals in which rests ultimate responsibility for policy and decisions affecting the government of the museum's service' (Museums Association 1995a). In the case of national museums, this is the trustees appointed by central government, while in local government museums, it is the full council of the municipal authority. In a company limited by guarantee, the governing body is the board of directors or council of management, while in a museum service run by an independent trust, it is the full board of trustees. The governing body therefore has considerable influence over the policy of the museum, and may at times clash with the demands of the funding body. Again, the only curb on the governing body is that nation's Museums Association Codes of Practice.

Independent museums have tended to fare better than other museums in defining their own policy.

> Independents are not subordinate to administrative and political committees over which they have little influence. They often have severe financial problems but they are not at the mercy of unpredictable, restrictive public sector requirements, rigid accounting procedures, and the arbitrary spending limits which affected so many public sector museums in the last decade.
>
> (Middleton 1990: 16)

Often though, independent museums tend to be controlled more rigorously by their trustees. The degree of interest and participation of the trustees can be far greater, with the trustees shaping the museum's culture. In voluntary-run museums, in particular, where some of the trustees are also staff members, the trustees can be the guiding force behind the museum, dictating, with minimal interference from outside the organisation, the direction that the museum's policy should take. Clearly, the task of a museum that is semi-independent but with some local authority control is more complex, where the demands of the different trustees may clash. Justifying its existence may require a different stance for each of the governing parties. Building relationships with each of these governing bodies is essential.

The dominance of the staff, particularly those who manage the museum, has been demonstrated by Bradford (1991) and McLean (1993). Bradford has affirmed the curator to be the pivot around which the rest of the museum operates. The curator's supremacy lies in his or her power to make and enforce decisions, and in shaping the culture of the museum. The curator either instigates decisions or enforces those made by the museum's governing body. The personality of the curator, his or her motivation and management style, as well as attitude to the collection and the public, and relationship with the staff and other stakeholders, all contribute to the nature of the museum. The curator determines the degree of participation of the rest of the staff in the decision-making process, and enables action and change in the museum. Many curators take their lead from professional bodies, such as the UK and US museums associations, at whose annual conferences and in whose monthly journals the museum debates are aired.

Other members of the museum staff may also be instrumental in shaping the nature of the museum. Key support staff, such as designers and educationalists, focus the activities engaged in by the museum. The image of the museum projected to the public could equally be determined by the attendants and cleaners. Developing relationships with members of staff, through internal marketing, can help ensure that the staff are motivated by the museum's goals; this ultimately benefits the museum as a whole. Similarly, volunteers and Friends can shape the nature of the museum as it is projected to the public, as they are often the main point of contact between the museum and the public.

The degree of influence of funding bodies, governing bodies, and staff varies according to the organisational structure of the museum. However, the internal organisational structure, which has overall influence over the museum, acts as a frame of reference, imposing its influence. The indirect influences, which tend to come from external agencies, may also prompt action or change in museums, particularly where these agencies are opinion-formers or can exert coercion on museums. In the UK, for example, the Museums and Galleries Commission's registration scheme is a means of dictating the shape of the museum culture. Funding mechanisms may prompt change, either through refusal to fund initiatives that are deemed inappropriate, or through funding schemes, such as the Museums and Galleries Commission's marketing scheme, which offered additional funding specifically for marketing initiatives.

Other external organisations, such as tourist boards, societies, and sometimes corporate sponsors, may influence museums through more indirect means. Their impact is more often social and cultural in nature, although they may also offer financial benefit for museums. The Northumbria Tourist Board in the north of England has influenced the Captain Cook Birthplace Museum in Middlesbrough, by including it in the Tourist Board's publicity campaign on 'Cook's Country'.

Moreover, as Mayo (1992) demonstrates, the corporate sponsor can also advance its own agenda, and censor what it regards as unimportant. The Museum of American History developed an aggressive fundraising campaign which ran for over five years, in an attempt to secure corporate sponsorship for two exhibitions on the history of women, namely 'From Parlor to Politics' and 'First Ladies: Political Role and Public Image'. The museum failed in its attempts, and so resorted to alternative sources, while the exhibitions were delayed and ultimately aspects of each had to be curtailed or jettisoned (Mayo 1992).

Finally, the media can be significant stakeholders in museums, through their decisions to print, or broadcast or withhold information about the museum. Their interest and support for a museum can often be crucial to its success in attracting the public. The withering press reviews of the Smithsonian's National Museum of American Art exhibition, 'The West as America', for example, represented an attempt to, 'defuse the impact of the exhibition's historical content' (Mayo 1992: 51).

Ultimately, if a museum is to develop relationships with its various stakeholders and nurture and maintain support, it must keep close to them (Peters and Waterman 1982). In other words, the museum must keep up to date with developments in these organisations, and also recognise their needs in terms of the museum.

COMPETITION

All organisations are competing for a consumer's money and/or time. Competition is defined as: 'those firms that market products that are similar to, or can be substituted for, its products in the same geographic area' (Dibb *et al.* 1991: 49). For a museum, competition can consist of direct competition (such as other museums and attractions) and indirect competition (or other activities that may occupy a person's time). Moreover, it has been argued that increased competition has intensified the speed of change in museums (Middleton 1985).

Disney-style theme parks and heritage centres have customer care and entertainment values at the forefront of their ethos. Museums have been seen as competing for the increased leisure time of their clientele. Museums operate in the leisure industry; their main competition coming from other leisure products. The general trend is for more home-based activities, with more direct competition coming from out-of-home activities such as retailing and leisure centres, new heritage attractions, and theme parks (Middleton 1990). Theme parks, learning from museums, are combining education and entertainment by offering educational and cultural experiences, which previously were the preserve of museums, even to the extent where they provide services to educators (Mintz 1994). Moreover, these themed environments – which offer a leisure outing for the family (often including shopping and food with the entertainment) – are attractive and enticing, and are often more relaxing and easier environments to enjoy than museums.

Museums not only need to address competition, but also need to assess the impact of that competition in terms of their social goals. This can complicate the notion of competition for museums. A museum, for example, which opens a catering or retail facility, may have to consider if this will create unfair competition for other local catering and retail facilities. If a museum is supposed to be for the public good, how does this reconcile with unfair competition with other local companies? Do economic goals override social goals?

Davies (1994a) found that the museum's main competitors, namely historic properties and gardens, were proving more popular than museums. Although 30 per cent of all consumer spending in the UK, for example, is accounted for by 'leisure', only 15 per cent of all leisure spending is on the arts and culture, with museums accounting for an even lesser proportion (Myerscough 1988). Davies (1994a) also found in his study that demand in the museum sector is likely to grow very slowly, since competition between museums and other attractions is likely to increase. As more museums open in the future and other museums undergo refurbishment or are extended, this will serve to take visitors away from existing museums. Consequently Davies (1994a) maintains that museum visits have reached a plateau.

Competitors exist not only in the user market but also in other relevant markets. The most obvious competition will be for funds, where a number of organisations will be competing for a limited supply of grants or sponsorship income. There may also be competition for other resources, such as volunteer labour or donations of equipment, or even objects.

Museums appear to have little appreciation of competition. They regard their product as unique and do not feel themselves to be competing on an equal footing. Many smaller museums are feeling the squeeze and are beginning to form consortia-type relationships with other local museums and attractions, to encourage, for example, holiday companies to make trips to the area, hence enhancing any competitive advantage they may have. Museums need to be clear what they are competing for. It may be for income, for objects to add to the collection, for volunteers, for status, or for a number of other criteria. Ultimately though, they are competing for the leisure time of visitors, and they need to recognise this as the currency for competition.

TECHNOLOGY

Technology is developing so quickly that as soon as this book is published the technological discussion will already be out of date! New developments in environmental controls, security mechanisms, preservation techniques, and documentation, are of significant benefit for the collection. Computers and electronic media also enable the time-consuming and repetitive job of market research to be simplified with market research software; mailing lists to be retained in a database; word processing to simplify administration for copy letters, reports, and press releases; graphics for sponsorship proposals and labelling; and so on. CD-Rom and CD-I publications with sophisticated images can be used to provide information to visitors. Multimedia with videos and computers are now being joined by the information superhighway on the Internet. It is possible to make the museum collection available over the Internet, including those items held in store. The Internet can be used for publicity purposes: for example the Netherlands Tourist Board has an on-line presence for every museum in the country.

In 1995 the National Museum of Science and Industry (NMSI) launched its World Wide Web pages for the Science Museum, the National Railway Museum, and the National Museum of Photography, Film, and Television. The Web pages provide a comprehensive introduction to the NMSI and a constantly changing guide to current attractions and events (Booth 1995). As Bowen states, 'individual museums should decide when, rather than if, it is worth their while providing on-line information concerning their facilities and collections' (Bowen 1995: 25).

Computer technology is also being more widely used for interactive displays. The Natural History Centre in the Liverpool Museum uses computers to stimulate interest by providing enlivening ways into the information embodied in the objects. The technology also gives access to the total documentation system of the museum's mineral collection. Video disc technology has also recently been introduced, in order to assemble in-house image databases (Orna 1994).

No museum can afford to ignore computer technology. Our daily working lives and leisure time are increasingly revolving around the use of the multimedia. Computer technology is here to stay.

CONCLUSIONS

In order to effectively monitor and assess any changes in a museum's environment, it is important to conduct an environmental analysis. This requires the gathering of information pertinent to each of the issues, through secondary sources such as government publications, museums journals, even general interest publications, and market research. This information can then be assessed and interpreted. It should then be possible to describe current environmental changes and to predict future changes. Armed with this analysis

> the manager should be able to determine possible threats and opportunities linked to environmental fluctuations. Understanding the current state of the marketing environment and recognising the threats and

opportunities arising from changes within it help marketing managers assess the performance of current marketing efforts and develop marketing strategies for the future.

(Dibb *et al.* 1991: 33)

Museums need to keep abreast of the changes in their environment, to build up relationships with their stakeholders and public, and to respond to these changes through their marketing efforts.

4

Museums and the public

Marketing's concern with the customer requires an understanding of the market potential. As museums are 'for the people', this assumes that the potential is limitless. Museums have in fact been lauded for their relevance to everyone, for their all-encompassing scope to attract any market sector (Jenkinson 1989). Enshrined in their purpose, to undertake various functions 'for the public benefit' (Museums Association 1984), this democratic *raison d'être* raises the museum above other leisure activities that reach out only to specific sectors of the population. But this notion of public service has not always been the case, and is not inherent in the structure of many museums. Any analysis of the history of museums would ascribe to the public only a secondary role to that of the preservation of the collection, while the public had only minimal influence in the initial creation of museums (Adam 1939). The shift in emphasis from the private to the public domain is only recent and in many museums the private still dominates.

BARRIERS TO ACCESS

The fundamental barrier to access in museums is psychological access, where certain sectors of the population or a number of the public feel disenfranchised, because of a sense of alienation from the dominating societal discourse of the museum. The other form of barrier to access arises from structural issues such as physical access and age. These barriers are true of any cultural institution, but museums have the added problem, summed up by the American Association of Museums in *Museums for a New Century*: 'Stated quite simply, the concerns of preservation and the demands of the public are a contradiction lived out in every institution' (American Association of Museums 1984: 58).

Thus, not only the affirmation of the dominating social strata but also the demands of preservation have exacerbated the entrenchment of the alienation from museums. In fact, it seems as though the whole nature of the museum has conspired against the public, since, 'ever since their inception, museums have been associated with the elite, and their imposing architecture and their glass cases have symbolically and literally excluded large sections of the population from them' (Merriman 1991: 2).

Despite their relevance to everyone (Jenkinson 1989), access for all has not been achieved, with the elite subordination of the museum affirming the status of the educated classes, alienating those who are not of that status. According to a survey undertaken by Merriman in 1985 (in which he investigated people's attitudes towards the past and their visiting preferences), museums 'divide the population into those who possess the "culture" or "competence" to perceive them as a leisure opportunity and make sense of a visit and those who do not' (Merriman 1991: 219). Merriman suggests that these findings confirm Bourdieu's thesis that 'A work of art has meaning and interest only for someone who possesses the cultural competence, that is, the code into which it is encoded' (Bourdieu 1984: 2). In order to have this 'cultural competence', to understand certain forms of cultural production, it is necessary to have experienced certain forms of socialisation, through upbringing and education, which endows 'cultural capital' that distinguishes those who have 'taste' from those who do not. Merriman's results affirmed this thesis by showing that museum visitors tend to come from higher-status groups, and have either stayed on at school or had a tertiary education (Merriman 1991). The increase in those aspiring to be middle class in our societies is paralleled by an increase in those visiting museums precisely because it reflects their changed status, and enables them to accumulate cultural capital (Henley Centre 1989).

Despite moves to create a forum out of the temple, where the museum is a place for 'confrontation, experimentation and debate' (Cameron 1971); despite opening the doors wide, and encouraging dominated groups to participate not only in gazing at the objects but in creating the displays; and despite a genuine concern in many museums, to widen the population base from which it attracts visitors, museums present psychological hurdles too high for many to surmount. Merriman (1991) suggests that if museums are to succeed in removing cultural barriers, they need to open museums up to the local community. Thus, increasingly replacing the longstanding notion of democratising culture (facilitating access to it), is the policy of promoting cultural democracy (creativity and participation) (Janna 1981). Although this does not preclude a large sector of the museum-visiting population, in tourists, it does not directly remove cultural barriers beyond the local. Urry (1990) considers that tourists, far from looking for authenticity, are seeking the difference between their place of residence/work and the object of the tourist gaze. Compare this with the success of Springburn Museum in Glasgow, where a number of projects have been organised where local people take their own photographs and mount their own exhibitions about themselves (O'Neill 1990). This 'cultural empowerment', defined as 'transferring skills to others and providing opportunities for them to present their own points of view within the institutional context' (Ames, P. J. 1990: 161), would run counter to a view of 'the gaze', which requires difference from one's own home and workplace setting. Perhaps we need museums of 'aura' for tourists, such as the great national institutions, and local museums for local people. Yet it would be wrong to suggest that tourists by implication have different museum needs to that of the local population. A tourist can equally enjoy a local culture. A lot more consideration needs to be given to the needs of tourists, and on how these compare and contrast with the needs of local people.

Merriman (1991) suggests that two separate senses of the past exist – the personal and the impersonal – where those who feel excluded from museums are most interested in the personal and the local. Thus, Merriman warns that by emphasising the representation of 'the personal' in their exhibitions, museums

> run the danger of destroying the very precious qualities of a personal
> sense of the past by appropriating for public consumption in an institu-
> tion, where it is scrutinised by others for whom it is not a personal past
> . . . To colonise it in this way would be to destroy it.
>
> (Merriman 1991: 133)

Instead museums should find ways whereby this personal past can be sensitively used 'to illuminate, in a personal way, aspects of impersonal history' (ibid. 133).

Hemmings (1992) found that if subordinated groups are to be enticed into museums, then exhibitions need to be related to areas of particular interest to them. Sheffield's City Museum and the Mappin Art Gallery staged an exhibition, 'Reflections to the Future: Black Lifestyles in Sheffield 1955–88' which attempted to portray the experiences and lifestyles of the city's Afro-Caribbean community. The involvment of members of the community in the development of the exhibition was felt to be a priority. The exhibition was also toured as a mobile museum to stimulate interest and to reach audiences who would not otherwise visit the museum. The exhibition has since been followed up by a succession of exhibitions and residencies involving local ethnic minority communities (Robinson and Toobey 1989). A further initiative is the Museum of London's 'Peopling of London' project, which saw the representation of visitors from the ethnic minorities rise from 4 per cent to 20 per cent during the exhibition (Merriman 1995). Shanks and Tilley (1987) also suggest that museums introduce political content into their displays; this shows how the past may be manipulated and misrepresented for present purposes.

Another interesting initiative is the Open Museum, which was set up by Glasgow Museums and Arts Galleries. It produces small touring exhibitions and handling and reminiscence kits which are used in non-museum venues, attracting around 200,000 visitors a year. The service is committed to working with communities which are 'under-represented, deprived or otherwise marginalised' (Edwards 1995: 22). In collaboration with *The Big Issue*, a newspaper that represents homeless people, the exhibition was designed so that it could be erected outside on the street, and be folded away into carrying cases. *The Big Issue* vendors were trained to install it, and the exhibition has been staged throughout Glasgow and Scotland. It told the stories of homeless people in their own words and using photographs. Other projects undertaken in collaboration with different groups have considered food, poverty, and architecture.

The project does not stop there, but has encouraged all museums in Glasgow to forge links with local people, and Glasgow Museums is even building this into their employees' job descriptions (Carrington 1995). As Edwards claims, 'we can only truly preserve our heritage by involving people' (Edwards 1995: 24).

It is important, though, that the community is involved in exhibition design when the exhibition relates to their culture; or at least, that the museum is sensitive to community concerns. In Edmonton, Alberta, for example, some local Ukrainians have expressed their displeasure at the Ukrainian Village outdoor history museum, for focusing on the poverty of Ukrainian immigrants. Instead they believe that the museum should address the more positive aspects of their culture as well (Adams 1995).

From an assessment of a variety of survey research, Davies (1994a) discovered the public's own perception of why they do not visit museums. The findings indicated lack of awareness, lack of time, and lack of interest, as well as structural reasons. It has been suggested that four factors dictate the decision to visit museums: awareness, accessibility, relevance to the visitor, and perceptions of the museum (Moore, R. 1988). Relevance and perception (the psychological factors) can be overcome, according to Merriman (1991), once the cultural factor of being a museum visitor, that is perceiving the opportunity to visit, is overcome.

Merriman's recommendations for ameliorating the psychological factors place museums in the context of community centres: serving the community rather than being 'a main building which is a repository of Truth' (ibid. 133). He suggests using oral history, devolving to a local scale (introducing programmes geared to the interests of local residents), and opening up the collections, possibly by introducing a Discovery Centre, such as the National Museums and Galleries on Merseyside's Natural History Room, which has an activities room and a collection room.

These kinds of initiatives are also being called for throughout the cultural community. The *Charter for the Arts in Scotland* (1993), for example, also seeks to widen the audience of the arts. The Charter was the result of an extensive consultation (paralleled by a consultation in England and Wales), overseen by a steering group comprising representatives of the Scottish Arts, Museums and Film Councils, and the Convention of Scottish Local Authorities, which sought to identify the main challenges facing the arts in Scotland. Although dealing with the arts in general, museums are included in its remit. The scope of the consultation included the question of audience, that is of the whole social, psychological, and market environment in which cultural activity takes place. From research conducted by System Three it was found that large sections of the Scottish population are disenfranchised in relation to public cultural provision, and comments that: 'this schism in our cultural life between high and popular forms damages cultural activity on both sides, and militates against the interests of the audience in both cases' (*Charter for the Arts in Scotland* 1993: 51). Museums, admittedly, fared rather better than other art forms, with 53 per cent of those surveyed occasionally visiting a museum. It was also found that museums tend to have a more positive image, as being popular, democratic, and accessible. This offers museums the opportunity to help break down the cultural barriers for other art forms, since they are ideal venues for activities related to the arts and culture.

The Charter process identified two areas of need in relation to potential audience for the arts: empowerment to enter into the cultural life of the nation and play a part in shaping it; and for more immediate forms of access to cultural activity. The main mechanism for empowerment, apart obviously from money, is education in the widest sense of the term, to include all types of formal and informal education. As the Charter comments,

> One of the particular strengths of museums, as a point of access to cultural education, is that their collections tend to embrace crafts and design work as well as painting and sculpture in a thoroughly catholic manner, so that they overcome many of the psychological barriers which exist, for example, between craft shops and art galleries.
>
> (*Charter for the Arts in Scotland* 1993: 58)

It then goes on to say that

> The imaginative recent work of Scottish museums on popular cultural artefacts is increasingly recognised by teachers and educationalists as a key resource for schools . . . [it] brings the full apparatus of historical and intellectual analysis to bear on phenomena like the history of football or 1950s design.
>
> (ibid.: 58)

Museums are seen as ideal venues for entering into direct partnership with local arts organisations, providing venues and back-up activity for local arts activity. Artists in residence schemes offer opportunities to empower the public in relation to the arts, developing long-term and sustained relationships between the artist and the community. Educational and outreach work can act not only as a service to the community or as a means of building future audiences, but can be a powerful mechanism for transforming and strengthening the relationship between the museum and the community (*Charter for the Arts in Scotland* 1993).

If museums are truly to act 'for the public benefit', then they need to take into account the demands of society (Davies 1994a). Community projects are closely linked to the issue of enabling ordinary people to take control of their own lives both economically and socially (*Charter for the Arts in Scotland* 1993). It is possible to become involved with wider social programmes in collaboration with municipal authorities, development agencies, or other government programmes. The banners now housed in the Kelvingrove Museum and Art Gallery in Glasgow were a joint initiative in which 600 people took part in sewing twelve banners for 'Keeping Glasgow in Stitches', covering every aspect of the city's life, from socialism to football.

Psychological barriers will only be broken down if attitudes within the museum community change. Enabling increased participation and community involvement can only succeed if those who work inside museums also see their role as participants, albeit enabling participants. They are there not to educate, but to assist in the learning process. As Birney (1986) suggests, learning as a purpose is perhaps more effective than education, since it can then incorporate curiosity and the urge to explore. Museum workers need to share and not guide, and to remember that they will only be regarded as a community facility if they are seen as equal partners, not as superior guardians of what is ostensibly a people's past. Barriers of 'cultural competence' are created and sustained by museum curators – they must be the first to break them down. This though may take time; since as Wright comments:

> On present evidence I fear that many curators do not view the overriding goal of their institution as being to communicate and share knowledge with its visitors, and thus to bring about a diffusion of power and knowledge from the specialist to the non-specialist.
>
> (Wright 1989: 134)

As with psychological barriers, where attitudes can build barriers, so too attitudes to disabled people, 'can be as impassable as physical and sensory barriers' (McGinnis 1994). McGinnis suggests that in the UK about one in four people have some kind of disability. Considerable progress has been made in providing wheelchair access, induction loop systems, and 'hands on' exhibitions for people with visual impairment, while links are being forged with local societies of and for disabled people. However, as McGinnis warns:

> Access means not only physical access, but conceptual, intellectual and multi-sensory access as well. A lift will not help a person with a learning difficulty or a partially sighted person to understand a museum's collection; but clearer layout and larger print on labels and signs will.
>
> (McGinnis 1994: 27)

Municipal authorities and other funders generally have policy commitments to improving physical access, while many authorities and organisations offer staff awareness training on the needs of people with disabilities as users of cultural facilities. Often the problem is exacerbated by museum staff simply being unaware that a person has a disability. Museums need to take the lead in developing strategies for the disabled.[1]

The Merseyside Society for the Deaf runs one-day workshops addressing the basic issues involved in communicating with deaf people. They suggest that written labels and signs can help, although staff need to be made aware of signals that can assist, such as facial expressions, eye contact, and body language (Fewster 1992). Another initiative was the launch of an art album for the blind and partially sighted in the Royal Academy in London. Ten works from the gallery's permanent collection have been recreated as 'thermo-forms' (raised images of parts of paintings), which are accompanied by a tape which is available both to individual visitors and for use in workshops. A touch tour is also available in the Wolfson Galleries at the British Museum (Pearson, A. 1989). The 'Art on Tyneside' exhibition at the Laing Art Gallery in Newcastle-upon-Tyne had a rubber mat on the floor to indicate the route through the exhibition. There are endless possibilities which are being added to as technology is harnessed to improve the facilities for the disabled.

Other structural factors such as age and geographical location can also act as barriers to visiting. Falk and Dierking (1992), for example, found that ease of access and availability of parking may determine visitor attendance as much, if not more, than the nature and quality of the museum's collection. The barriers for older people, though, are compounded by psychological factors, where the cohort effect means that attitudes and habits acquired in youth remain with people for the rest of their lives (Davies 1994a). Museums have a considerable number of barriers, both psychological and structural, to overcome if they are to provide literally for the whole population (Jenkinson 1989).

WHY VISIT MUSEUMS?

Having considered the reasons why people do *not* visit museums, consideration should be given to why they do. A good starting point for such a review is Falk and Dierking's *The Museum Experience* (1992), which draws on a number of studies undertaken in the US, in order to develop an understanding of the way the public uses museums. Falk and Dierking conceptualised the museum visit in what they term the 'Interactive Experience Model', where the museum visit involves three contexts: the personal context, the social context, and the physical context:

> The museum experience occurs within the physical context, a collection of structures and things we call the museum. Within the museum is the visitor, who perceives the world through his [*sic*] own personal context. Sharing this experience are various other people, each with their own personal contexts, which together create a social context . . . At any given moment, any one of the three contexts could assume major importance in influencing the visitor. The visitor's experience can be thought of as a continually shifting interaction among personal, social and physical contexts.
>
> (Falk and Dierking 1992: 5–6)

The principal findings of this study are extremely useful for museums in creating museum experiences for the different types of visitors. Falk and Dierking break down the visitors into casual visitors and organised groups. It may be helpful to break these down even further into constituencies that represent distinct styles of perceiving exhibits: groups containing children; singletons; couples; and adult social groups (McManus 1991). The museum public is increasingly fragmented with different publics wanting to learn and do different things at different speeds (Wright 1989). Consequently, Falk and Dierking's recommendations may need to be further broken down to accommodate this fragmentation of experiences.

Falk and Dierking set out a number of principles which will increase effective communication with the public. They regard exhibitions as the major media through which museums communicate with the public, and so their recommendations refer to ways in which exhibitions can be designed 'to reinforce both the experiences the visitor has inside the museum and those outside, before and after the visit' (Falk and Dierking 1992: 151). It is worth looking at each of the principles in detail.

The first principle is that each visitor learns in a different way, interpreting information from their previous knowledge, experience, and beliefs. Related to this is a further principle: that visitors have different learning styles, with their previous experiences affecting what they learn from the museum. The creators of the exhibitions need therefore to have an understanding not only of what the museum wants the visitor to take away from an exhibit, but also what the visitor already knows. This entails building 'structures that enable visitors to traverse the path from current knowledge and experience to hoped-for knowledge and experience' (Falk and Dierking 1992: 137). Along with other commentators such as Radley (1991), they suggest that consideration needs to be given to ways in which mixed media and other kinds of images can help audiences acquire information. Another approach could be to layer the exhibition, with parts for the expert and other layers for the visitor spending only five minutes; or designing exhibits specifically for the novice and others specifically for the expert. Connections should also be sought between the museum experience and the visitor's life outside the museum. If the visitors can relate to the exhibition in some way, they are more likely to remember and use the information given by that exhibition.

Another principle outlined by Falk and Dierking is that all visitors personalise the museum's message so that it conforms to their own understanding and experience. They confirm Radley's (1991) suggestion that the context of the objects is highlighted. They also suggest that museum visitors tend to compare an object on display with an object they have seen before. Consequently, they should be encouraged to personalise the exhibit through using such techniques as living history displays, labelling, videos, and the contextual arrangement of the displays. Then the interpreter can begin with the familiar and move to the unfamiliar. As McManus (1991) warns, curators should beware of defining the exhibition using their own agenda and understanding of the objects. A further suggestion not considered by Falk and Dierking could be to tell the public what the museum's goals are and the principles behind the organisation and display of work, which may also bridge the gap between previous knowledge and the exhibition's message (Wright 1989).

A third principle is that every visitor arrives with an agenda and a set of expectations of the museum which will strongly influence their behaviour and learning. To a large extent, people go to museums because they want to have fun, a word more often associated with Disney. The fun that people want from museums though is related more to seeing unique and unusual objects,

82

of being visually stimulated and intellectually challenged. As Falk and Dierking stress, 'Making museums entertaining does not mean trivializing exhibits, but it does suggest designing exhibition spaces that encourage a variety of emotional responses' (Falk and Dierking 1992: 142). In order to facilitate learning, then, exhibitions should be designed to incorporate the visitor's perceptions of the exhibits rather than the exhibition designer's ideas. As MacDonald has commented,

> Visitors bring to any exhibition particular preconceptions – particular tendencies towards certain imaginings. Clearly, the more that exhibition-makers can manage to detect of these predispositions, the better they will be able to work with them . . . exhibitions can at least shake preconceptions which visitors may hold.
>
> (MacDonald 1992: 407)

However, this is not to suggest that the professional does not have a significant input to the exhibition, since 'The idea that the public are better judges than curators about exhibition contents seems to me like saying that the patient will make a better diagnosis than the doctor' (Borg 1984: 47). Instead there should be a partnership, informed by the preconceptions of the public and the knowledge of the professional.

Falk and Dierking found that most visitors come to the museum as part of a social group; and that consequently, what visitors see, do, and remember is mediated by that group. Numerous surveys have discovered that people find museums uncomfortable places to visit. Museums therefore need to encourage socialising, since this 'creates a personal comfort zone that enables visitors to learn' (Falk and Dierking 1992: 157). The physical setting needs to be understood to enable social interactions, with examples being suggested, such as displays designed to be seen from both adult and children's heights, and exhibits created specifically for particular groups.

Related to this is the finding that the visitor's experience within the museum includes the museum staff and other visitors. In living history displays, for example, the staff can play an integral role in the display, helping visitors to appreciate the scale of an object and its relation to the world. Consideration also needs to be given to ways of overcoming crowding and queuing within the museum. Visitors are further influenced by the physical aspects of the museum, including the architecture, ambience, smell, and sound, as well as the location of exhibits and the museum's orientation. Wright (1989) gives some useful suggestions for ameliorating some of these problems, such as catering for 'museum fatigue' by offering opportunities for recollection by having separate rest rooms.

Although not referring to the 'authenticity' debate which engages the interests of numerous other commentators, Falk and Dierking do recognise the visitor's sense of awe and the legitimacy that the museum provides the objects in its care. Drawing on Graburn's (1977) discussion on reverence, they cite Shelton (cited in Weil 1991), who considers that the public has no difficulties when the legitimacy of an object is obvious and historical. Where they do encounter difficulties is when the legitimacy is not immediately obvious or is recent in origin. Consequently, Falk and Dierking suggest that the museum does not allow these 'value' discrepancies to discredit the exhibition.

Falk and Dierking go into further detail, most notably in terms of the social context, and finding ways of making the experience of group members more effective. Their study, although it could have been further developed and broken down into more distinct constituencies, nevertheless offers a number of useful indicators for assessing and improving visitor experiences. It has brought together a wealth of research and has lent it a coherence which gives a number of useful insights. Falk and Dierking drew on material which investigated the museum visitors and their reactions to the museum as a whole and to the exhibitions in particular. It is worth considering the types of research that could be used for these investigations.

Seagram and her colleagues (1993) have constructed an approach to audience research in terms of three models of exhibit development. The traditional model, the 'mandate-driven model', is a construct where

> the display of collections and the expository transmission of facts as selected by the museum's academic staff have been the predominant means of fulfilling the mandate to educate visitors. What the visitor makes of these education opportunities is up to him or her.
>
> (Seagram *et al.* 1993: 30)

A more recent approach is the 'market-driven model', whereby 'the audience is given a central role in determining what museums offer in their exhibits' (ibid.: 30). Instead, Seagram and her colleagues advocate that museums adopt the 'transaction approach' which was originally developed by Ashley (1989) of the Canadian National Historic Parks and Sites Services. This approach enables the staff who are planning an exhibit to 'try to represent the needs and characteristics of the audience *at the same time* as they work to meet the goals of the institution' (Seagram *et al.* 1993: 30). This approach overcomes the fundamental problems of the other two approaches. Mandate-driven research has excluded questions about how to enable audience participation and investigations of current museum-visiting experience, as well as ignoring current non-visitors. The market-driven approach, on the other hand, overcomes the problems of the mandate-driven approach but tends to undermine the role of the professional staff, where the direction of the museum's educational role has been handed over to the audience. Instead, the transaction approach allows the museum to balance the merits of the mandate and market approaches.

This unifying conceptual framework should enable a coherent programme of audience research to develop. Seagram and her colleagues (1993: 34) stipulate that the goals for such an audience research programme should be:

1 the building of effective, economical exhibits through research into an audience's interaction with the museum, and in particular, its exhibits

2   the establishment and continual refinement of standards that define effective museum exhibits
3   the building of a better relationship between a museum and its communities, particularly communities not traditionally represented in museum audiences, by informing exhibit development with knowledge gained through community consultation
4   the dissemination of knowledge gained through audience research to all museum staff and the wider museum community.

In order to achieve these goals, both basic and applied studies need to be conducted. Basic research includes: general demographic surveys of visitors and non-visitors; studies of audience attitudes and expectations of museums and their exhibitions; and more specific projects that relate to gallery clusters (such as, assessing how one can effectively convey the importance of current issues or principles).

On the other hand, applied research assists museums in examining the effectiveness of museum exhibits at communicating their intended messages. Thus evaluation takes place at three main stages of the exhibition process, although these do overlap (Griggs 1992). Front-end evaluation is carried out at the beginning of a project when ideas are being developed for an exhibition. Formative evaluation tests these ideas and exhibits while in production, before they are too firm to be modified. Here pre-testing takes the form of mock-ups of the exhibits and considers communication effectiveness on a sample target audience. Summative evaluation assesses the effectiveness of the exhibition after it has opened. Here information is sought to inform the creation of further exhibitions. Few museums employ all of these methods, preferring to concentrate on one particular evaluative method, although some museums, such as the Royal Ontario Museum, have consistently used all three of these methods over a number of years (Lockett 1991).

The National Museum of Natural History in the US, on redesigning its Marine Life Hall, used front-end evaluation to reveal the public's understanding of ecosystems and their attitude and understanding of the preservation of ecosystems. By talking to the public, the museum discovered not only that they had little understanding of the meaning of an ecosystem, but that although they considered that marine systems should be preserved, they did not know why. As a consequence, the new exhibition did not focus on convincing the public to preserve marine environments, but concentrated on why it is important and on how the public could help the effort (Falk and Dierking 1992).

Formative evaluation also demands dialogue with the visitor. Gallery 33 in the Birmingham Museum and Art Gallery assessed their new labels by asking colleagues, friends, family, schoolchildren, and target group members to read the text aloud. They were then asked to describe what they understood, thereby giving the professional staff some indication as to the flow of the text (Hooper-Greenhill 1994). More formal methods can also be used, such as using small groups of people to discuss their reactions to, for example, a preliminary video which is to be used in a display.

An alternative formative evaluative method is observation, where visitors are watched and their movements tracked, looking at where they stop and the length of time they view an exhibit. The main disadvantage of this method of evaluation is that the evaluation is based purely on observation, and cannot assess the underlying motives of the visitor. Why did the visitor stop at that exhibit? What made them stay there for that particular length of time?

Summative evaluation was used by the Discovery Room at the National Museums of Scotland. Using 'structured video recall', a video of the eight themed areas of the Discovery Room was shown to visitors on leaving the room. The ensuing conversation was recorded, and an analysis undertaken of their reactions and meaning of their experiences. The research proved invaluable in demonstrating how the project had worked, and was instrumental in developing the project as a travelling exhibition (Stevenson and Bryden 1991).

The importance of evaluative research is increasingly being recognised, since according to Seagram and her colleagues,

> museums have a choice. They can support new models of community consultation, of which audience research is a part, and transform their functions and modes of operation such that they can continue to serve pluralistic societies with new priorities while maintaining their expert functions of research and education. The alternative is for museums to remain as they are, serving steadily diminishing audiences, and becoming increasingly marginalized institutions, or to suffer intervention that will undermine their expert functions.
>
> (Seagram *et al.* 1993: 38)

Such a prediction is as relevant to evaluative research as it is to the whole museum approach to the public and the issue of public access. To enable access a museum needs to understand its public, the subject of concern for the next chapter.

Part II
The practice

5

The museum's markets

The starting point for any marketing activity is to meet the needs that consumers seek to satisfy. By researching and understanding the needs of the public, a museum will be able to develop its products accordingly to facilitate the exchange process. As Hooper-Greenhill remarks, 'the relationship between the museum and its many and diverse publics will become more and more important. And this relationship must focus on genuine and effective use of the museum and its collection' (Hooper-Greenhill 1994: 6).

Although the museum's public will also include stakeholders and other influencing organisations, this chapter will focus primarily on the museum's users. The term 'visitor' is a limiting concept, referring only to those who passively visit the museum. However, there are a variety of other 'users' of a museum's service, whether it is through answering enquiries about objects and specimens, assisting with research, supplying information to journalists, or assisting schools with projects. The variety of uses for museums include:

- sightseeing and tourism
- education, formal and informal
- historic site visiting, general and specific
- entertainment
- gift shopping
- catering
- research: academic and amateur
- collecting and recording
- social and community work
- personal entertaining of family, friends, or business associates
- fulfilment of personal, political, and social objectives
- loan of material
- creation of employment
- volunteer employment
- image-building: local, regional, or national
- location work, television, film, and radio
- product launches
- community involvement
- skill and craft training

- leisure and recreation
- club and membership programmes
- club, society, and enthusiast activities
- corporate hospitality
- special events.

(Adapted from Bryant 1988 and Wilson 1991)

Depending on the size and scope of the museum, all or only a few of these uses can be offered, while the demand from potential users will also differ depending on the circumstances.

Museum audiences are far from captive, and so it is vital that the museum understands what it is that attracts them to museums (Moore, R. 1988). Moreover, if a museum is effectively to serve the public, it needs to know who that public is, both visitors and non-attenders. Market research can help the museum to learn about and understand the public, while at the same time fulfilling other needs of the museum.

Seagram and her colleagues (1993) have recognised three fundamental reasons why museums need to undertake market research. As the funding debate places increased emphasis on accountability, so a museum needs to know how it can fulfil its public mission. Second, they stipulate that museums need to formalise their programme of market research, instead of conducting *ad hoc* studies. Finally, as attendances decline, museums need a better understanding of their audiences' needs, interests, expectations, and motivations. Munley (1986) has suggested five further uses of market research. Research can justify the institution, in terms of its worth and its choice of exhibitions and public programmes, while at the same time the process of gathering information assists in long-term planning. Research can also assist in the formulation of new exhibitions or programmes as well as in assessment of their effectiveness. Finally, with this increased understanding of how people use museums, it will be possible to construct theories. A museum, then, would undertake research for any or all of the following reasons:

- To know who its visitors are; what is the profile of their age, their occupations, interests, and so on.
- To keep in touch with the needs and wants of the visitors; how can the museum's service best be improved to meet these needs and wants?
- To elicit visitor opinions: what do they like or dislike? Did they find the museum easily? Would they recommend the museum? What do they think of the shop, café, staff, and so on?
- To discover who are not visiting the museum; how they could be persuaded to visit.
- To assist in developing marketing plans: Where should the museum advertise? Should special groups be targeted? How might more visitors come at quiet times? Are new exhibitions needed?
- To help establish priorities: Should the museum invest in upgrading the labelling or is there a greater need for baby-changing facilities?

- To define and solve problems: Why does the temporary exhibition attract only a small percentage of visitors? Is it the content, location, admission fee?
- To prove the museum is doing the best it can.
- To make a case for additional funding; there may be strong audience demand for additional facilities.

MARKET RESEARCH

There are two types of research that will elicit this information: qualitative and quantitative. Qualitative research is less common, but is invaluable in exploring how people feel or believe about particular things. It enables a much more in-depth understanding to attitudes. Qualitative research takes the form of either in-depth interviews or focus group research. In-depth interviews are one-to-one interviews. There is usually an agenda set for the conversation, although it is not fixed, the conversation usually following topic areas. The conversation is taped and subsequently analysed by extracting the main points and assessing trends with other similarly conducted interviews. In-depth interviews are more often used in exhibit evaluation. They are time-consuming and are probably not as useful as focus groups.

Focus group research

Focus groups usually consist of between six to twelve people who have been pre-recruited to meet defined characteristics to discuss topics on the research agenda (Chandler 1954; Banks 1957; Burgess 1982). For example, if the museum is keen to learn why the public is not visiting the museum, then it would recruit current non-visitors. The group format aims to capitalise on group dynamics in order to throw light on the research topics, where participants often exchange ideas in a dynamic way (Robson 1989). A moderator guides the discussion, which usually follows a set agenda. The moderator's role is quite skilled, since some members of the group may dominate and others may be overwhelmed. It is the moderator's job to ensure that all members of the group get a chance to air their views. The discussion usually lasts for one to two hours, and is videoed or tape-recorded. The discussion is then analysed to draw out the main points according to the set agenda. Usually around six groups are run, in order to assess trends, and to compare responses in terms of characteristics. For example, are there any differences between men and women or younger and older people?

Conducting focus groups involves a number of techniques, and ideally should be undertaken by a professional. However, if finances do not permit this, it is worth at least sitting in on a professionally run focus group to assess how it works. Volunteers can be recruited by using a short questionnaire to match them to the profile that is being sought. It is a good idea to recruit more than are needed, since there will always be those who do not turn up. The volunteers will need to be reimbursed their travelling expenses, and usually refreshments are served before or during the discussion.

Focus groups are an increasingly favoured method of seeking information for market research, although they have rarely been used in museums. An exception is the research conducted by the Susie Fisher Group (1990), outlined in *Bringing History and the Arts to a New Audience: Qualitative research for the London Borough of Croydon*. Here a market research company conducted focus group research with current non-attenders to museums – those who 'wouldn't be seen dead in a museum'. The objectives of the research were to develop an insight into these attitudes, into people's interpretations of experience and personal meanings. The London Museums Consultative Committee, which represents the interests of all museums in London, also commissioned qualitative research from Mass Observation. This research entitled *'Dingy Places with Different Kinds of Bits': An attitudes survey of London museums amongst non-visitors* (Trevelyan 1991) had a London-wide museum application.

An illustration of the running and consequent use of the findings of focus group research would be recent research undertaken at the University of Stirling. The sample for the focus groups was drawn from a population of university employees, with a quota set for occupational category. This quota was set as a result of previous research (Cheek *et al.* 1976; Duncan 1978; Hood 1983; McLean 1992), which has shown that museum visiting is often directly related to social classification. There were no criteria for splitting the groups into regular museum visitors and non-regular museum visitors, since it was felt that a mixture of regular and non-regular visitors may encourage debate on visiting patterns within the groups. A total of six groups were conducted: five groups with eight participants, and one group with five participants. Each of the groups consisted of a mix of professional and non-professional workers. All of the groups contained a mixture of regular museum visitors (that is they visited museums at least twice a year) and of non-regular museum visitors. Each group session was run by a moderator following a structured set of topics, and lasted between one and one and a half hours. The units of analysis consisted of the groups' ideas, experiences, and viewpoints, and the reported and logical relationships between them.

The discussion focused on the following issues: reasons for visiting/not visiting; the types of museum visited; interaction with other museum visitors; interaction with museum staff; improvements to museums to increase attendance. The discussion was tape-recorded and transcribed. From these transcripts it was possible to analyse the findings and relate them to the objectives of the research. The findings were written up in a report format, using the discussion topics as subject headings. The main trends were reported often using the participant's own words to illustrate. The report recognised the limitations of the research, mainly due to the use of university employees as a population to be sampled. The whole exercise gave considerable insight into the underlying reasons for non-attendance at museums, which was largely a consequence of bad experiences during school visits, and the perceptions of museum attendants as security guards. Interestingly, the perceptions were similar in all social classes, although the lower social grades were more likely to be deterred from visiting a museum as a consequence.

Focus groups address the questions of what, how, and why. They deal with information too difficult or expensive to quantify, such as subjective opinions and value judgements. It is also possible to probe and learn about feelings, experiences, attitudes, and ideas. It allows flexible questioning, and is responsive to what is being said. However, there is a technique to conducting the groups: while it is important that the aims and subject areas of the discussion are very clear (or little will be gleaned from them), their value lies in their ability to probe and delve more deeply into attitudes. Moreover qualitative research can help to interpret, illuminate, illustrate, and qualify empirically determined statistical relationships.

Survey research

Quantitative research is the method used to determine empirical, statistical relationships. In other words it answers the questions of who, where, when and how: the quantity questions. It collects quantitative data, that is, numbers. These can then be used to tell how many people fall into certain categories and hold certain attitudes. For example, how many people arriving by car had difficulty in finding the museum; or how many adults who came with children felt there was too much information on the labels. Quantitative research uses surveys, usually through questionnaires, to extract the data.

Ideally a market research agency would be commissioned to undertake the survey. This can be extremely costly, though, and for many museums is only worthwhile if a consortium is formed, particularly if a survey is being undertaken of non-visitors, to assess who they are and why they are not visiting. Often surveys are derided for confirming what is already known. This may be the case, but if the museum already knows that its visitors want improved parking facilities, then it will be easier to make its case to a funding body if it has the statistics to confirm its hunch. The overall purpose of a survey is to make decisions based on evidence, to identify opportunities, and to help resolve uncertainty and risk. Usually there are some surprises in the findings. The success of a survey, though, lies in the design – it should be well planned and carefully executed (Conybeare 1991).

There are four main areas of information that can be extracted from a survey:

1   *Levels of use*
    This includes both variations in levels over time and levels of use over space. For example, levels over time would include seasonal, weekly, and daily totals. When do most people visit? Are Fridays quiet periods? (And would they perhaps be quieter than the usual day for closure of municipal museums – Monday?) Variations in levels of use over space would

consider the distribution of visitors over the site. Are there too many people in the shop? What areas are not being visited? Much of this information could also be extracted from the museum's records, and from observation of, for example, the number of visitors at entry and exit points, and the formation of queues.

2 *Characteristics of the visit*

There are two aspects to this: the characteristics of the trip and the characteristics of the visit itself. When considering the trip, a museum might want to find out the journey time, journey distance, form of transport, type of route. How far did the visitors travel? How did they get to the museum? Does the museum need more car parking facilities? The characteristics of the visit would consider how often the respondents visit. Are they regular visitors? Do they use all the facilities? What do they do once inside the museum? Do they visit other museums or leisure attractions?

3 *Characteristics of the visitors*

This is where the museum learns about the profile of its visitors. Surveys have traditionally looked at the socio-demographic characteristics and the attitudes of the visitors. Socio demographics would consider the following: Who are they? Who do they come with? Where do they come from? Questions could also be asked on their age, gender, group composition, occupation, education, and geographical origin. Attitudes would consider what the visitors think of the museum, what their likes and dislikes are, and what improvements they would like to see.

4 *Publicity information*

The media profile could be ascertained for publicity purposes. What papers and magazines do the visitors read? What television programmes do they watch or radio programmes do they listen to?

Decisions would need to be made on what information is required. Obviously the extent of the information that can be extracted will be restricted by the museum's resources to undertake and analyse the survey and by the type of survey to be used. Below are outlined the steps for scheduling a survey. A sample self-completion questionnaire is included in Appendix 1.

1 Analyse the problem.
2 Undertake secondary research.
3 Finalise objectives of survey.
4 Decide what areas to cover from:
   ● visitor identification
   ● facilities development
   ● programme development
   ● visitor development (non-visitor survey).
5 Decide on the sample.
6 Decide on duration.
7 Decide on type of survey:
   ● self-administered (site or mail survey)

- personal interview
- telephone interview
- non-visitor survey.

8   Design the questionnaire.
9   Pilot the questionnaire.
10 Print questionnaires and observation schedules.
11 Recruit and train staff.
12 Undertake fieldwork.
13 Prepare data for analysis and undertake analysis.
14 Report on survey findings.

First the museum needs to analyse the problem. Is the museum trying to increase the profile of its visitors, or is it trying to improve its facilities to match the needs of its visitors? It is then worth doing some exploratory research looking at secondary sources. This is existing information that is available either internally, in the museum's own records, or externally, from such sources as tourist or government publications. The information needed to solve the problem may already be available. Decide whether a survey is in fact the best means of obtaining the information needed. If it is, obtain surveys conducted by other museums or leisure attractions, and learn from them. Decide what resources are available to undertake the research. Can the museum afford a market research agency, or does it have enough willing volunteers, and access to a personal computer to analyse the data? As Conybeare warns, do not be over-ambitious, 'It is better to do a limited survey well, than to attempt something more elaborate and fail to complete the project' (Conybeare 1991: 4).

The next stage is crucial – clear, well thought-out objectives will make the analysis simpler. Consult with colleagues and the museum's trustees to be sure the most pertinent areas are being assessed. Once the objectives are set, the museum should be clearer about the areas that will need to be covered in the survey. It is likely the questionnaire will be used to identify the visitors, their demographic characteristics, and so on. Will the survey need to consider the development of the museum's facilities – what are the visitors satisfaction levels with the current facilities, and what additions have they asked to be included? Does the museum wish to consider its programme development by consulting the visitors on exhibitions and the activities programme? Finally, if one of the objectives is to find out why people do not visit the museum and what would make them visit, then a non-visitor survey will need to be undertaken.

The sample should ideally be an accurate cross-section of the visitors to the museum or of the general public. Either question all visitors to the museum over a given period, or decide to choose every nth visitor for interview. Decide who is to be excluded, for example, children under 16 years of ages. It is important to be consistent. Specific visitor types could be targeted, such as all elderly visitors, if the museum wishes specifically to learn about older visitors. This would require a question on age before the survey takes place. Often a museum will want to learn about groups of visitors, so the group leader should be targeted and a sample of group members. The size of the sample will depend on the number of visitors to the museum – obviously a small museum would not be able to survey as many visitors as a museum attracting hundreds of thousands of visitors. A small sample, though, is rarely valid, and has little value. Aim for a minimum of 200 responses. The larger the sample, the more statistically significant the result.

A decision then needs to be made on how long the survey should run, and at which time of the year. The days of the week on which it will be undertaken also need to be determined. Ideally the survey will be conducted at different times of the day, on different days of the week and the year, depending on the museum's resources and the objectives of the survey.

Once the content of the survey, the sample, and duration have been decided, it should be easier to determine the type of survey. Self-administered and personal interview questionnaires are the most common; telephone interviews are rare, only being used if the museum has the telephone numbers of visitors. Self-administered questionnaires can be completed in the museum, usually at the exit at the end of the visit, or via mail surveys, using a return post-paid envelope if the museum has a mailing list. Mail surveys are more expensive, and would normally only be used if the museum was wanting to find out about, for example, the museum's Friends. Alternatively a telephone survey could be undertaken. Self-completion site surveys are the cheapest survey method and the easiest to administer. They have their limitations, though, since there is no control over who fills them in. Moreover only simple questions can be used; and there is the risk that the form may be completed inaccurately.

Personal interview surveys are usually carried out at the museum exit. This method enables large amounts of data to be collected, and also offers personal contact between the museum, in the form of the interviewer, and the visitor. The results generated from this type of survey also tend to be more reliable than other methods. The disadvantages are the cost, particularly of staff time and expertise.

The non-visitor survey – or more accurately population survey, as some of the respondents may in fact be visitors although they are not currently on the museum site – is conducted either in-home or on the street. These questionnaires can be long and detailed, particularly if conducted in the respondent's home. However, they are extremely costly and require considerable expertise, and so are best left to the experts. It would be advantageous to form a consortium of other museums and attractions with similar requirements from a questionnaire to conduct this type of survey. These surveys can be extremely informative, and if possible, should be conducted periodically.

The questionnaire should be concise and have clear instructions for completion. The questions should be in everyday language and should be kept simple, avoiding ambiguity. They should be specific and to the point, and should not be leading, such as 'Do you find the displays interesting?'! The question sequence usually starts with an introduction, briefly outlining the purpose of the survey, and possibly also mentioning its anonymity. This is followed with some warm-up questions, which are simple and innocuous in order to build up a rapport. The main body of questions should be grouped in related subjects, and ensure that answers to earlier questions do not influence later questions. It is usual to keep the demographic questions until the end, since they can be sensitive, but by that time a rapport should have been built up with the respondent. The only exception is when particular groups of visitors need to be filtered out, for example if the intention is to confine the sample to older people, their age being ascertained before the questionnaire is started. Finally, remember to thank the respondent.

The question format will vary depending on the information required. However, to simplify the analysis it is worth using well-structured, multiple-choice questions from which the respondent chooses from a series of options. Remember to leave an 'Other' option where possible, in case the list is not exhaustive. In opinion-seeking questions, as well as the 'Yes' and 'No' responses, include 'Don't know' or 'No preference', since the respondents may not have any opinion on the subject. Keep the open-ended questions (questions which the respondents complete in their own words) to a minimum, since they are time-consuming to analyse. For attitude questions it is worth using Likert-type scales, which enable the respondents to judge the question on a scale of 1 to 5, the maximum 5 for example being 'agree strongly', and 1 being 'disagree strongly'.

A self-completion questionnaire would rarely have more than twenty questions or fill more than two sides. An interview-administered questionnaire could be longer. It pays to pre-code the form, so that the respondent or interviewer can circle the printed numeric code. This increases the speed at which the data can be entered into the computer, and therefore reduces error.

The next stage is essential, but often neglected. Pilot the questionnaire by testing about a dozen on the general public, to test the respondents' and the interviewers' reactions. It is highly likely that as a result amendments and adjustments will need to be made in the layout or wording.

Once finalised, the questionnaire can be printed up. Brief staff on the procedure for the survey. Attendants will need to know if they are to hand surveys out to visitors either at the beginning or end of the visit. An area needs to be set aside with tables and chairs and a supply of pens for the questionnaire to be completed. Interviewing staff need to be thoroughly briefed on the procedure and the importance of their role. It can be helpful to offer an incentive, such as putting the respondent's name in a prize draw, or possibly even offering a free cup of coffee in the café. Keep a record of when the surveys were conducted, and such conditions as the weather or special events either inside or outside the museum; this will help to monitor fluctuations. Finally, if the survey is a street or door-to-door survey, the police need to be informed.

Once the fieldwork is undertaken, each questionnaire should be checked over, to ensure it is correctly dated, and then numbered in sequence, to enable them to be identified later, if necessary. Discard the inevitable spoiled questionnaires. The results can be processed either manually, which can be a long tedious process, or ideally on a computer. Each response option should have a numeric code, which can simply be entered into the computer for that question. It is usual to type in '9' for no response. There are various computer software packages for processing the data. Depending on the sophistication of these packages, it should be possible to supplement the percentage frequency data with cross-tabulation. This enables the assessment, for example, of whether a preference for workshops is favoured by one age group over another. There is a huge range of possibilities depending on the capabilities of the computer, the software, and of course the museum's needs in terms of the stated objectives.

The findings should then be set out in report form. The report should be concise, and should include a summary of the main findings as an executive summary, for quick and easy reference. The data can be laid out in tables, bar charts, pie charts, and so on. Admit any limitations in the survey method, and any possibility of bias, if, for example, the survey was undertaken in a school holiday period, when the profile of the visitors may differ from the norm. Use other sources of information, such as demographic data for the region, to assess how the museum's visitors match up to the regional profile. Assess trends from previous surveys undertaken at the museum and compare with surveys undertaken at other local museums. Do not let the report gather dust on the shelf. It should be used at every opportunity: to assess the strengths and weaknesses of the museum; to anticipate threats and opportunities; to understand the visitor, and implement change; to make decisions on which media to use for publicity; and also for segmentation and targeting purposes. Finally, repeat the process. Surveys should become an integral aspect of the marketing effort. Ideally they should be conducted every season, although an annual survey will suffice for most museums. There should not be too long a time lapse between surveys, or inevitably the museum will lose contact with the public.

SEGMENTATION, TARGETING, AND POSITIONING

Most museums today recognise the need to segment their markets. By breaking the public down into constituent groups that have some characteristics in common, museums should be able to anticipate their needs and accordingly decide where to place efforts for audience development. It enables museums to focus resources and effort on the market segment(s) that are most appropriate for meeting the museum's aims and objectives. Most museums are aware of their current market constituency but have not evaluated their needs and wants or the potential target audiences who do not currently attend. Whilst undertaking research into museums, Diai (1994) discovered that only half of the museums surveyed claimed to have identified specific target markets, while only 30 per cent had developed marketing plans. Although ideally museums wish to meet their mandate of operating 'for the public benefit', their resources and appeal to individuals' interests preclude the 'something for everyone' ideal.

Segmentation effectively subdivides a heterogeneous market into identifiable homogeneous submarkets. Market segmentation 'is the process of splitting customers into different groups, or segments, within which customers with similar characteristics have similar needs. By doing this, each one can be targeted and reached with a distinct marketing mix' (McDonald and Dunbar 1995: 10). Since buyers in a market differ in their wants, resources, geographical location, buying attitudes, and buying practices, any of these variables can be used to segment a market (Kotler 1967). The theory of market segmentation is well developed, embracing what Kotler (1967) refers to as 'STP' marketing, namely Segmenting, Targeting, and Positioning. Once different segments have been identified, it is then possible to target one or more segments which the organisation wishes to attract. Finally, the organisation competitively positions the product offering in each target market. This involves describing to customers how the organisation differs from current and potential competitors. Ultimately, effective segmentation should increase an organisation's profitability and reduce the competition it faces (Frank and Wind 1972). Market researchers tend to apply up to four variables to segment a market: geographic, demographic, psychographic, and behavioural (McGoldrick 1990).

However, as Davies has pointed out, 'traditional segmentation (as employed in the commercial marketing sector) is not always appropriate for museums and galleries' (Davies 1994a: 50). It is worth considering the problems that museums will encounter in segmenting their audiences, because unlike commercial organisations, museums are services, generally small, usually public and non-profit organisations, which are heterogeneous rather than homogeneous.

Because of the inseparability of service organisations, there is a high level of customer contact where the consumers themselves become part of the product (Carmen and Langeard 1980). The visitor becomes a part of the product through the experience in the museum. Thus, because of the closeness of the production–delivery process, mixing segments can lead to different groups influencing each other's experience (Lovelock 1984). Equally, because of their heterogeneity, museums provide a variety of different services, which appeal to different segments. This requires some skilled balancing. Alton Towers, the UK's top theme park, maintains its lead over its competitors by identifying a variety of target segments, such as families with children, young adults, annual general meetings, and product launch events. A separate marketing mix is then set for each segment with separate price policies, promotional tactics, product offerings, service levels, and so on (Dibb and Simkin 1993).

Museum visitors segment to a large degree according to the subject area of the museum (McLean 1993), to the extent where, for example, railway enthusiasts would visit railway museums but would not consider visiting a museum of another subject type. This reflects the notion of benefit segmentation first articulated by Haley (1968), where segments can be grouped according to benefits sought, in this case a special interest. Segmenting by special interest would require a greater understanding of the potential visitor than merely their demographic characteristics. Huie (1985) has pointed out that prediction of behaviour patterns on the basis of demographics alone is becoming increasingly difficult. Nevertheless, museums still tend to segment predominantly according to geodemographic bases, paying lip-service to the attitudes and opinions of visitors. Although there is a place for geodemographic segmentation, it may be that lifestyle characteristics need to play an ever-increasing part in the segmentation process.

There are, however, more influences at play in museums when choosing market segments than merely selecting the most appropriate segment. Municipal museums, in particular, are subject to political control. Here the market segment is often defined for the museum by the municipal authority, which, for example, has a policy of practising equal opportunities. Museum market researchers tend to give little consideration to the political influences that can dictate the choice of market segment.

Because of the nature of perishability, many service organisations, and particularly museums, experience significant variations in demand over time (Rathmell 1974), suffering from over-capacity and under-capacity at certain periods. The importance of the time dimension is particularly acute in leisure services (Stone 1990). Many potential visitors fail to visit museums because of lack of time, whereas others visit in order to fill in some time, particularly when they are on holiday. Holman and Wilson's (1982) explanation of shopping preferences in terms of a time dimension may be relevant for museums. They suggest that most consumers seek to restore one of two types of 'time equilibrium'. Some suffer too much obligatory time (time scarcity), while others have too much discretionary time. In the museum context, catering for visitors with discretionary time could include provision of lectures, guided tours, and maybe even museum clubs. Visitors whose time is scarce may need extended opening hours in the evening, the opportunity to be given guided tours of only one aspect of the museum, and so on. Museums may need to take more account of the two types of 'time equilibrium' in their decisions on segmentation and throughput of visitors.

The concept of intangibility means that the consumer's experience is variable, and is also more difficult to assess than the consumer response to manufactured goods (Zeithaml 1981). The variability involved creates difficulties in delineating segments. Heterogeneity refers to the difficulty of achieving standardisation of services that have the potential for high variability in their performance (Regan 1963; Rathmell 1966). Homogeneity of the consumer base therefore is not always possible or even desirable for many service organisations. Two or more distinct market segments may each contribute importantly to the organisation's success, yet they may not mix well. Ideally, potentially conflicting segments should be separated in their use of the facility (Lovelock 1984).

However, because of the perishability of services, this is complicated by the desire to increase the number of niche markets to fill capacity through diversification of the service offering. In art galleries, attempts are made to change the conceptualisation of the service by means of temporary exhibitions which attract a new market segment. An illustration of this would be the 'Art on

Tyneside' exhibition at the Laing Art Gallery in Newcastle-upon-Tyne, which sought to attract a wider socio-economic profile of visitors than its traditional market segment with a 'popular' exhibition aimed beyond the traditional art gallery attender. However, according to Carmen and Langeard (1980), the service provider will encounter difficulties in changing the conceptualisation of its core service to fit the new market segment. Equally, the provider will need to find some method of isolating the existing market segments from exposure to information about a new conceptualisation. The temporary exhibition that seeks to attract new market segments to the museum can encounter a number of problems. The new market segment, attracted initially by the temporary exhibition, may return when it has terminated, only to feel excluded from the social milieu and the traditional exhibition style, which is the normal practice of the art gallery. Equally, the current customer segment might be alienated by the addition of new market segments that do not fit into their social milieu. Market researchers tend to give little consideration to the stability of segments over time, particularly as new segments are introduced.

Davies (1994a) in *By Popular Demand*, includes a useful discussion on market segmentation. He suggests that for museums the principal ways of segmenting the market will be by demographics (which he breaks down into age, gender, class, and educational attainment), lifestyle, geography (broken down into residents, day-trippers, and tourists), schools, and special interest.

Demographic segmentation is the most commonly used form of segmentation. Clearly, choice of age and gender segmentation will depend on the nature of the museum and on the museum's own objectives. Segmentation by stage in the life-cycle, which considers age and family composition, is probably one of the most useful segmentation variables for museums. The needs of parents with young children will differ markedly from older couples whose children have left home. Young families will require crèche facilities, children's facilities, children's workshops, and so on, whereas an older family will have more time and a greater attention span, with demands for more information and inter-action with museum staff. A science museum is likely to attract more men than women, while a museum which is keen to widen its appeal to elderly people will segment according to age. Education attainment can also be a significant segmentation sector, the more highly educated being more likely to visit museums (Hooper-Greenhill 1994).

Social class as a basis of segmentation can be a minefield, and although post-modernists claim that social class is being eradicated, with the result that high and low culture begin to meet, the reality is that many museums are still subscribed to as an activity along social divide lines. Social class is determined by occupation, income, and sometimes ethnic origin and education. Classifications will vary from country to country; social class being considerably more fluid in the US than in the UK, where there are quite rigid guidelines on social class determination.[1]

Geographic segmentation can be broken down into local residents, day-trippers, and tourists. The factors that will define the museum's catchment

101

area will be the distance that people are willing to travel to the museum, and the time that it takes to travel that distance (Davies 1994a).

Referring to lifestyle or psychographic segmentation, Middleton, in *New Visions for Independent Museums in the UK* (1990), summarises the classification devised by Applied Futures Ltd: sustenance-driven groups; outer-directed groups; and inner-directed groups. Sustenance-driven groups include those who are low down on Maslow's hierarchy of needs (1970), their attitude and behaviour patterns being organised around fear for their future and their need for security. They tend to be older and disadvantaged people, or those who are relatively affluent, but are afraid of redundancy or debt. Outer-directed groups are further up the hierarchy of needs, and are striving to achieve social esteem and status. They tend to be materialistic, often in the 20–40 age group, and are constantly seeking to impress in order to belong to the 'right' group. Finally, the inner-directed groups are seeking self-actualisation. They are happier with their lot, have achieved a level of self-confidence, and feel in control of their lives. They are typically well educated, over 40, and often provide the museum with potential volunteers. Spiritual and aesthetic values, together with creativity, are strongest in this group.

Middleton suggests that museums should concentrate on the most prevalent group in contemporary society, the inner-directed groups. However, this clearly depends on the objectives of the individual museum. It may be that the inner-directed groups will represent the most appropriate 'fit' for museums. Some museums though will want to target segments which may belong to one of the other groups, particularly the sustenance-driven groups. Thus, for example, the Boston Children's Museum has developed a work programme for disadvantaged teenagers, called 'Kids at Risk', which was designed in collaboration with the schools, the criminal justice system, and social service organisations. Another museum, conscious that it should serve the needs of all members of the community, targeted people with learning difficulties. St Helens Museum developed a project in conjunction with Carousel, a Brighton-based organisation which specialises in creative arts by and with people with learning difficulties (Moore, K. 1993). Workshops using visual arts, drama, and music were held to explore the participants' feelings about their own home lives. A study visit was also arranged to Merseyside Maritime Museum. The participants then developed an exhibition consisting of a series of room sets, and followed this with a performance within the house, using music and drama. The participants kept a diary detailing their work in creating the house and the performances, which along with photographic records formed the basis of an accompanying exhibition. The project was found to be 'a highly rewarding experience for both the clients and their carers. It was also a highly positive experience for the museum staff, as much a learning process for them as for the other participants' (Moore, K. 1993: 19).

Schools are the next segmentation variable suggested by Davies (1994a), since they offer the museum hard data. It is a simple process to locate schools and discover the number of children at each school. Moreover, 'a thorough understanding of the relevant curricula and an analysis of past visiting experiences can enable the museum to construct a very precise and focused strategy for capturing a significant market share' (ibid.: 60). In the UK, schools account for a third of all visits to museums (*Sightseeing in the UK* 1992), offering an extremely lucrative market. There are other group combinations which a museum might choose to target, such as groups with children; singletons; couples; or adult social groups. The Boston Children's Museum, for example, has extensive family programmes, including a discovery kit that can be rented and taken home.

Finally, many museums are in the most fortunate position of being able to entice subject specialists. Thus industrial and transport museums may have a broad appeal, but a significant proportion of their visitors will comprise subject enthusiasts. The importance of themed museums is enhanced by the growth of associated leisure interests, including local history and amenity groups, conservation societies, and adult education classes (Davies 1994a). Themed museums are particularly attractive to researchers, students, and collectors, which could offer considerable latent potential for segmentation (ibid.). This type of segmentation equates with benefit segmentation, devised by Haley (1968), which divides the market according to the benefits that the consumer wants. It is a technique which has been used predominantly in both the tourism and leisure industries. In museums then, benefits will often accord with the attraction of the museum's collection.

A further segmentation variable could be added to Davies's (1994a) list: product-related behaviour or usage segmentation. A significant proportion of a museum's visitors will be accounted for by repeat visitors. These repeat visitors can form a loyal base of museum users, and will act as advocates for the museum. The concept of people 'belonging' to a museum is deeply rooted in the US. Building up loyalty and maintaining relationships with these repeat visitors is a mainstay of the concept of relationship marketing.

Although most museums tend to focus on demographic and geographic socio-economic segmentation, there are clearly a number of alternative bases for segmentation which could be more useful. Lifestyle, benefit, and usage segmentation should also be considered as a menu of possibilities, with ultimately the most appropriate choice depending on the individual museum and its goals.

To be effective, market segments need to be measurable (easy to identify and relatively homogeneous); substantial (large enough to justify developing a marketing mix aimed at that segment); accessible (easy to reach through promotion); and stable (the segment will be around long enough for action to be taken) (Dibb *et al.* 1991). Choice of which segmented markets the museum wishes to target should be based on the segment's compatibility with the museum's mission and its resources. The museum could opt for a concentrated strategy which focuses on only one segment in the population, or more likely would choose a differentiated strategy, selecting several segments to serve and developing tailored marketing programmes for each chosen segment (Lovelock and Weinberg 1988). The tendency is to consider every member of the public as a target, since it is only through attempting to reach everyone that the museum will fulfil its role as serving the public. As Davies comments, 'The concept of "something for everyone" is an attractive one because it encapsulates the fact that very few people in the UK have never visited a museum or art gallery and no socio-demographic group has been entirely marginalised as visitors' (Davies 1994a: 90). However, as Davies goes on to warn, 'the optimism of "something for everyone" should not deceive managers into either forgetting about marketing altogether or resorting to "spray and pray" strategies' (ibid.: 9). Segmentation and targeting are important if the museum is to ensure that it achieves its mission while maximising the use of its resources.

Positioning is the final stage in Kotler's STP strategy. This is where the organisation attempts to differentiate itself from its competitors in attracting an audience. Each organisation has a position or image in the consumer's mind which influences the decision to use the service. Each organisation has a set of attributes or benefits which can be compared to competitive offerings. The task is to find out how consumers feel about the service compared to its competitors in terms of the benefits offered. The organisation can then adopt a competitive strategy for its core positioning. A museum would also perhaps highlight a range of specific benefits for different aspects of its programme. Benefits in a museum might include links to curriculum studies, the reputation of the collection, or ease of access by public transport.

CONCLUSIONS

The relationship between the museum and its public is paramount in the contemporary museum. The role of the public has altered quite dramatically, while in the future public demands on museums are likely to increase. The response of museums has been wide and varied, from inviting full participation to interpreting their role as providing for the disadvantaged in society. The extent to which this response has been built on research of the market has also varied widely, with some museums undertaking continuous research of their visitors, while others have made no, or only token attempts to learn about their visitors. The customer is paramount in the concept of marketing, and meeting the customer's needs while meeting the goals of the organisation is the starting point of any marketing strategy. If museums are to maintain existing interest and increase their appeal, they need to look to their product. Ultimately the product will need to be matched to the market, which will assist in decisions on development of the product and choice of target market. Thus, segmentation, targeting, and positioning cannot be undertaken in isolation. Consideration of the benefits offered by the product also needs to be taken into account. The next chapter looks at the product and decisions on matching that product to the market.

6

The museum product

Goods can be defined in terms of their physical attributes but services are intangible, which complicates the concept of the product. Although there is a physical product (the collection), what is really being marketed is an intangible – the temporary use, generally by display, of the product. There may also be tangibles associated with the service, such as the facilities and promotional literature. These 'physical support' elements are often the only aspect of a service that can be viewed prior to purchase. The service product is also often equated with the service provider. Thus, the employees, or 'people', and their performance, or 'process', are also important dimensions of the marketing effort.

Most service organisations, including museums, provide a portfolio of different offerings. However, according to Lovelock and Weinberg,

> new products are often added without regard for their impact on the organization as a whole or for their interrelationship with other products in the portfolio. Old products sometimes continue to be offered, long after they have ceased to be useful to fulfilment of the institutional mission or to match the needs and concerns of potential customers.
> (Lovelock and Weinberg 1988: 201)

Since products form the focal point for an organisation's effort in satisfying its customers' needs, it becomes apparent that the museum needs to match the product and the target users. Getting the product right is possibly the single most important marketing activity. No amount of promotion or price incentives will encourage demand, let alone repeat demand, if the product is inferior. The task of creating demand is more complicated for museums, since there is no identifiable 'need' for a museum (Van der Vliet 1979). Moreover, to a large extent, the 'product line' is predetermined. The museum is not creating a product to meet an unmet need of the public. Rather, it has a fixed product, its collection, and the building in which it is housed. The product may be altered (by acquisition, new displays, or temporary exhibition) or enhanced (through additional facilities) but to a large degree, the museum product is fixed.

What is the museum product? The product is a bundle of images in the mind of the user, with the nature of the reaction to the museum product being psychological, rather than physical. The user aggregates impressions of the product (the museum experience), with all inputs (be they the display, the appearance of the attendants, or the atmosphere) being equally important to the composite product received by the user. It is only relatively recently that the museum product could legitimately be considered as the 'experience' of the museum. In the past, the product was the preserved collection; the significance of the relationship of that collection with the public was negligible (McLean 1995). Collections were not put together by the public, but by single individuals, in most instances for their own purposes and not for the gratification of the masses. The intrinsic character of museums, even today, still portrays the individuals who produced them. To the extent that a collection might have been developed without reference to society, its relevance may need to be assessed. Thus, according to Vergo:

> This notion of the dual function of collections as places of study and places of display was inherited both as a justification and as a dilemma, by the earliest public museums . . . the dilemma is complicated still further today by the entrepreneurial notion of museums as places of public diversion.
>
> (Vergo 1989: 2)

The tension between, on the one hand, the collection and its value to the public and, on the other, the attitude of the museum's staff and stakeholders, both to the collection and to the public, should not be underestimated. The nature and display of the collections are crucial factors for the public in choosing to visit a museum, and therefore the essential determining feature of the marketing thrust (Falk and Dierking 1992; McLean 1993; Hooper-Greenhill 1994). However, in stressing a relationship between the collection and the public, the museum is prey to raising expectations and to disappointing in reality. This can only be avoided if the museum has a sense of the visitor's and the potential visitor's expectations and what would meet them.

If products are the focal point for satisfying users' needs, it is worth considering what these needs may be in terms of a museum. Graburn (1977) has identified three human needs that the museum can fulfil: the reverential experience, an associational space, and the educational function. The reverential experience equates with Horne's 'aura' (1984), where the museum experience is higher than everyday experience, where the spirit is uplifted by the beauty and inspiration of the objects. The museum is a place for contemplation; it is the personal context of Falk and Dierking's interactive experience model (1992). The associational space is the social context of Falk and Dierking's model, because a visit to a museum may be a social occasion, where friends and family can interact together and with the objects. In order to fulfil this function, Falk and Dierking's physical context comes to bear, where the physical aspects of the museum (such as seating, labelling, and routing) need to be amenable. Finally, the educational function appeals to those visitors who wish to make sense of their world, where the objects can be translated into the context of personal values. Consequently,

> each of us may be, in different times and moods, any one of these types of museum visitor. The point is that museums provide a variety of

experiences that fulfil a spectrum of human needs and that are not, in quite the same way, available anywhere else.

(American Association of Museums 1984: 59)

The museum, then, through its products, should be striving to fulfil the needs of its various publics.

In marketing parlance the collection, its conservation, and exhibition, could be termed the 'core' product, that is the product that is central to advancing the institutional mission. The other products or services provided by the museum are the 'secondary' or 'augmented' products, which complement or facilitate consumption of the core product(s). The augmented product also includes products that are termed 'resource-attraction' products, which are designed to generate funds and other donated resources (Lovelock and Weinberg 1988). Often the museum products have been augmented for financial reasons rather than as a response to public demands, although they do add value for the public.

The Audit Commission in its report on local government museums in the UK, *The Road to Wigan Pier?* (1991), makes a useful breakdown of the products that could be provided by museums:

- conserving the heritage (stewardship)
- support for scholarship and research
- information
- education
- general visitor and other services.

The exhibitions and visitor support services are typically aimed at a wide audience, whereas the other services are targeted at specialised segments, such as academic scholars. It is worth considering each of these products in turn.

STEWARDSHIP

In terms of its first role, that of stewardship by conserving the heritage, the museum is firstly responsible for preserving objects for current and future generations. As the UK Museums Association's *National Strategy* points out,

> much of the material that museums collect was not designed for a long life ... The principle of maximising access to collections is in direct conflict with the welfare of the collections and it is therefore essential to work a balance between the two.

(Museums Association 1991b: 10)

The various interests involved in the service, which is direct (to the public) and indirect (to future publics) can cloud the issues involved in providing a service (McLean 1994). Where are the museum's limited resources channelled? To active conservation of artefacts for future generations, or to display and provision of support services to the present public? This dilemma is largely being answered by the demands of funding bodies, which, on the whole, require the museums to perform a function for the current public. Future publics tend to take second place in this new thinking, where there are considerable cost implications in curation and conservation of museum collections. To many within the museum profession, though, the preservation of the objects in their care supersedes any notion of public service (Morris 1990).

Often marketing is blamed for this false economy, where resources are diverted from care of the collection to public service. The one hundred redundancies of curatorial staff at the Natural History Museum in London have been blamed for precisely this public emphasis (Murdin 1991). However, only a short-sighted marketing person would promote short-term gains in visitor numbers from visitor facilities at the expense of the long-term benefits to be accrued from careful preservation and restoration of the collection. Rather than marketing being at fault, often it is a lack of a co-ordinated visionary policy for the collection which exacerbates the dilemma of resource allocation. It is acknowledged that there are high cost implications in the conservation and curation of museum collections, where on average two-thirds of the gross revenue cost of a museum relates directly to the collection, its security, storage, conservation, and so on (Lord *et al.* 1989). Often there is inadequate information about the storage, documentation, and conservation requirements of existing collections. Collection audits should be undertaken by all museums, which should include, 'an assessment of the continued relevance of the collections, and museums should be prepared, if necessary, to reallocate objects to other collections' (Museums Association 1991b: 11).

Some collections do not have clear themes, often through no fault of the curators, the collection having been amassed from various sources, being the gifts of various benefactors. Consequently, it may be difficult to create an informative exhibition from the items held by the museum or to create any kind of theme between displays. This is further complicated by displays being regarded as the 'territory' of one member of staff, with a number of different colleagues possibly being responsible for each of the displays (Hooper-Greenhill 1994).

Equally, museums have only about 13 per cent of their collections on display at any one time (Lord *et al.* 1989). Reserve collections are retained for a variety of purposes: as reference collections and primary evidence for scholarship; as objects that are likely to deteriorate if on display; as objects that are being held for future use; or too often because the museum lacks exhibition space (Audit Commission 1991). These reserve collections may be 'drawn upon to create an exciting, attractive and cost effective temporary exhibition programme. Such temporary exhibitions can help encourage people to make return visits' (ibid.: 16).

Similarly, the Audit Commission (1991) recommends transfer of objects and collection rationalisation between museums. Material that is superfluous to requirements or unrelated to the theme of the museum can be referred to other museums, as can potential donors or benefactors. Thus, for example,

Kirklees has collections agreements with other metropolitan districts in West Yorkshire, while Birmingham has been rationalising its storage arrangements and implementing a computer-based records system. New acquisition policies should also be outlined, particularly since it can be difficult to dispose of gifts if they are held in trust. Moreover, decisions should be made on the cost implications of any new acquisitions in advance, a policy that is already being pursued by the Victoria and Albert Museum in London.

Disposal of collections is also regarded as a marketing ploy for asset stripping simply to generate income. However, disposal of objects that lie outside the collecting policy may generate income (but not always), but will also free up storage space and conservation and other resources which can be used to look after and acquire new objects that are related to the museum's collection. It might not be in the interests of marketing to sell off important items of the collection: items which would be an attraction for visitors. Tastes and fashions may change, and objects that currently may be of little interest, may acquire significance in the future.

A marketing-oriented museum, then, would have a designated collections manager who would oversee the collection, its conservation, documentation, acquisition, disposal, and so on. This is an area where co-operation between museums is advisable, not only for rationalisation purposes but also for such initiatives as joint storage facilities. The need for adequate collections management can easily be overlooked, or resources may be transferred from collections management to visitor management. A collection is the linchpin of the museum, and it is essential that the collection is managed efficiently and effectively, if it is to best meet the needs of its users.

The second aspect of the stewardship function according to the Audit Commission (1991) is the preservation of the museum building. Many museums are housed in historic buildings, which have associated costs for maintenance and refurbishment for adequate conservation and storage facilities. Historically, museum buildings were not constructed with the public in mind, but to display artefacts in a manner befitting them – in buildings resembling the stately homes wherein they were originally collected (McLean 1993). The national museums in London are vast, imposing buildings, mainly erected in the nineteenth century. Their appearance is awesome, but perhaps because of their national status, they can project a palatial regality. The Gothic style of architecture of many museums also resembles Christian churches, promoting a religious reverence for the exhibits (Cameron 1971). Often buildings are used as museums because there is no other use for them, or because the municipal authority is obliged to preserve the building (Audit Commission 1991).

Research conducted by Merriman (1991) has shown that although half of the museums in Britain have opened since 1971, many people equate museums with these early buildings, and some groups of people are intimidated by them. Exacerbated by the association of museums with high culture and dominant values, museums have been regarded as havens of knowledge and scholarship.

> Modern museums may be suffering from the fossilisation of this outdated image, whereby, despite improvements in displays and facilities they are unfairly seen to be irrelevant to the concerns of the contemporary world and of interest only to those who are initiated into the mysteries of these silent cathedrals of learning.
>
> (Merriman 1991: 88)

On the other hand, for those seeking a reverential experience, such buildings offer the overawing aura that is required.

The contemporary demands made on museum buildings for improved display, conservation, and so on have resulted in increasingly sophisticated design demands. As Smith comments, 'there is and ought to be a symbiotic relationship between a building and its contents' (Smith, C. S. 1989: 18). Modern, purpose-built museums are in a better position to incorporate such techniques. Clearly though, museums housed in older buildings need to ensure that their maintenance and refurbishment allows them to conserve the collection adequately and meet the needs of the users. Survey research has discovered that the principal area of criticism of museums is the general state of repair of the building (Touche Ross 1989). It may be prohibitive, though, to offer the facilities required by users, where, for example, space may not be available for a café or shop. However, rarely does lack of space preclude a refreshments or sales point in a museum. An awesome appearance can be softened: for example, the Victoria and Albert Museum has erected large banners and advertising hoardings on its frontage in an attempt to brighten it and make it more accessible. The appearance of a building can, on the other hand, offer advantages. The Lady Lever Art Gallery in Port Sunlight has an uncanny resemblance to the Taj Mahal. An advertising campaign capitalised on this, promoting the museum as the 'Taj Mahal of Merseyside'.

The collection then can be viewed as the core product of the museum. The museum building though is also an integral part of the museum product and needs to be accorded appropriate significance. The building and its location may even determine the nature of the museum for the visitor (Brawne 1965). A potential visitor may turn away when confronted by a closed door, or may walk past the elitist 'temple of culture'. It is up to the museum to address the physical image created by its building.

SUPPORT FOR SCHOLARSHIP AND RESEARCH

Although scholarship and research may appear to be far removed from the world of marketing, nevertheless this is, or should be, a fundamental concern of marketing in museums. Traditionally, the role of the museum has been to conserve artefacts for the purpose of scholarship and research. Museum professional staff tended to be subject specialists, academics devoted to the cause of the artefacts. This emphasis has been diluted, not so much by marketing as by the demands of education. Now the learning in museums is less specialised and more accessible to a more general public. Marketing has continued this new tradition but it was not the cause of this shift. Nevertheless, any general education needs to be informed by more academic rigour. Many of the new independent museums that were established in recent years lack the curatorial expertise of the long-established museums, and often have recognised that they need to turn to specialists for advice, if they are truly to develop. Thus, although the main focus may no longer be on scholarship, it will always have a fundamental place in the museum's mission.

Research in museums needs to be conducted on two fronts: research that advances knowledge, and research to develop and expand the collection. The museum has a role in society which transcends its own singular purpose. The national museums and university-run museums, in particular, need to fulfil this role, for it is to them that the public turns for knowledge and understanding. Their reputations may depend on their contribution to learning, which often manifests itself on the public stage through interviews with the media and publication of learned texts. A spokesperson for the Natural History Museum on a natural history television programme, for example, reinforces the public perception that the museum has a significant contribution to make. Equally, stakeholders wish to be associated with an institution that has a reputation and can prove that it justifies support. Central and local government, in particular, need constant reminders of the fundamental necessity for funding a museum service. Similarly, if the collection and its display are to be enhanced, then it is imperative that museum researchers are able to conduct research into objects, both those in the care of the museum, and those that may be acquired to add value to the collection.

Museums can also support external research, both by publishing specialist catalogues and textbooks about the collections, but also by providing access to the collections. Particularly where only 13 per cent of the collection is on view at any one time, museums have an obligation to permit access to the reserve collections. A scholar who is studying the paintings of S. J. Peploe, for example, needs to view the original painting. Obviously safeguards need to be put in place, both for security and for preservation purposes, but if museums are to serve society, they need to limit any restrictions on access. Scholars and researchers are a target market segment of any museum, and museums need to ensure that the product they offer matches the needs of that market segment.

INFORMATION

Related to the support of scholarship and research is the provision of information. Only through scholarship and research will a museum be able to provide a service for the public who require information. The popularity of television programmes about antiques has increased public awareness of object identification by specialists. Some museums now charge for such services, while others consider object identification to be part of their service to the public.

Usually the public go to the museum empty-handed, but if a museum has the scholarly expertise, it may be worth encouraging individuals to bring their treasured heirlooms for identification, perhaps by running its own version of the antiques programme.

Other publics also require the services of museums from time to time, for example, outside publishers requiring photographic illustrations, and responses to planning enquiries. Maintaining databases documenting the museum's collection will further support the scholarship function of the museum as well as ensure the museum has up-to-date records on all of the objects in its care. Finally, on a more general educational level, museums can provide information by producing publications, such as pamphlets and guides for use by the general visitor. Such guides can be retained as further sources of learning, and for use on return visits. Even a simple guide can enhance a visit, particularly where space for explanatory labelling is restricted. The guides can also cross-reference displays, thereby creating theme tours around the museum. Separate guides can be produced for separate theme tours.

The National Maritime Museum in London has established a Maritime Information Centre, which responds to written and telephone enquiries. It also arranges for people to consult personally with curators and to view items that are not on public display (Orna 1994). The museum also holds Hidden Collection seminars, which give specialists access to each other's knowledge and to the curators' knowledge of the reserve collections.

Multimedia provides an exciting opportunity to integrate the museum's catalogues with interpretative and education services, thus enhancing the powers of the museum to inform the visitor (Arts Council of Great Britain 1992). The National Gallery in London links laser printers to its system, producing black and white reproductions. This has proved extremely popular, and since there is a charge for use of the facility, it provides a source of income (Hoffins 1992).

A recent initiative, which attempts to enable this type of intellectual access through multimedia, is the Mosaics interactive computer system being developed in Edinburgh as part of the new Museum of Scotland project (Orna 1994). The aims of the project are:

- to provide levels of information both about the objects, and about the themes presented in the museum, beyond what is available in the core displays
- to help place the Scottish collections into their regional, national, and international context
- to offer the user guidance in exploring the evidence of Scotland's past that lies outside the museum
- to improve significantly the accessibility and value of the national collections for disabled visitors and remote communities
- to permit tailor-made tours and briefing/work packages for specialist visitors and school parties.

If museums are to enhance and encourage learning, then they need to make the learning experience interesting, stimulating, and worthwhile. Any prop that can assist in this task can only contribute to the museum's mission.

EDUCATION

Education is now the main driving force in any museum's mission. For many though, there is still little consensus on the place of education within the museum, and little recognition that education is an essential element both of access and of communication (Museums Association 1993). Many museums have been left behind by the rapid changes and developments in education in recent years. As Wright points out:

> It requires museums to change their approach and methods in order to accommodate the needs and styles of learning of today's visitors, because the clock cannot be turned back to the spirit, and the attitudes, of early nineteenth century museum visiting.
>
> (Wright 1989: 138)

The American Association of Museums (1984) suggests that there are a number of ways in which museums can accommodate this new educational agenda. First, they need to reassess the educational function in the internal structure of museums, ensuring that it is an integral part of all museum activities. They propose new organisational structures where education is not seen as an isolated function, but where there is a breakdown of the structure to enable better co-ordination of the collections-related functions with the public programmes. It also recommends collaboration with other museums and cultural institutions, universities, and continuing education providers.

Children make up a substantial proportion of visitors to museums (*Sightseeing in the UK* 1992). Most children visit museums for the first time with a school group, 'and those experiences have a profound effect on their attitudes toward museums' (American Association of Museums 1984: 66). Focus group research conducted amongst employees at Stirling University found that non-museum attenders tended to have had bad experiences of museum visits while at school, which had coloured their image of museums. They remembered 'being dragged around', 'being told off by dragonian guards', and 'boring lessons' in the museum. Many museums are trying to ensure that learning is now provoked through active enjoyment followed up by reflection and analysis, for 'learning is best achieved in circumstances of enjoyment' (Hooper-Greenhill 1994: 140). Moreover, even exhibitions designed principally for entertainment are educational in a wider and more profound sense (Vergo 1989).

Museums need to keep abreast of changes in school education; for example, the national curriculum in England now emphasises practical experience. Museums can capitalise on this, but only if they publicise their facilities and collaborate with schools to produce the right materials for an educational visit.

Museums also have the potential to fulfil the increased demands of life-long learning. As more adults enter tertiary education, they develop an instilled desire to continue their learning, and will turn to museums to enrich their experiences and broaden their horizons (American Association of Museums 1984). Museums themselves have recognised that they need to go out into the community, into community centres, hospitals, prisons, and so on, to share their expertise. Consequently, the American Association of Museums recommends that:

> Museum professionals must consider ways to introduce their institutions to the adult public as sources of intellectual enrichment, as places where learning can be spontaneous and personal and as opportunities for growth and thinking as well as being.
>
> (American Association of Museums 1984: 71)

A commitment to life-long learning can demonstrate a positive social role for a museum, and can also meet the demands from funding bodies for demonstrating public benefit and greater public accountability (Museums Association 1993).

The Audit Commission (1991) outlines the main initiatives that can be undertaken by museums to promote learning: organised visits; teaching materials; tutorial rooms and meeting rooms for special interest groups; curriculum-related lectures; and loans. Collaboration with schools and teachers in pre- and post-visit activities, on the appropriateness of teaching materials, is essential. The organised visit does not start and end at the museum door; it should be integrated into the school's education. It should also be enjoyable. Very little research into either the school group or children has been undertaken; often this is because it is difficult to assess meaningful results. However, if museums are to ensure that museum learning is not acting as a 'turn off' for children, it must know how they feel about the museum.

Recent educational initiatives by Fife Regional Council in Scotland have included the launch of a teacher training video demonstrating how recording and observation skills can be developed through museum collections; a museum bus which tours throughout the region to schools and to local communities; and loan box schemes for reminiscence groups (*The Scotsman*, 1 February 1995). In Glasgow an initiative for life-long learning takes the museum into the learners' own communities. The open-museum scheme operates through an alliance between the city's museums and community education service.

The North Yorkshire Science Advisory Team has developed projects covering national curriculum programmes of study. Children and teachers carry out some preparatory work, visit the museum, and then follow up ideas with investigations and project work back at school. A local primary teacher is seconded to each activity site, and is trained by the project team to stimulate discussion and explain difficult ideas. All visiting primary school teachers are also offered training and receive packs of activities for use in preparation or follow-up to the visit. The first of these projects, which are now held every autumn, took place in the Yorkshire Museum in 1992. Entitled 'Earth and Space', it made use of the museum's building and grounds, while the lecture hall was turned into a spaceship for children to fly through the solar system.

Education goes hand in hand with marketing (Ames, P. J. 1993), for as the American Association of Museums (1984: 63) commented, 'everything that occurs in . . . museums to show and interpret the collection to the public or create and promote the museum's image is considered part of the museum's educational function'.

GENERAL VISITOR SERVICES

The principal general service offered by museums is access to the collection through exhibition. However,

> To examine how, and why, exhibitions are made means taking a magnifying glass to any number of sensitive, often problematic, sometimes fraught relationships: between the institution and its Trustees, its paymasters and sponsors; between the museum (or gallery) and its public; between the public and the objects on display; between conservation staff and curators on the one hand, and imported (by which I mean specially commissioned) makers of exhibitions (sometimes referred to as 'guest curators' – usually scholars or experts in some particular field) on the other; between the avowed or unspoken policies of the institution, and the ambitions and enthusiasms of the individual scholar or curator or designer.
>
> (Vergo 1989: 43–4)

This situation is further exacerbated by the increasingly vast array of technological innovations where models, dioramas, and simulations can either be integrated into or supplement the display. The collection is also the subject of various debates between its educative value and the demands from some visitors for entertainment, and between the use of the collection for research and its public display. Even more problematic is the assumption that there is a link between viewing objects in a museum and the acquisition of knowledge (Jordanova 1989). Labelling and interpretation decontextualise the object which is contextualised in the display.

However, beyond the internal debates on the collection, its display, and inter-pretation, stand the public. Their understanding and appreciation of the objects should be the singular purpose of the museum. How that understanding is elicited depends on the museum's individual approach. This requires a complex melding of the experts' guidance and the users' perceptions. Careful analysis and study are demanded through behavioural and attitudinal research into the use of the museum by the public. Decisions need to be made on how much information to give and how it is given; the reaction of users to the methods of presentation – the words, forms, colours, and sounds. The People's Palace in Glasgow explains to the visitor how the material displayed was selected and grouped in different ways (Porter 1988). Photographs of the curators who created the display can be used to emphasise that the exhibition was a human creation, with all the limitations that that implies (Weil 1995).

Techniques for developing thematic routes and queue avoidance need to be developed. The Van Het Rijksmuseum in the Netherlands pioneered thematic routes, by producing a leaflet that described forty walks, each with an appropriate theme, covering around fifteen objects (Vos 1975). All of this requires a clear understanding of user needs as related to the artefacts.

Decisions also need to be made on whether it is appropriate to enhance the core product through such techniques as living history, behind-the-scenes open days and special events. The use of performance in museums has escalated: for example there are history re-enactment workshops at Oakwell Hall Museum; Platform 4 Theatre Co. performances at the Keighley and Worth Valley Railway; and living history interpreters in permanent employment at Beamish Museum. Some museums have gone further:

> Dan-Yr-Ogof Showcaves in the Brecon Beacons, south Wales, has hired a caveman to bring some interactive excitement to the educational attraction. Former security guard Alan Jones lives in a reconstructed Iron-Age hut and dons animal-skin tunics to help children understand what it was like to live with the dinosaurs.
>
> (*Leisure Management*, August 1992)

An evaluation study of live interpretation found that over 90 per cent of visitors thought it was a good idea, and that over 80 per cent said it made them look at the displays more closely (Price 1993). Museum curators differ widely on their attitude to live interpretation, with some considering it to be too much like live theatre for museums.

However, if the performance is compatible with the aims of the museum, and if it enhances and does not detract from the collection, then it can only contribute to the product.

Such responses to user needs reflect the increasing demand and requirements for democratisation of museums. Community participation, where the local community is closely involved in the preparation of exhibits, and maybe even the organisation of the museum, is increasingly popular. The Museum of Liverpool Life was developed with the help of the Liverpool Life Advisory Group. This group was established to involve the local community in the museum, and consists of representatives from trade unions, community arts and adult education groups, as well as local, regimental, and academic historians.

As the Audit Commission (1991) highlighted, there are a number of types of exhibition – permanent, special, travelling, and outreach. Permanent exhibitions can be rotating exhibitions of the permanent collections, so that the reserve collections can be aired. Special exhibitions include blockbusters, such as the recent spate of dinosaur exhibitions, and community exhibitions, such as the Victoria and Albert's tent project (a huge South Asian tent designed as an exhibition centrepiece). Local communities, such as a group of Asian women in Birmingham, designed and worked on the panels of the tent. Outreach enables the museum to be taken out of the confines of its walls, to the community, through mobile museums, and exhibitions outside the museum building (for example, in shopping malls). In Michigan, Arttrain takes exhibits from town to town, while in a number of American cities the Rouse Company's 'Art in the Marketplace Program' brings museum exhibits to shopping malls (American Association of Museums 1984). Museums can also become part of a theme trail, where for example, the Captain Cook Birthplace Museum in Middlesbrough is part of the Tourist Board's 'Captain Cook Trail'.

It is the collection which differentiates museums from any other leisure attraction. The collection is unique and offers a piece of the authentic in a hyperreal world. Museums need to capitalise on this asset, making the key aspect of their collection the Unique Selling Proposition (USP). In order to stand out from the noise of all the competing attractions, museums have a particular niche in their core product. This USP needs to drive the rest of the decisions in the marketing mix, from the image that is communicated through publicity, to the price that is charged to enter the museum. The core product can be used to position the product, that is position it against other attractions in terms of how users perceive its value. The core product is the key to the marketing effort, and any attempts to enhance the core product, as long as it develops the organisation's mission *vis à vis* the public, can only enhance the marketing effort.

The Audit Commission highlights other areas of general visitor services, namely support and information. To this could also be added infrastructure:

> Since all the surveys of the patterns of museum visiting demonstrate that visitors spend extremely little time inspecting any of the contents, except in the museum shop, it is arguable that the overall environment is of greater importance than what is actually displayed.
>
> (Smith C. S. 1989: 18)

Support services come in the form of catering and retailing. Cafés or restaurants and sales points or shops enhance the experience for the visitor, while sometimes being the source of lucrative funds for the museum. Too often, though, these support services have been developed almost exclusively for financial reasons. Consequently, because their development has taken little account of the needs and wants of the public, they have frequently achieved only limited success. The shop, in particular, can send out different messages from the collection and cause confusion and conflict in the mind of the user. Often the shop sells a range of products of dubious taste and quality, that bear little relation to the museum's fundamental purpose. Consequently, it may confuse or cancel out the central message. As with all aspects of the augmented product, support services should integrate into the total marketing programme, reinforcing it while still providing needed revenue. The relationship between the museum's collection and its support services should be symbiotic.

The provision of information about the collection and associated topics traditionally takes the form of formal lectures and publications. Techniques such as workshops can also be adopted, particularly for children or for teaching adults new skills. The Victoria and Albert Museum's tent project has helped to revive half-forgotten skills of embroidery, taught to the younger South Asian women by the older women.

The infrastructural concerns are too often overlooked, although they can sometimes be more important than the collection itself in creating a satisfactory visit (Falk and Dierking 1992). Infrastructure includes seating; picnic areas; car parking; baby-changing facilities; enquiry points; toilets; furniture; furnishings; equipment; ambience; lighting; heating; signage; language provision; and physical provision. Research carried out by Touche Ross (1989) discovered that when respondents were asked what additional facilities they wanted in museums, the principal responses concerned additional or better seating; better cloakroom facilities; and better directional signage and floor plans. Infrastructure can also enhance the collection through the use of, for example, audio aids.

The programme of events and activities which a museum could organise is limited only by the imagination of the museum staff, and of course their relevance to the museum's mission. They do not need to be based in the museum and can be organised as joint events with other organisations. Ambrose in *New Museums: A start-up guide* (1987), has listed a number of activities which could be programmed:

- object/specimen of the month temporary exhibition, focusing attention on an item from the collection, a loan or a new acquisition
- videos/film showings
- touring exhibitions from the museum
- workshops for children on themes and objects in the museum's collections
- print and picture loan schemes
- family workshops
- coffee mornings organised by Friends' groups to help increase membership
- museum stands/stalls/exhibitions at local fêtes or shows
- lecture and talk programmes
- volunteer conservation group meetings
- recorded music programmes
- meetings
- fieldwork
- photo-recording training and photographic surveys
- multi-ethnic arts festivals
- oral history recording training and oral history collection
- talks and demonstrations by visiting conservators or other specialists
- competitions and quizzes; prizegivings and associated exhibition of work
- craft fairs
- publication launches
- previews of exhibitions

- hospital visiting programmes
- dance and drama programmes
- education programmes
- pageants.

Finally, museums provide a service for, and receive a service from, volunteers and Friends. The relationship can be twofold: the museum receiving much-needed assistance, while at the same time the volunteer can pursue an interest or even just get out of the house and meet other people. The volunteer can also assist in augmenting the product for the general public by acting as a tour guide.

This is not an exhaustive description of the techniques of enhancing the product. The list is probably endless, particularly as more technological innovations and attempts to democratise the museum are introduced. It is also possible for museums to become over-enthusiastic when introducing all of these innovations and lose sight of the public. The product should only be augmented if it supports the mission of the museum in terms of the needs of its public. This should remain the driving force behind any decision on the collection.

The product is an agglomeration of a vast array of core and augmented products. If the museum is not to be perceived as disparate but holistic, it needs to ensure that it is communicating the same message through all of its products, a message that reinforces its mission while at the same time meeting the needs of its users. This is no easy task and requires careful management of each of the parts if it is truly to form a whole.

MANAGING THE PRODUCT

She climbs the steps to the door of the museum. Suddenly the door swings open, held aloft by an attendant. The attendant, dressed in a grey uniform, says hello with a disdainful scowl. She steps in the door, tripping on the strategically placed doormat. Looking around, she sees what looks like a cloakroom, but on approaching finds it is a ticket booth. The unsmiling woman behind the cash desk demands £3. Having handed over the money, she looks around the vast foyer, hoping to find some indication of where to go next. Approaching the attendant and asking directions, she is met with a grunt and a pointed finger showing the direction of a closed door. On passing through that door, she enters a room packed full of display cases and crammed full of people. Shutting the door, she rushes down the long corridor, and on going down some stairs comes to a peaceful room with a few pictures on the wall. She wanders around the room glancing at the labels which give the name of the picture and the artist. Soon, she leaves the room and walks into . . .

This is not an atypical account of a visit to a museum. Each sentence depicts a 'moment of truth', a phrase originally coined by Carlzon (1987), denoting each individual encounter of the customer with the service provider. Each of these moments of truth make up the service encounter, defined as, 'a period of time during which a consumer directly interacts with a service' (Shostack 1985). The moments of truth are each critical incidents, opportunities for the user to evaluate the museum and form an opinion on the quality of its service. They occur every time a user interacts with the service provider, be it the infrastructure or equipment, or between users and service firm employees (Bitner *et al.* 1990). All employees are influential in forming satisfactory or dissatisfactory critical incidents, whether they are front-line and have direct contact with the user, or work behind the scenes, and should be treated as part-time marketers (Gummesson 1991).

There are three issues at stake when considering the service encounter: the maintenance of service quality; the purveyors of that quality, the employees; and developing relationships with users. Service quality and internal marketing (marketing to employees) are both recent concerns of marketing, service quality paralleling the burgeoning general management literature on total quality management, which has already been adopted by some museums (*Museums Journal*, January 1994). To some, they would appear to be outside the remit of marketing, coming under the jurisdiction of operations management and human resources management respectively. However, if a museum is to achieve its mission in relation to its users, then obviously the critical incidents of the user–museum encounter are crucial and need to be addressed. Relationship marketing is an even more recent consideration of marketing, where service organisations attempt to replace casual transactions with ongoing relationships, building a loyal customer base. This has real implications for museums and in particular the development of relationships with the local community.

SERVICE QUALITY

Quality must be seen from the user's viewpoint and not the museum's. Quality needs to be measured from the user's perspective and not from what museum managers think their users' views are. Quality itself is a difficult concept to define, at its most basic being defined as conforming to requirements (Crosby 1984). Since quality should be considered from the viewpoint of the user, an analysis of quality as outlined by Grönroos (1984) could be particularly useful for museums, since it can be easily measured by both the customer and the provider of the service. Grönroos identified 'technical' and 'functional' quality as being the two principal components of quality. Technical quality refers to the relatively quantifiable aspects of a service, for example the length of time a user needs to queue at the enquiry desk. Because services involve direct consumer–producer interaction, consumers are also influenced by how the technical quality is delivered to them. This is what Grönroos describes as functional quality, and cannot be measured as objectively as the elements of technical quality. For example, in the case of the queue at the enquiry desk, functional quality is the environment in which the queuing takes place, and the manner in which the staff handle the user's enquiry.

If quality is defined as the extent to which a service meets customer requirements, the problem remains of identifying just what those requirements are. Zeithaml and her colleagues (1990) suggest that there are five general dimensions that influence customer assessment of service quality. The first is reliability, that is, performing the service dependably and accurately, which they claim to be at the heart of service marketing excellence. Organisations undermine their reputation for service excellence when their service performance is lacking, and when they make avoidable mistakes. When an organisation makes alluring promises to attract customers which it fails to deliver, it can only disappoint. From the customer's perspective, flawless performance is the proof of the service. This is undeniable in the museum: a recognition of the need for accuracy in promotional material by not exaggerating the museum's performance, of being open when publicised, and of having a clean café, are all proof of a quality performance.

The second dimension suggested by Zeithaml and her colleagues (1990) is tangibles, such as the appearance of the physical facilities, personnel, and communications material. Because of the nature of intangibility in services, customers cannot see a service, but they can see various tangibles associated with the service. Tangibles such as the employees' uniforms, the decor of the organisation's building, the publicity leaflets, offer 'clues' about the invisible service. Prospective customers place great emphasis on tangibles, because they cannot see what they are buying before they have made the purchase decision, and they need to understand what the service is that they are actually buying. If the tangible clues are not managed, they can communicate the wrong message about the service. Museum attendants dressed in uniforms, glossy promotional material, dusted cases, and even management of the flow of visitors, can convey specific messages to the visitor and prospective visitor.

The third dimension isolated in the service quality literature is responsiveness, that is the willingness to help customers and to provide prompt service. Related to this are the other two dimensions: assurance and empathy. Assurance means the knowledge and courtesy of employees and their ability to convey trust and confidence. Empathy refers to the provision of caring, individualised attention to customers. Each of these three dimensions emphasises the crucial role of staff in the performance of the service. Training in customer care for staff at all levels, not just the customer contact staff, is equally relevant in museums. It should inculcate a recognition by all staff, not just front-line staff, of their role in delivering a quality service to the customer. The person writing the labels for the exhibits, the cleaner dusting down the cases, the demeanour of the attendant at the entrance, are all crucial in defining the quality of the service.

Zeithaml and her colleagues (1990) maintain that to achieve each of these dimensions in influencing customer assessment of service quality, service organisations need to pursue a number of guidelines. The prerequisite for service quality is that senior management take a central role in delivering excellent service. Strong management commitment to service quality leads and motivates an organisation to improve service performance. The key is genuine service leadership at all levels of an organisation, which emanates from the top. This was recognised by both Bradford (1991) and McLean (1993), where the role of the leader or museum director is considered critical in creating a service quality environment.

In order to make tangible the service performance, Zeithaml and her colleagues (1990) place considerable emphasis on managing the tangible evidence such as the building, the personnel, and promotional literature, and particularly on one form of evidence – the service brand. The essential purpose of a brand is to distinguish one organisation's offering from that of another organisation, using names and distinguishing features such as slogans and symbols. Brands provide customers with an efficient mechanism for identifying a particular organisation. In goods marketing, the product brand is the primary brand; whereas in services marketing, the corporate brand or corporate identity is the primary brand, because there is no actual physical product which facilitates packaging, labelling, and display. Few museums to date have recognised the importance of corporate identity. This may necessitate a change of name, to distinguish the museum from other similar or local museums; to reflect the content of the collection; or to convey an attractive, quality product. Once a strong corporate identity is established, then the logos, labels, and so on need to be devised to communicate it.

Zeithaml and her colleagues (1990) also emphasise the importance of marketing; first, to existing customers to build strong and long-lasting relationships, and second, to employees to empower them to assume responsibility for providing service quality. Finally, there is a recognition in the quality literature of the increasing importance of the effective use of new technology, particularly computers, in enhancing service quality, by speeding up the service performance and increasing its efficiency and effectiveness. Some museums now utilise computers for interpretation and educative purposes, while there are clearly benefits in computerised documentation and administration.

The quality literature suggests that the organisation should be striving to attain service quality excellence as perceived by the customer. This reflects a highly populist approach, where it is what the customer, not what the museum director or staff deems to be excellent, which is crucial. There are implications here for the museum's cultural leadership role. It is possible, for example, that some exhibitions of contemporary art might provoke hostility amongst visitors and cause a fall in attendance. Should the museum abandon the exhibitions that carry this risk, and choose only ones that would be deemed 'excellent' by the customer? Equally, no two people view an exhibition in the same way; it is a matter of personal taste. Which visitor's impression does the museum adhere to as the 'excellent' one? Admittedly, in terms of the augmented product aspects, such as the café, shop, and toilets, the museum can take this concept literally and attempt to provide a service that is deemed excellent by the visitor. However, the nature of the museum prohibits the achievement of excellence for every visitor. Thus, the museum can attempt to achieve an 'excellent' rating for its building's structures and facilities, but it will always be constrained by its collection. To suggest that the museum director should choose and display a collection that all visitors would consider to be excellent would be nonsense. However, the museum director should not discount the views of the visitors.

Responding to visitors' demands for the collections, though, is not necessarily so straightforward. For example, if the museum is a natural history museum, and the visitors appear to be demanding that the museum adopt an environmental conservation stance in its displays, whereas the museum's aims state explicitly that it is to educate the public on the history of species, a decision needs to be made. Should the museum incorporate more conservational issues or should it retain its history of species stance? The director will need to assess the museum's position through discussions with employees and stakeholders. Strong leadership will be required whichever course of action the museum chooses. The museum will also need to ensure that if it does reposition itself, it reflects this in its corporate identity.

A quality orientation in a museum's marketing will assist it in anticipating and meeting the needs of its users. However, if too strictly adhered to, it could result in a market orientation rather than a marketing orientation. Museums may need to tread warily, and beware of taking too literally the notion of quality being equated to the visitor's rather than the museum's perception of it. It may even be that the visitor's perceptions are misinformed precisely because the museum itself has not clearly articulated its purpose in its communications, and is not conveying an identity that equates with its own goals. For the notion of quality to be effective, a museum must first address its own goals and reconcile them with the public's perceptions of the museum. It is essential that the museum does not lose sight of its own mission when pursuing service quality as perceived by the customer.

DEVELOPING RELATIONSHIPS

Relationship marketing is a recent development in marketing theory which has largely been developed by European theorists such as Gummesson and Grönroos. It contrasts quite markedly from the cut and thrust approach to marketing developed in the US. Recently a number of US marketing theorists, such as Kotler, have embraced the notion of relationship marketing, and produced their own interpretations. It remains, though, a European perspective on marketing practice, one that is more sympathetic to the specific context of the organisation in developing a marketing orientation. Because of this, it is a particularly important development for museums, since it takes a new approach to marketing, one that recognises that an organisation has multiple publics, and that it needs to forge relationships that it can sustain with each of these publics. The theory itself is in its initial stages, and so museums would be wise to follow its development and assess its application in the museum situation.

Relationship marketing, as with service quality, has the dual focus of getting and keeping customers (Christopher *et al*. 1991). Traditionally, much of the emphasis of marketing has been directed towards the getting of customers rather than the keeping of them. According to the relationship marketing perspective, marketing is concerned with the exchange relationship between the organisation and its customers, where quality and customer service are key linkages in this relationship. The challenge to the organisation is to bring these three critical areas – marketing, customer service, and quality – into closer alignment.

For most services, existing customers represent by far the best opportunities for profit growth, where it may cost up to five times more to get a new customer than it does to keep an existing one (Grönroos 1990). The central tenet of relationship marketing therefore is the creation of a 'true customer', that is 'customers who are glad they selected a firm, who perceive they are receiving value and feel valued, who are likely to buy additional service from the firm, and who are unlikely to defect to a competitor' (Berry and Parasuraman 1991: 133). True customers make favourable referrals, spend more money on a per-year basis with an organisation, and may even pay a premium price for the perceived benefits offered by a service.

Many museums are in a position to create loyal visitors, through such schemes as Friends organisations. Those museums with computer technology can build up a database of visitors and regularly mail them publicity literature. However, the notion of beating off the competition to retain these customers is only partly applicable. Clearly, if one local museum won over loyal visitors at the expense of another local museum, then there would be a sense of competition. However, most loyal visitors are regular museum-goers, and will not confine their visits to one museum alone. This has to be recognised, and should be exploited by museums by linking together, perhaps through consortia. This is already occurring in local government museums services, where visitors to one museum are encouraged to visit another museum in the service.

The relationship marketing theorists have devised a six-market model (Christopher *et al.* 1991) which encompasses customer markets, referral markets, supplier markets, employee markets, influence markets, and internal markets. The primary focus of marketing remains on the customer, but with increasing emphasis on building a long-term relationship with that customer. Referral markets basically means word-of-mouth, that is to get your customers to do the marketing for you, although there are other referral sources as well, such as tourist information bureaux. With regard to supplier markets, the relationship marketing literature refers to evidence of a movement from the traditional adversarial relationship between suppliers and their customers, towards a new form of relationship based on co-operation. This has only limited relevance in museums, with, for example, suppliers of goods for the museum shop. However, it could also refer to the building up of relationships with prospective donors to the museum, of nurturing agencies and individuals who may donate or lend to the museum or enable the creation of a temporary exhibition. Employee markets refers to potential recruits: increasingly, organisations are finding strong competition in their efforts to attract a sufficient number of suitably motivated and trained employees. The organisation needs to ensure that it is attractive to the candidate, either through the quality of its recruitment advertisement, the support material it sends with its application form, or even the response to expressions of interest. Influence markets are additional markets, such as local and central government, which may need to be addressed. Museum directors and staff need to build up personal relationships with the influential players, to convince them of the value of the museum. This six-markets model addresses the problems encountered by any museum, of having multiple markets. It is a useful development which can guide museums in their marketing strategies for each of these markets.

Clearly, there are a number of issues that need to be taken into account if a museum is to adopt such an approach to its marketing. Such initiatives will require the input of marketing into the whole process of the management of the museum, but this is easier said than done. Office bearers and function-holders can be quite territorial about their own domain, and may resent the encroachment of marketing on issues that would normally come under their jurisdiction. Co-operation is essential – a co-operation led, but not imposed, by senior management. Internal marketing should facilitate such an approach; employees who are conscious of their role in terms of the public are more likely to be willing to adopt a customer focus. The development of relationships with users should also bring the staff closer to the users, and help them to recognise that if they are truly to serve the public while promoting the goals of the museum, then they need to listen to the users and take their needs and wants into consideration.

PEOPLE

Customer service and internal marketing have become key concerns of service organisations in recent years. Services that rely particularly on considerable staff contact with the customer need to ensure that their staff are well versed in customer care. Contact with staff is usually kept to a minimum in museums, where attendants are the only visible personnel. Museums with live interpretation will clearly have more personal contact with the visitors, while contact will also be relatively high in the museum's café and shop.

Customer care came to prominence in the 1980s with the highly publicised customer care campaigns of Disney theme parks. The rigorous training used by Disney Corporation emphasises that the job of employees is to bring satisfaction to the customers. Strict standards are set, with employees conforming to dress and conduct rules. As Payne comments, 'the success of marketing a service is tied closely to the selection, training, motivation and management of people' (Payne 1993: 163).

The regal splendour of the nineteenth-century museums required a warding staff whose demeanour was consistent with the grand manner of such institutions. Moreover the need to guard the collections, despite increased use of sophisticated deterrents, is a tradition which has become entrenched. The attendants stalk the corridors like wardens in a prison. While intimidating the poor visitor who has dared to penetrate into these inner confines, the attendant is bored, and is probably following the visitor's every move to stay awake: 'all dressed up and nowhere to go, most attendants have about as much to look forward to as an underemployed sub-policeperson' (Leishman 1993: 30).

Compare the prison warder scenario with the scene at Ironbridge Gorge Museum, where demonstrators dress in character as locksmiths, candlemakers, and so on, and chat to the visitors. Rather than watch the visitors, they welcome them and answer their questions. According to Falconer, 'attendants are a largely untapped resource for museums struggling under funding constraints to provide an ever improving service to visitors' (Falconer 1995: 21). As well as providing guidance to visitors and participating in school visits, attendants could also, suggests Falconer, provide curatorial and technical assistance, by helping out with environmental control, collections, and exhibitions.

Colchester Museums pioneered a new role for attendants, beginning with the premise that, 'alert, informed and valued attendant staff, closely involved with visitors, are better able to meet both customer care and security needs' (Seaman 1995: 28). Their job title was changed to museum assistants, under-lining the fundamental shift in their role in the museum. Their remit includes formally welcoming school groups with a short introduction to the museum; promoting the service and the town of Colchester, as well as giving directions; and participating in museum activities, 'rather than be ill-informed invigilators' (ibid.: 28).

The front-line personnel are closest to the visitor, have most contact with them, and are able to learn how the visitor feels about the museum. Consequently, they have an essential contribution to make, in keeping the museum informed about its visitors. Attendants need to be fully integrated, by also keeping them informed of what is happening in the museum. If they are excluded from infor-mation about developments, they will feel they are unimportant. There needs to be a regular exchange of information, both up and down the staff hierarchy. Tullie House Museum in Carlisle, for example, regularly arranges temporary closures for in-house training of staff.

Customer care, though, has an image of 'smiley campaigns', of insincere, 'have a nice day' comments. Consequently,

> Managers should encourage human rather than mechanical responses, and give attendant staff the confidence to relate easily to visitors. This will help them to remain interested, alert and welcoming and to convey through their attitude the message that all questions will be dealt with politely, that information or assistance is there if needed and that complaints will be taken seriously.
>
> (Leishman 1993: 32)

This can also be facilitated by taking some of the onus off the staff. The Museums Association (1994) recommends that public suggestion boxes be placed in the galleries. A complaints procedure should also be established and publicised to the public. Staff should be well briefed on how to deal with complaints, and it is essential that every complaint is responded to.

However, it is not enough merely to train and motivate front-line personnel to care for the customer. Since activities undertaken behind the scenes can also impact on the quality of the service provided, it is essential that all staff members are satisfied with their job. Internal marketing

> recognizes the importance of attracting, motivating, training and retaining quality employees by developing jobs to satisfy individual needs. Internal marketing aims to encourage effective behaviour by staff which will attract customers to the firm. The most talented people will be attracted to work in those companies which are seen to be good employers.
>
> (Payne 1993: 163)

The purpose of internal marketing is to ensure that all members of staff make an effective contribution to the marketing of the organisation. Their impact on the visitors also needs to be highlighted. The National Museums and Galleries on Merseyside produces articles on conservation in the museum to be included in its own publicity for visitors and in press releases. This has the dual function of validating the role of the curatorial staff and of making the collection and its care more accessible to the public.

People are a fundamental aspect of the museum's product, both directly in the form of the visible attendant or shop assistant, but also indirectly as behind-the-scenes support staff. Museums are increasingly recognizing the importance of the front-line staff, but have been less responsive to internal marketing. Internal marketing is still at an early stage in its development in any organisation. However, it is likely that museums will begin to recognise its relevance in motivating and retaining employees.

CONCLUSIONS

The museum product is immensely complex, potentially involving scores of different activities and events. It encompasses both the collection and the staff, and is augmented by a variety of support services. The number of ways in which the product can be enhanced is endless, particularly as the speed of technological innovation increases. The diversity of initiatives which can be adopted to develop a customer focus in the product is also increasing. A museum needs to understand and anticipate the needs of its public, assess its resources, and develop products that reflect those needs, while at the same time reflecting the mission of the museum. As Wright comments,

> An alert museum would already have been in advance of its public, asking itself questions, aware of the changing habits of visitors in other contexts,

and seeking to complement them on its own terms, instead of bewailing change, or pandering in a half-hearted way to populism with hastily cobbled-together gimmicks, as a means to lull visitors into liking what those who work in such institutions hold to be good – that is to say, what those museums already happen to own and wish to study.

(Wright 1989: 145)

7

Communicating the museum product

Museums are instruments of communication, a museum display being a branch of the mass media (Brawne 1965; Hudson 1977; Hodge and d'Souza 1979). As Lumley argues, 'The notion of the museum as a collection for scholarly use has been largely replaced by the idea of the museum as a means of communication' (Lumley 1988: 15).

Communication in the museum includes 'those aspects of the institution that impinge either on the museum's image, or on the general experience of the visit' (Hooper-Greenhill 1994: 50). In other words, communication is reflected in the entire experience of the museum. The museum's core product, its exhibition, together with its information functions, its infrastructure, and its support services, are all communicating a message to the public. The management of access to the museum also contributes to the overall image of the museum, both through physical and psychological access, and through promotion of information concerning the museum. The image of the museum develops attitudes in the public which in turn is the agglomeration of the product, accessibility, and promotion.

Communication, then, is a museum-wide activity, not just a series of isolated functions. A holistic approach needs to be adopted, not only to the communication of the product, but to every aspect of the museum that communicates in some way to the public. Each function of the museum needs to collaborate, which may even require a reassessment of the organisational structure of the museum. For example, the Milwaukee Public Museum has only two divisions – programmes and operations – each of which is headed by a deputy director. This system was introduced in order to improve co-ordination between the collection-related functions of the museum and its public programmes (American Association of Museums 1984). Whatever the decision on organisational structure, communication will clearly permeate throughout, and will need to be co-ordinated.

Communication of the product was largely dealt with in Chapter 6. This chapter will concentrate on communication through management of access and promotion, or in other words, the 'place', 'process', and 'promotion' aspects of the marketing mix. Clearly though, as it is the 'product' which is being promoted and is being made accessible, aspects of the 'product' and 'people' will also need to be taken into account.

MAKING THE MUSEUM ACCESSIBLE

'Place' in marketing parlance means 'distribution'. Distribution is concerned with making desired products available to consumers in a location and at a time that is convenient – delivering the right product, at the right time, in the right place. This requires delivery of the product through distribution channels. It is important that these delivery systems are designed in such a way that user needs are met. Decisions also need to be made on the appropriate channels of distribution. Although channels of distribution are less relevant in the service situation, they are important in the distribution of goods, for example, merchandise in the museum shop. The implications of distribution and its focus on time and place benefits for users of services is the management of demand and supply. Since services are produced and consumed at the same time, they cannot be stored for use at a later date: their use is therefore perishable. In order to ensure that a museum is not empty one day, and the next the public are queuing to get in, demand and supply need to be managed. Finally, distribution also includes the distribution of promotional information. Since this relates to promotion it will be considered below (see p. 000).

Grönroos (1982) suggests that although distribution is important for goods, the focus for services is also on accessibility. Rathmell (1974) classifies services by location in three ways: where location may be irrelevant; where the services may be concentrated; and where the service may be dispersed. Museums' services are concentrated in their location, mainly through tradition as opposed to supply. The concerns of location are crucial in museums, where it can be a key factor in the final purchase decision (Davis *et al.* 1979). It is rare that a museum can move to a location where it can improve its service performance. Museums attempt to overcome this restriction through touring exhibitions and turnaround of the permanent collection. A major national exhibition of paintings by Cézanne, for example, will attract crowds to a municipal museum. Locational factors may, however, be beyond the control of the museum. Often the building is in an inaccessible location, or it prohibits the incorporation of additional facilities or extensions. The building itself may not be ideal for creating an image, being housed in a nineteenth-century structure built to imitate a stately home, which is intimidating and uninviting. The message of 'do not approach' is reinforced by the guards at the door, which is often closed. The whole museum is a security area, protecting the valuable objects in its care. There are alarms, security cameras, and guards on patrol. The museums are often dark and humid, environmentally controlled for the benefit of the objects housed in them (Hooper-Greenhill 1994).

What is at stake here is accessibility through time and place. There are a number of issues to be considered. First, the overall management or design of the delivery system, in order to meet user needs in terms of time and place.

Place as location needs to be addressed, as does availability of time through demand and supply.

DELIVERY SYSTEM DESIGN

The delivery system design begins with the users' needs. These are then matched to the skills and capacity of the museum, to the products that it can make available. Because of the inseparability of the service, the users will often perceive the service delivery system as part of the service itself. The processes by which the service is created and delivered will be a major factor in the users' perception of the service. Thus, 'process', or decisions on operations management in the services marketing mix, are of great importance to the success of marketing. Continuous co-ordination between the operations and marketing is essential.

A number of factors need to be taken into account when designing a delivery system. Physical factors of the product, the tangibles, influence service delivery. They can 'help attract the attention of prospective users, suggest the quality and the nature of the services offered, and provide support or evidence that promised benefits will be forthcoming' (Lovelock and Weinberg 1988: 286–7). Few consumers are willing to devote much time and effort to obtain and use a service (Claxton *et al*. 1974). If an organisation has distinctive product offerings, which users would view as special, then it is likely that users will make more effort and travel longer distances. Thus a museum could introduce attractive products, such as blockbuster exhibitions, to entice the visitor. It must always be remembered that museums are competing for users' time and effort. Time and place utility are particularly important in the decision to use the service, which has to be consumed on the site of the provider. Patronage of museums tends to decrease among more distant prospective users (Lovelock and Weinberg 1988). A response to this could be outreach, where the museum may put on programmes in facilities such as school buildings or community centres, or use mobile transport. Such a strategy would attract potential users who are unwilling or unable to travel any distance to the museum venue.

Process involves all the activities undertaken to deliver a service to a consumer. It includes policy decisions on the degree of customer involvement, and the extent to which employees can use discretion in the service delivery. However, it is not just customer contact employees and their activities which are important, but also those employees working behind the scenes. Thus, the museum must address process in both the 'front office' and the 'back office' (Mudie and Cottam 1993). Shostack (1984; 1987) devised a process-oriented approach to services, through a flowchart of the service process. By blueprinting a service, each of the activities or elements of the service organisation, including the moments of truth, their sequencing and interaction, can be visualised.

Stage in process	Enters door	Pays for ticket	Asks for directions	Follows signs to exhibition	Enters gallery
Is incident critical?	N	N	N	N	Y
Participants	Visitor	Visitor Ticket seller	Visitor Attendant	Visitor	Visitor
Visible evidence	Layout of foyer	Cash-collection procedure	Appearance of attendant	Signs	Ambience of gallery
'Line of visibility'					
Invisible processes	Cleaning of foyer	Accounting procedures	Training of staff		Presentation/ cleaning of gallery

Figure 7.1 Blueprint of part of a museum visit

Source: Adapted from A. Palmer, *Principles of Services Marketing*, McGraw-Hill, 1994

There are a number of steps in blueprinting a service:

- All the principal functions of a service are identified, so that it can be seen clearly and objectively.
- The fail points are identified, where things might go wrong.
- Execution standards regarded as acceptable by a user are set for each function. These represent the quality targets of the service.
- All the evidence or moments of truth that are available to the user are identified.

Figure 7.1 shows the service process of part of a museum visit up to the stage where the visitor enters the first gallery, in a time sequential order from left to right. The blueprint is also divided into two zones: a zone of visibility (processes visible to the user and in which the user is likely to participate) and a zone of invisibility (processes which although necessary to the efficient distribution of a service, may be hidden from the user).

Blueprinting is an exercise which can help the museum director take a fresh look at how the museum operates. The aim of such scrutiny is not only to meet customer needs but also to utilise the museum's resources more effectively. The blueprint allows all the employees to see their role in the process, while consultation on the activities undertaken may give the front-line employees, in particular, a voice in how the service should be delivered. Too often the customer-contact personnel, those who have an insight into the users' needs, are not consulted. However, as Mudie and Cottam suggest, 'Mapping out the process is as much a test of the validity and endorsement of management's belief as to how things do and should work' (Mudie and Cottam 1993: 55). The views of management, employees, and users should be solicited when reviewing a museum's process.

Blueprinting is an extremely useful way of improving service quality. As Payne remarks:

> The blueprint is a valuable tool in helping visualise the service process, understanding what can go wrong and setting performance standards for improvement in service quality. This helps not just with solving potential problems but also in designing ways to deal with service recovery.
>
> (Payne 1993: 229)

The blueprint enables marketing to be integrated with operations.

However, museums have to overcome a considerable amount of hostility to marketing before facilitating co-operation between marketing and operations. Museums are not alone in meeting resistance from within the organisation to the co-ordination of marketing and operations. Lovelock (1992) found that many operations executives in service organisations resist the introduction of a marketing orientation, regarding it as a costly add-on function, and an interference in their activities. However, each operational issue affects both operations and marketing. Thus the interplay between processes, marketing, and human resources is critical (Payne 1993).

Ultimately, the performance of the museum itself will need to be measured relative to: goals and objectives; competitors; user expectations; and resources deployed (capital, labour, materials, information). Quantifiable measures should be used wherever possible, although some measures will need to be qualitative or involve simple Yes/No measures (Audit Commission 1991). For example, the following indicators could be met:

1   *Education*
    - number of courses/workshops arranged and their take-up
    - number of school visits
    - percentage of schools in the target areas reached
2   *Enquiries*
    - number of enquiries dealt with each year
    - percentage of total enquiries successfully dealt with
    - average time/cost per specific enquiry
3   *Access*
    - length of stay
    - number and type of visitors
    - return visitors
    - percentage from a given catchment area
    - relative performance with competition
    - measurement of visitor satisfaction

(Source: Museums Association 1991c)

The problem with such an approach, though, is that qualitative measures are often glossed over or neglected (Marsan 1993a). If it is difficult to identify precisely the output of a process, then a surrogate measure may be used. For example, the true output of a museum could be its contribution to expanding the knowledge base of, and entertaining, the local community. Since this is difficult to quantify, a proxy measure of 'number of visitors' is used. How well the service is delivered though is a more realistic and expedient measure for museums. Although overseeing performance measurement is an operations rather than a marketing task, it is essential that marketing is involved. If the process of delivery of the museum service is to be effective, then marketing and operations must collaborate.

LOCATION

Location, that is convenience of location and ease of access, is an important determinant of usage. There is considerable inflexibility, though, in the location of a museum. Only new museums can have the luxury of choosing a location. For the rest, location is pre-determined, and often far from ideal. Accessibility requires good transport links. Museums can encourage public transport improvements, but cannot control a structural effect outside their control. Car parking can also be a limitation – many museums are located in a town centre, where car parking is at a premium. Surveys can ascertain how users actually travel to the museum, and frustrations can often be voiced. This is where signage is important. Potential users need to find a museum; whether it be centrally located or in a remote corner, signposts should direct them to their destination. Signs should be placed on roads at appropriate entry points, while pedestrian signs should be placed in appropriate walkways, including heritage trails, tourist trails, and so on. If car parking is limited, then signs should indicate where parking may be available. Promotional literature should include information on transport access, possibly with a map. Location can be a hindrance to facilitating accessibility, but a museum can do much to overcome these problems.

Outreach has already been suggested as a means of overcoming locational problems. As the Museums Association noted in its *National Strategy*: 'many people only attain access if museum resources are brought to them; for example, by loans, by touring facilities (whether through exhibitions or through mobile museums); and by other forms of outreach' (Museums Association 1991b: 13). As was also discussed earlier, access includes physical access for those who are physically disabled. The museum should not unintentionally debar the disabled, but instead should attempt to provide for their needs.

Movement of collections for outreach should be tempered with caution, since there is considerable inflexibility in the location of the collection. Whatever the size of the collection, the risks and costs involved in transporting items may prohibit its movement. It may not always be realistic to distribute the product itself. Information about the product can be distributed instead. Thus, augmenting the product and informing about this can increase the propensity to travel. Expanding the range of products or introducing temporary block-buster exhibitions, for example, can attract users who would not normally take the time or make the effort to visit a museum.

Museums need to have a unique appeal, and as Bryant suggests, museums in out-of-the-way places can actually capitalise on this by making this a distinctive appeal attraction. As he comments, 'it is not essential to be at the very heart of things' (Bryant 1988: 23). Being different, by having an interesting location, can make the museum an appealing destination in its own right.

Location and the physical infrastructure of a museum can impact on a user's orientation once inside the museum building. Many museums are vast, maze-like buildings, with labyrinthine corridors. Small museums may become overcrowded, while some museums prefer to move their users round the museum in one direction. This is a method favoured by the United States Holocaust Memorial Museum, where the exhibition is linear, so that the visitor has to follow the route offered, or risk jettisoning the whole experience (Linenthal 1995). Signposting in the museum can be important in ensuring that the users can orientate themselves easily. At the same time the signposts can contribute to the experience, since they can enable thematic routes to be created, and can also filter visitors and ensure that they visit specific areas of the museum. During its dinosaur blockbuster exhibition, the Hancock Museum in Newcastle-upon-Tyne placed giant dinosaur footprints on the floor to guide visitors through the corridors to the exhibition. Signs may also be used to explain to the visitor why, for example, the galleries are in darkness, or why an object has been removed from the display for preservation. Keep the visitor informed. (As British Rail have learned, telling the passengers why the train has stopped can often diffuse frustration and anger!)

Introductory information for orientation can include a map of the museum on printed leaflets, leaflets on theme trails, and posters strategically positioned detailing the locations of galleries throughout the museum, rather like the alphabetic store guide in department stores. Directional signing can be placed throughout the building in the form of posters and even banners, and such techniques as footprints on the floor. The museum must always consider the messages that signs transmit. Negative signs should always be avoided, such as 'Gallery Closed' – an explanation with an apology should always be given.

Decisions on the construction and layout of a museum, or the timing of its refurbishment, should take visitor needs into account. Overcrowding (for example, in the shop) should be avoided, while toilet facilities should be located for ease of access for disabled people, and also close to refreshment facilities, not at the other end of the building. Many new museums take the opportunity to filter visitors through the shop as part of the visit, to maximise sales. The Museum of the Moving Image (MOMI), for example, has its shop located at the end of the visit, and has ensured that all visitors must pass through it before leaving. Beamish Museum has its shop located before the turnstile, so that non-museum-visiting customers can purchase souvenirs. Some may consider such initiatives to be too commercially oriented, but if they do not detract from the museum's mission, and are in fact achieving that mission by offering a service while at the same time as netting much-needed income for the museum, then there should be no conflict of interests.

DEMAND AND SUPPLY

Matching capacity to the timing of demand is a problem for all service organisations, where the perishable nature of services means that they cannot be stored for later use. In addition to this, users participate in the creation of the service and may create variability in capacity. For example, a school party may crowd around a picture in a gallery, blocking it off from the view of other visitors. There may also be large demand fluctuations over time, with a museum being crowded over a lunch-hour but empty first thing in the morning. Providing capacity to meet demand is clearly a distribution problem, but often the full range of the marketing mix is used to deal with, or alter, the timing of demand.

Demand in service organisations can be tailored to fit capacity (Sasser 1976). Demand can be shaped through manipulation of the marketing functions. Thus, in terms of the product, decisions need to be made as to whether the service provided is always appropriate at all times. There are two approaches to this: first, radically altering the service and, second, adding value during trough periods. Altering the service could include the hiring out of the museum for hospitality during the evening, while adding value could include price reductions at certain times. For example, the Science Museum drops its charges and allows free admission after 4 pm, when the museum is quieter.

Delivery can be altered in terms of the location and timing of the service. Outreach initiatives can change the location. Opening hours could be altered to meet the preferences of users. Many museums restrict opening hours on a Sunday, are closed on a Monday, and open from 9 am to 5 pm Tuesday to Saturday – inconvenient hours for most working people. The Royal Scottish Museum is now opening on a Tuesday evening until 8 pm to enable working people to visit. However, such responses will be subject to the willingness of employees and volunteers to work different hours.

Promotions can be used to manage demand. For example, Deep Sea World at North Queensferry indicates in its leaflet that it is busy at certain times of the day, thereby encouraging potential visitors to visit outside these times. Promotion can also be used when it is known that the museum will be quiet, maybe in the winter season; whereas promotion may not be necessary or even fortuitous when the museum is busy, for example during a festival. The Natural History Museum in London postponed an advertising campaign when its new permanent dinosaur exhibition proved so popular that queues were forming to see it.

Price, where admission is charged, can also influence demand. For example, Beamish Museum uses price elasticity, with a range of prices for different seasons of the year, with lower prices at off-peak periods. Alternatively, capacity can be tailored to meet demand. According to Armistead (1988), there are a number of approaches to vary capacity to meet short-term demand fluctuations. The first is to change the number and hours of personnel, usually by using part-time or temporary staff who can be brought in at peak times, such as during the summer season. Part-time and temporary staff, though, may not be so committed to the organisation. It may be preferable to build flexibility into the working hours of full-time staff. They could then work more hours when necessary, although this may also result in high labour costs through overtime payments. Multiskilling could be introduced where staff can perform more than one task. For example, museum attendants can act as guards, help with the information desk, and answer questions about the displays. It may also be expedient to schedule downtime, where periods of low demand can be used for staff training or to catch up on paperwork.

Finally, particularly if a museum is scheduling a popular exhibition, it is inevitable that queues will form. The user will regard waiting in a queue as time wasted. Queues therefore need to be managed if a negative and frustrating experience is to be avoided. If the wait is going to be particularly lengthy, it is better to give an indication of how long the wait will be, with an employee periodically going up and down the line advising of the length of waiting time. Anxieties can be allayed if the museum can reassure everyone that they will get in. Boredom may set in, which could be alleviated by such initiatives as street entertainment. Lovelock and Weinberg (1988) have also suggested that queuing could be ameliorated by introducing a reservation system. Museums that are offering popular blockbuster exhibitions can reduce, or even eliminate queues, lessen crowds at peak times, and increase attendance at off-peak times, through a properly designed reservation system. Clearly, this last initiative is confined to the larger museums, which have the resources and technology to administer such a system. Finally the queue can represent an opportunity for the museum to inform the user of the facilities in the museum. Leaflets can be distributed to members of the queue, the reading of which will fill in time.

CHANNELS OF DISTRIBUTION

Decisions need to be made on who participates in service delivery in terms of the service provider's personnel, any intermediaries that might be used, and the user (Lovelock and Weinberg 1988). Thus, customer service, the use of intermediaries, and the degree of involvement of the user all need to be addressed.

Customer service is becoming increasingly important in service organisations, as consumers become more demanding and sophisticated and as competitors see customer service as a competitive weapon for differentiation. Dissatisfied customers will tell on average ten other people about their bad experience, while satisfied customers will tell five people about their positive experience.

It has also been shown to cost five times more to attract a new customer than to keep an existing one (Grönroos 1990). Thus, customer service is also integral to the relationship marketing perspective. Customer service 'is concerned with the building of bonds with customers and other markets or groups to ensure long-term relationships of mutual advantage which reinforce the other marketing mix elements' (Payne 1993: 175). As with all aspects of distribution, customer service requires the integration of operations and marketing.

The use of intermediaries is relatively rare in museums, apart from circumstances where tickets to exhibitions may be sold at tourism outlets. Instead, accessibility with co-production is more often used, where services are made available with other goods or services. For example, Beamish Museum uses travel companies to sell tickets to Beamish as part of a holiday package. Tickets may also be sold as part of a rail travel ticket.

Finally, the degree to which the consumer is included in service delivery can vary depending on the museum. Self-service is the main use of consumers in service delivery, but this has its limitations in museums, apart from self-service in the café. It may be possible, though, to encourage self-service through technology, where for example, computers are set up to provide information on the museum, thereby eliminating the need for an enquiry desk. Leaflets describing the layout of the museum, and tape-recorded tours of the museum, eliminate the need for guided tours. High consumer involvement in service delivery can reduce problems of staff contact, although it can also lose the personal touch of interaction with a member of staff.

PROMOTING THE MUSEUM

Promotion plays a vital role in building and maintaining audiences. It should also be used in building relationships with other critical markets, particularly employees, funders, and sponsors. Promotion is the means by which a museum communicates with its target markets. At the very least a museum should tell people it is there and describe the products it can provide (Hannagan 1992). Research has found that lack of awareness is one of the key reasons why people do not visit museums (McLean 1992). There is a large variety of alternative methods of communicating which can be used in a communications programme. Developing a communications programme involves four key tasks: identification of the target audience; determining promotion objectives; development of the message; and selection of the communications mix.

The target audience should already have been defined in the market segmentation process. It is important that each audience is clearly defined, since 'this audience determines what is to be said, when it is to be said, where it is to be said, and who is to say it' (Palmer 1994: 272). However, it may not be the target audience alone who are made aware of the product. The museum may be brought to the attention of other members of the public through its promotional activity. They will also form impressions of the museum from this; lack of experience does not preclude opinions being voiced!

Promotional objectives need to be determined under three broad headings: to inform; to persuade; and to remind. Objectives then may include:

- developing and enhancing the image of the museum
- informing potential users about the museum and its relevant attributes
- reminding users about the museum on an ongoing basis
- reminding funders of the value of the museum
- developing motivation and commitment amongst employees.

Once the objectives have been set, decisions then have to be made on the message. A number of models have been devised showing how marketing communications can ultimately result in a decision to use the service. One of the most popular for services is the AIDA model, which suggests that the user moves through stages of Attention, Interest, Desire, and Action. Another model is the hierarchy of effects model (Lavidge and Steiner 1961), where the user moves through a number of sequential stages:

1 *Awareness*, where the potential user becomes aware that he or she has a need that must be satisfied and that there are ways of satisfying it.
2 *Knowledge* is when it is known that the need exists, and an interest is developed in learning more about it.
3 *Liking* is when the potential user begins to understand what is on offer, and recognises the benefits involved.
4 *Preference* is when alternatives have been compared, opinions and preferences are formed.
5 *Conviction* is when the potential user not only has a preference for a course of action, but also a conviction for demanding it, although he or she has not yet decided to act.
6 *Action* is the 'clinching' of the sale, when conviction becomes action.

The promotion task is to move the target audience from one stage to the next. Development of the message will involve consideration on which of these stages to emphasise. It will also depend on how well known the museum is, and on the users' perceptions of it. Development of the message involves four issues:

- *content* – what to say;
- *structure* – how to say it logically;
- *style* – creating a strong presence;
- *source* – who should develop it.

The museum then needs to decide what proportion of its budget should be earmarked for promotional activity. In the UK most museums spend less than 4 per cent of their income on publicity, although both the Museums and Galleries Commission and the Arts Council of Great Britain recommend that the figure should be nearer 9 per cent (Runyard 1994). Consideration also needs to be taken of the cost of staff time and salaries, both of salaried staff and volunteers,

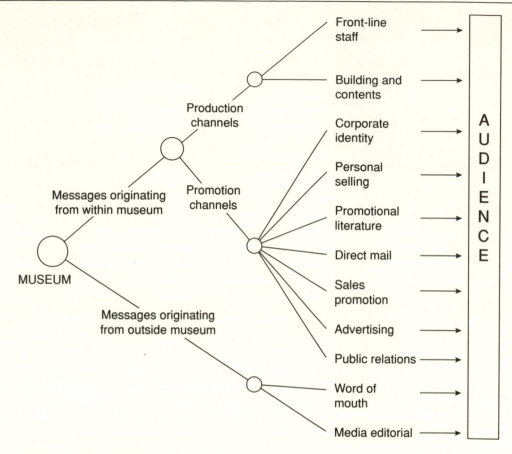

Figure 7.2 Communication channels for a museum

Source: Adapted from A. Palmer, Principles of Services Marketing, McGraw-Hill, 1994

in running a promotional campaign. The budgetary implications may seem extremely high, but if a museum is truly to meet its mission and serve the public, then the public must know about the museum and its activities.

Finally, the communications mix needs to be selected. The communications mix is the combination of channels that an organisation uses to communicate with its target audiences. Figure 7.2 illustrates the communications channels for a museum.

There are two principal sources of communication – those within an organisation and external sources. The external sources – word of mouth and media editorial – tend to have high credibility in the evaluation of alternative services (George and Kelly 1983). The museum cannot control the communications generated by external sources, although it can seek to influence them. Equally, the museum's front-line staff, its building, and contents, project a message about the museum over which the museum cannot have total control. The personnel can be trained and dressed appropriately to convey the message, but ultimately it is the individual who will manipulate the message. Similarly, the museum can add facilities, and adjust the decor and atmosphere of the building, but inevitably the structure with all its connotations cannot be changed. It can update its displays and introduce temporary exhibitions, but much of the content is predetermined. The communications generated from within the museum but over which it has control, form the promotional mix.

The museum needs to decide on the relative emphasis on the different promotional mix elements. The choice of combination will depend primarily on the target market and how best to reach it. Competitive activity may also help in making this decision, as will the cost of the various channels. A new museum is more likely to use advertising and public relations to inform prospective users, and possibly sales promotion to stimulate trial. A more established museum will need to make less use of promotions, relying to a large extent on word of mouth communications and possibly direct mail. However, where there is considerable competition or where visitor numbers are less buoyant, a museum would increase the distribution of its promotional literature and possibly advertising, and would encourage more publicity from the media.

Little has actually been written specifically on promotion in services. However, one article, 'Guidelines for the Advertising of Services' (George and Berry 1981) is particularly insightful, and is relevant for all communications, not just advertising. George and Berry highlighted a number of guidelines which should be considered when developing communications:

- *The role of personal selling*
  Because of the inseparability of production and consumption, the museum's front-line staff can become critical communication variables, their manner and appearance being important tools for personal selling.
- *Provide tangible clues*
  In order to reduce the risk of choosing an intangible product, tangible clues should be given to the potential user. These clues come from all aspects of the museum's corporate communication.
- *Make the service understood*
  Again because of their intangibility, services may be difficult to grasp mentally. Tangible attributes of the service can help make it easier to understand the service. For example, the Science Museum used an effective advertising campaign which focused on specific tangible objects within the museum.
- *Communications continuity*
  It is important to be consistent in the corporate image of the service, unifying all the communications. It can help differentiate from other offerings. A museum should use its logo and typeface on all its literature and correspondence.
- *Promising what is possible*
  Museums have a tendency to overpromise, hoping that it will entice potential users. This will result only in short-term gains if the user is

disappointed. The museum must deliver on its promises. It is important to manage expectations, since most problems about customer satisfaction relate to expectations exceeding delivery (Czeipel *et al.* 1985).

● *Capitalising on word of mouth*
The variability of services encourages people to seek out recommendation from friends and relatives. Word of mouth is a vital communication tool and should be encouraged.

● *Direct communications to employees*
Promotions for employees, such as staff newsletters detailing the activities of the museum and achievements of staff members, can help build their motivation and commitment to the organisation.

It is useful to keep these guidelines in mind when devising a communications campaign for a museum.

THE PROMOTIONAL MIX

Communications in the museum have tended to be left to chance (Hooper-Greenhill 1994). Communications activities have taken place, but usually in isolation from each other, and rarely in any co-ordinated fashion. However, as Bryant states:

> Once the message is determined it must become the focus of all communications directed by whatever means to the market place and its constituent segments. There has to be a common hymn sheet and everyone, just everyone, has to know the tune.
>
> (Bryant 1988: 23)

Although the museum should select the most appropriate promotional mix elements, there is one function which every museum should undertake, that of developing a corporate image. From the image comes the predominant message, which then needs to be used throughout all the other promotions, even though each individual promotion may have its own message to communicate. To ensure consistency, there must be an overall message underlying specific individual messages.

CORPORATE IDENTITY

Corporate identity is created by a range of factors including: the style and content of a museum's exhibition programming; the 'culture' of the museum, that is how it feels both to outsiders and those working within it; and the many different forms of information it produces (Arts Council of Great Britain 1993). Corporate identity is most obviously expressed through a museum's logo and the graphic style of its printed information. Every museum has its own personality, which is the image that it projects to its audience. The individual characteristics of the museum, expressed in its mission statement, need to be understood. This then needs to be reflected in its name. The change of name from the British Museum (Natural History) to the Natural History Museum is much more appealing, while the North of England Open Air Museum has found that people refer to it as Beamish, the name it now uses to promote itself. This then becomes the brand name of the museum, similar to brand names such as Pepsi and Bank of Scotland. Brand names are becoming increasingly significant since it has been suggested that corporate branding will, in the future, become the main discriminator, and that the consumer's choice will depend less on the perceived benefits of a service, and more on their assessment of the organisation and the people who run it (King 1991).

There are problems, though, with the notion of brand image in museums. To suggest that a museum's personality can be conveyed by its name should be treated with caution. Clearly, it is much more complicated than that. Museums such as the Louvre or the British Museum, could perhaps develop brand images; although the brand image of the Louvre reflects the content, such as the Mona Lisa, rather than any personality, while the British Museum is a national institution, with all the connotations that implies, rather than a brand. This does not preclude the museum from developing an identity, or 'corporate identity', but it should beware of the limitations of using brand names as promotional tools in the museum context.

It takes a considerable amount of time to develop a corporate identity, so it should be built to be long-lasting, not to reflect current fashions which will be out of date next year. It is worth investing in a commissioned design, which does not need to be expensive, and should be a long-term investment. The quality of the design will only be as good as the briefing given to the designer. Once developed, the logo and designated typeface should appear on as many aspects of the museum as possible: typography on stationery, advertising, mailings, posters, leaflets, catalogues, paper bags, and signposts. Always have photographic bromides of the logo available for the media and printers, and insist that the typeface is always used. Beamish Museum uses a typeface which was carefully selected to remind people of a past age when that typeface would commonly have been used. A pen and ink drawing of the familiar outline of the bridge is used by Tower Bridge in London to achieve instant recognition, while MOMI is a word created by the Museum of the Moving Image, which in its special typeface and promotion has also established instant recognition (Richards 1992).

From the corporate identity a corporate image is then developed – the way in which the organisation is perceived by outsiders. Uniforms are an excellent way of reflecting the museum's image. The attendants in the National Galleries of Scotland are now decked out in 'tartan trews' – very Scottish! In the Design Museum in London, the more approachable staff wear casual sweatshirts. It is essential to remember that image should be consistent and it should reflect the character of the museum, particularly in terms of the benefits it offers its users – a Scottish institution in the case of the National Galleries of Scotland, and a participative approachable museum in the case of the Design Museum.

This image is then projected to users, stakeholders, and employees, helping to reinforce the museum's role.

The corporate identity should be maintained until the museum shifts in character, or market research shows that it is projecting the wrong image to the public. The Royal Albert Memorial Museum in Exeter changed its logo from an illustration of a splendid building to a design incorporating illustrations that symbolise the museum's principal collections. The intention was to remind people of what was inside the museum rather than what the building looked like. The museum also wanted to attract more young people, and it was felt that the logo change was a logical step (Baker 1991).

A new museum will need to put a good deal of thought into its name since it will ultimately reflect its corporate identity. A recent museum initiative in Glasgow, which could have been named, 'The Museum of Religion', was called, 'The St Mungo Museum of Religious Life and Art'. After consultation with local religious communities in Glasgow, it was decided to name the museum after the sixth-century saint, St Mungo, who founded Glasgow. The name was friendly, memorable, and interesting, and referred to someone whom all Glasgow schoolchildren learn about, and who reflected the importance of religion in the life of the city. The second part of the title, 'Religious Life and Art', 'reflects the fact that the museum could only approach the spiritual domain through works of art or objects used by people in their daily lives' (O'Neill 1995: 52).

PERSONAL SELLING

Bateson (1989) found that personal selling and image-creating strategies are the communications tools most often used by service organisations. Often personal selling can be the most important variable in the development of expectations (Mudie and Cottam 1993). In museums the only personal contact that users have is usually with attendants or shop and café assistants, and so it is important that they are chosen carefully and are trained effectively. As Bryant comments, 'Every interface between museum staff, friends or committee members and an existing or potential museum user is a promotional opportunity to be taken advantage of' (Bryant 1988: 23).

Ideally, promotion would always involve personal selling. Since each potential user is an individual, they should be treated thus, with a well-trained salesperson in contact with one user at a time. The users' needs could then best be matched to the available products. Personal contact between museum employees and users is a personal selling experience for the user, reinforcing the importance of customer contact personnel. Contact should be a positive, not a negative selling experience, particularly since these contacts may be the only personal selling contacts the museum will be able to afford. This underlines the importance of recruitment and training, and of giving employees a sense of purpose as a positive part of the marketing of the museum product.

All museum staff are ambassadors for the museum, whether they are customer contact personnel or whether they go out to give talks about the museum and its contents to clubs and societies. They each contribute in their own way to the marketing effort of the museum. The staff should be trained to have a positive effect on the visitors, encouraging them to return and to recommend that their friends visit, perhaps by giving them literature to pass on.

PROMOTIONAL LITERATURE

Most museums rely on printed material to reach their target users. Leaflets are the most popular and effective material, while posters tend to be less effective, since,

> they are attractive to look at, and create a visible presence for the gallery, but most galleries have no idea whether a single image from an exhibition and its title, presented in isolation from other information brings people in. Surveys often show that posters are not actually given by people as a significant reason for attending a show.
>
> (Arts Council of Great Britain 1993: 5)

It is probably better to design an A5 brochure which unfolds to incorporate an A5 poster. Posters should not be larger than the A3 size, as notice boards are generally too small to incorporate large posters. The only exception is transport posters, if a campaign is being mounted on railway stations or bus sites, when four-sheet size posters are needed. Before deciding on use of print material though, it is worth assessing its effectiveness by examining museum surveys and whether visitors actually use promotional literature to find out about the museum's activities.

Leaflets can be as simple as single-sided fliers, but ideally, should be coloured with a range of photographs. They should convey the image of the museum with an indication of the quality of the experience, while giving details of opening hours and of the range of exhibitions and services. They should also include an indication of how to find the museum. Some leaflets will be produced for a special event or seasonal programme or possibly for group organisers, such as schools. Some will be used for mailing to the travel trade, while the rest will be used for display in information racks.

There are a number of ways of distributing print: for display in the museum or other museums or libraries; through distribution systems run by independent agencies, while some regions have arts marketing consortia offering this service; through other organisations' distribution systems, such as schools; through tourist information centres, hotels, organisations associated with a particular community group; and through direct mail. Ask retailers to make a window display of the museum's material, possibly in return for an incentive. It may be worth forming consortia for producing and distributing literature to pool costs and spread the effort. Many municipal museums already do this, although more museums should take the lead on such initiatives as the Edinburgh

Gallery Guide. Effective distribution of print material is essential. It is important to ensure that the print material will reach the target audience at a time when they will be most susceptible to the message.

The design of the print is crucial in attracting attention and ensuring that the message is read and understood. Professional help should be sought at this stage if possible. Producing literature can be a lengthy process, and it is worth allowing plenty of time for design, printing, and distribution, to ensure that the literature reaches the target market at the most appropriate moment.

Catalyst, the Museum of the Chemical Industry in Widnes, developed an effective promotional campaign using leaflets and posters for its launch in 1989. The main leaflet carried the slogan, 'Unusual . . . Possibly, Fun . . . Definitely', while a leaflet publicising special events used cartoons. The graphic design was consistent, intending to suggest an image of a distinctive and contemporary museum. The literature was reinforced with media advertising, where the museum was publicised as one of the 'Wonders of Widnes', the other being the Welsh rugby captain who had recently joined the Widnes Rugby League Club. The whole campaign was light-hearted, in order to overcome people's negative expectations of a museum of the chemical industry (Baker 1991).

As publicly distributed literature tends to be passive, it is important to try and elicit a response. Include a request to ring the museum for further information; monitor attendance at special events that have been publicised through posters and leaflets; attach a coupon to all leaflets for people to bring in for a reduction on a catalogue or a complimentary cup of coffee; encourage people to make a donation for a specific purpose, for example towards the organising of an exhibition of local artists.

There are alternative forms of literature which a museum could use, including newsletters for regular visitors. If the target market includes employees and stakeholders, then it is worth considering the use of print to convey the message to them. Newsletters for employees, updating on museum activities and staff achievements, can also help to build relationships with the staff, and increase their sense of belonging and ultimately motivation. Regular updates of the museum's activities and achievements through a magazine or newsletter for stakeholders is also a worthwhile consideration. If the intention is to remind them of the museum and impress upon them its importance, print material can be a powerful mechanism.

The effectiveness of the literature should be monitored where possible, through survey research, or merely by verbally asking visitors how they found out about the museum. A phone enquiry to the museum could be used to elicit this information, while staff on the information desk could be briefed to ask the visitors. The effectiveness of the distribution should also be monitored. It is worth offering an incentive to a volunteer to make spot checks on the stock of leaflets and positioning of posters in the venues where they were distributed. Using a special promotion on the literature, with a code for different locations for the leaflet 'drops', should enable the responses to be tracked.

As distribution of paper increasingly becomes obsolete with alternative sources for distributing information being sought, such as e-mail and the Internet, museums should be cognisant of these developments and ready to capitalise on them. The Internet may in the future become a regular source of communication on cultural activities and usurp much of the need for distribution of printed material. It is essential that museums are at the forefront of the technological revolution, recognising the imperative for communication by technology.

DIRECT MAIL

Direct mail is a relatively recent technique which has been eagerly adopted by performing arts organisations. It is an excellent way of promoting directly to specific target groups using printed material. It is popular both for targeting an audience and for fundraising, targeting prospective stakeholders. It is an expensive exercise, especially if mailing costs are involved, but if well targeted can prove to be the most cost-effective publicity medium.

There are a number of advantages in using direct mail. First, in terms of relationship marketing, it allows the museum to build continuing relationships with its users. If the museum keeps in touch with its users, makes them feel personally involved in the museum, then they are more likely to become loyal users. Direct mail also enables the measurement of response, and therefore the calculation of its cost in terms of numbers reached. For example, include tear-off slips, or phone-in responses, to private view invitations.

Direct mail can be included as a benefit for joining a Friends scheme – invitations to private viewings, receiving literature about up-and-coming events, and so on. It may also be used more generally, although it is important that a more general mailing list is kept up to date and reviewed regularly by asking those who have not responded to the mailing list if they wish to remain on it. Users can be encouraged to join a mailing list by including a request for further information in publicity literature. A campaign to reach current non-attenders could use data on addresses to reach a target profile with a similar profile to current museum visitors. Evaluating the success of such a widespread campaign is difficult, although a form of coupon response, either as a discount or other benefit voucher on presentation, is feasible.

It needs to be remembered that any mailing list held on a computer for marketing purposes needs to be registered. In addition, anyone whose name is held on the mailing list needs to be informed about who will be holding the data; the purpose for which it is likely to be used; and to whom it might be disclosed.

Direct mail lists can also be useful for finding out more about the museum's users, by sending them a questionnaire to complete. It can encourage users to visit the museum more frequently. It is also a good way of inviting regular users to bring a friend the next time they visit the museum. Use every opportunity to build up the mailing list. The Arts Council of Great Britain (1993) has suggested a few ways of doing this:

- Invite those already on the list to add friends who might be interested.
- Let users know about the list by prominently placing a notice, with a supply of cards and a box, so that users can leave their name and address.
- At special events and lectures leave notices and leaflets on chairs and place prominently, encouraging people to leave their name and address.
- Carry out special promotions.
- Borrow or rent mailing lists from other organisations. Share lists with other organisations, as long as users are informed, and give them the option not to be included in any other mailing list.

Direct mail is a useful tool, but clearly depends on the resources and capabilities of the museum. If few activities are organised or little promotional material is produced, then a mailing list may not be useful; alternatively only a minimal mailing list, for example to Friends, might be required. It also depends on the museum having the technology to hold a database, and the resources for mailing. Alternatively, a small museum with a small base of loyal supporters may wish to use the phone to contact them and advise them of any special events or special promotions – again it is the personal touch that counts.

SALES PROMOTION

A museum may choose to use special promotions, events, or offers that act as incentives to use the museum. Special promotions can help to attract new users, to encourage repeat visits, and to encourage purchases from the shop or catering facilities. Again, sales promotion is popular with a number of performing arts organisations, although to date has been little used in museums. It is associated with a 'hard sell' approach, which, particularly if it is seen as too commercial, can be inappropriate for the image of the museum. However, if used carefully and without being too pushy it can be an effective promotional medium.

Sales promotion includes: discounts and complimentary purchases, such as cups of coffee in the café, or discounts on entrance to exhibitions; free offers and competitions; special events; and joint promotions. The Arts Council of Great Britain (1993) lists a number of opportunities for devising sales promotions techniques:

- discounted exhibition catalogues
- publications at the shop
- food and drink at the café and restaurant
- exhibitions with an entrance charge
- appropriate merchandise, for example, carrier bags, pens
- prizes or gifts made available by sponsors and other organisations promoting their goods, for example, books, records, tape, tickets
- special events linked to specific exhibitions
- combined promotions with other venues.

The Royal Museum of Scotland in Edinburgh organised a 'Christmas Collection' to promote the museum over the Christmas period. It included a Christmas art competition for all ages; a festive tree trail, where visitors had to find ten Christmas trees hidden in the museum; and lantern slide shows, with coloured lantern slides featuring the stories of Peter Pan and Ali Baba. The promotions were advertised in local newspapers, along with a telephone number to call for further information.

If used sensitively, sales promotion can be an effective promotional tool, but only if it is compatible with the museum's image and is well integrated into the rest of the promotional mix.

ADVERTISING

Advertising is the most expensive and least cost-effective way to promote a museum. By contrast, editorial coverage is at least ten times as effective as paid advertising space (Runyard 1994). Advertising is any paid form of impersonal communication that is intended to inform and persuade. Museums may advertise to build a good corporate image; to increase usage; to counteract competition; and to inform of new exhibitions, events and so on. The main advantage of advertising is that complete control is retained over the content of the message, which is not the case in editorial coverage.

Before deciding on whether advertising will be an effective means of promotion, it is important to have clear objectives for the advertising. The objectives should determine what the advertising is intended to communicate. An analysis of the objectives may suggest that there is no need to advertise.

Govoni and colleagues (1986) have outlined a number of key elements in defining advertising objectives. These should include:

- a concise definition of the target audience
- a clear statement of the desired response or responses to be generated among the target audience
- an expression of goals in quantitative terms
- a projection of achievements attributable to advertising
- an expressed understanding of advertising's role with respect to the rest of the promotion programme
- an acknowledgement that the goals are demanding yet achievable
- a statement of time constraints.

Having defined the objectives, an advertising strategy can be developed, which would include:

- the purpose of advertising
- the target audience
- the budget
- the content
- the media to be used

- the frequency of the advertisement
- the measure of effectiveness.

The purpose of the advertising will determine the measure of effectiveness. However, it can be difficult to track effectiveness without some kind of response mechanism, such as a voucher or coupon. The advertising plan needs to consider a number of questions, that is: Why? What? To whom? How? When? Where? Why is advertising being carried out? What is the purpose and objectives of advertising? To whom is the advertising directed? What response is expected from the target audience? When is the best time to advertise? Where is the most cost-effective medium for advertising?

Advertising is best undertaken with the advice of an agency. Advertising agencies may be costly, but they are able to derive discounts from the media which are not available to the museum. With a clear brief, an agency will recommend a package of suggestions for approval. Be careful to choose the agency that shows an understanding of the museum rather than one with bright ideas and the seemingly least expensive proposal.

The advertising message needs to be kept simple, clear, and precise, since advertisements can only signal a very limited amount of information. The message should be supported with dates, times, address, and telephone number – where the museum is, and when it is open. The museum's corporate identity and use of logo also needs to be considered. Research conducted by the Arts Council of Great Britain (1993) found that people like to have exhibitions described in words. This gives the opportunity to use recommendation to support the message, such as a critic's comments, or it could express the responses of the target audience at seeing the exhibition.

In order to reach the target audience, the museum needs to know which newspapers, magazines, and programmes they read, watch, or listen to. The principal media include television, radio, cinema, newspapers, magazines, posters, and outdoor advertising. Each of these has specific advantages and disadvantages. Selecting which medium or media to use involves taking four factors into account: characteristics of the medium; the atmosphere of the medium; coverage of the medium; and comparative cost. The first, characteristics of the medium, includes geographical coverage; types of audience reached; the number of times they will possibly see the advertisement; the potential for use of colour, sound, and movement; and the power to reach special target segments in a credible manner. Assessing the atmosphere of the medium involves ensuring that the medium reinforces the image the museum is seeking to project. Coverage of the medium should be considered, in terms of the number of people reached and their characteristics. Comparative cost should also be taken into account, that is the cost to reach a specific audience size such as cost per thousand viewers or readers.

A number of reference works give the circulation numbers, type of market at which the publication is aimed, and the cost of advertising.[1] The idea is to use the medium that reaches the largest number of the target market in the most cost-effective way. To achieve impact, it is more effective to use display advertisements, that is large spaces in specified places, rather than classified advertising which is usually only single column width. Redeemable coupons can be used, such as discounts on entry, or two for the price of one, thereby helping to monitor the effectiveness of the medium.

It might be worth collaborating with other museums to pay for a page of advertorial, usually called an 'Advertising Feature'. The advertisement has the appearance of being part of the editorial copy of the publication, which tends to be more highly regarded by the readership. Or, it may be that advertising is not required or can be kept to a minimum in some magazines or newspapers which have listings pages. This provides the museum with free advertising and should be used as widely as possible.

Outdoor advertising on poster sites or in and around transport systems offers a variety of opportunities. It is possible to make a strong visual impact, although it can be costly. It is also open to vandalism, so care needs to be taken with the copy. The London Underground has been used by a group of museums in London who share the sites according to their requirements and means (Runyard 1994).

Television advertising is extremely expensive, and unless the museum can afford to pay to go on air at peak periods during the day, it will find its advertisements tucked away in the early morning or early afternoon. It is not just the cost of purchasing the time spots, but the production of the advertisement, which will take up a large proportion of the promotion budget.

Radio is a good way of reaching local and regional markets. It has the advantage of immediacy, being able to distribute new information about events or incentive admission charges. Radio need not be expensive but the advertisement should be made either by an agency or the commercial production department of the radio station.

Perhaps the most famous museum advertising campaign was the Victoria and Albert Museum's 'Ace Caff' campaign, which ended with the line, 'An ace caff with quite a nice museum attached'. Few other museums could afford to use the advertising agency Saatchi & Saatchi to develop their campaign, but some lessons can be learned from the process they used to mount this campaign. A survey of visitors to the museum indicated that a large proportion of the museum's visitors were young, relatively 'upmarket' adults who were generally culturally active. In order to attract more of this segment, it was felt that the museum needed to divest itself of its old-fashioned image as a museum devoted to Victoriana. Moreover the research found that people liked what they saw on display in the museum once they had been enticed in. The message that the advertising tried to get across was that, 'the V&A is a place which is engaged with communication now, and it is prepared to stick its neck out' (Baker 1991). The advertising took to task the attitudes towards the museum by being contentious and challenging.

A further campaign described by Baker (1991) is the Science Museum's campaign, which featured an individual exhibit in each advertisement, to suggest that the museum is a place full of things that 'make you think'. A television commercial featured various artefacts from the history of flight. Posters were also used which told the story about individual items in the collection, including the controversial Mr Crapper water closet. The approach required the co-operation and assistance of the curators in the museum in the selection of the items and the writing of copy, integrating operations and marketing, so that 'it's everyone's ad' (Baker, N. 1991: 25).

It is also worth remembering that the signs and banners on a building can convey messages about the museum, while the whole appearance suggests an image – an old building which has been cleaned will be more welcoming. The Scottish National Gallery of Modern Art uses banners across its rather imposing frontage to soften the building, and to clearly denote the building as a modern art gallery.

Once the decision has been made on the media to be used, an advertising or media-buying agency should be engaged, to buy the time or space, since they will be able to negotiate higher discounts. Always monitor the results of the advertising. Use a response device on the advertising, or survey users with a simple questionnaire. Always ensure that the advertising is integrated with the other methods of promotion being used.

PUBLIC RELATIONS AND MEDIA EDITORIAL

Public relations and those aspects not included in the promotional mix, media editorial and word of mouth, are extremely important methods of communication for museums. Public relations is defined by the British Institute of Public Relations as, 'the planned and sustained effort to establish and maintain goodwill between an organisation and its publics'. The 'publics' are all the groups of people and organisations that have an interest in the museum.

Public relations is concerned with a number of marketing tasks, including building or maintaining image; supporting the other communication activities; handling problems and issues; reinforcing positioning; influencing specific publics; and assisting the launch of new exhibitions, facilities, and so on. A number of tools are used in the design of a public relations programme (Payne 1993), including:

- publications, including press releases, annual reports, brochures, posters, articles, and employee reports
- events, including press conferences, seminars, speeches, and conferences
- stories that create media coverage
- exhibitions at museum conferences.

The UK Museums Association has produced a useful Briefing on *Advocacy for Museums* (Museums Association 1995c), which it defines as, 'creating a network of support whereby people of influence, outside a museum's direct responsibility, will choose to represent that museum's interests with a particular constituency'. Planning and partnership are the key to advocacy. It involves the skills of image-making, presentation, and identification of key players (Carrington 1995). Developing relationships with advocates such as politicians and business people is essential.

Buckinghamshire County Museum was closed in 1989, but in 1995 was re-opened thanks to the County Museum officer's campaign on its behalf by making contacts and winning support (Carrington 1995). Wealthy and influential personalities in the county were persuaded to support the cause, while the press was instrumental in persuading the county council that it needed the museum. The press publicised the closure of the museum and its subsequent dilapidation as a disgrace – to which the council responded with most of the refurbishment funds. The cultivation and subsequent support of an art critic and historian and former Member of the UK Parliament, Timothy Raison, was considered instrumental in saving the museum. Cromarty Courthouse, on the other hand, relies on the local community to provide a mutual support network (Carrington 1995). An independent museum, it depends on local volunteers both to work in the museum and to act as trustees. In order to be a community organisation, though, the museum needs to develop relationships with its local community. Clearly then, public relations is crucial in communicating not only with visitor markets, but also other target markets.

Publicity, or unpaid media coverage, is probably the most popular form of public relations work conducted by museums. It is not expensive and can be extremely cost-effective. However, there is no direct control over the content of the publicity, although often journalists transcribe word for word a good press release. The key to good publicity then is a good press release and developing relationships with journalists. It is important to have them on the museum's side, because, contrary to public opinion, all publicity is not good publicity. The media will be quick to give coverage when things go wrong. Try and avoid this by maintaining regular personal contact with the media.

Media coverage can be broken down into three areas: editorial, such as news, features, reviews; listings; and advertorial, that is editorial or listings space linked to paid-for advertising. Editorial is perceived as impartial and can be invaluable in promoting a museum. There is an art to writing a press release. It has to stand out to ensure that the news editor will read it, and take notice of it over all the other press releases that will be received every day. Richards (1992) has outlined some useful rules to follow in a press release. They include:

- Incorporate the museum's letterhead and clearly head it 'Press Release'.
- Date it.
- Use a catchy heading – but make sure it is not too clever, since journalists like to think they are clever too!
- Double space the copy.
- Highlight bullet points.

153

- If using a quotation, put the quote within inverted commas and give the source.
- Keep it simple and factual.
- Check the spelling.
- Say who to contact for more information and where they can be found easily at any time.
- If photographs or any other material are enclosed or attached, say so on the press release.

It is important that the press release is sent to a named journalist, and that the press release is customised for specific publications, if necessary. It is also important to know when a publication needs a press release – for example, some magazines work at least three or four months in advance. It is also worth following up the press release. A simple phone call asking if further information is required or mentioning another interesting detail can reinforce the message.

Other elements in a press campaign might include: a press preview, where interviews can be arranged as well as photo opportunities; a photo call, when for example, a well-known personality is opening an exhibition; a press launch, if there is something special to tell them, possibly asking a speaker to address the press and providing refreshments.

Listings are usually free, and are often included in both regional and local newspapers and magazines. Decide which publications will best reach the target market and find out what kind of information the Listings Editor requires and the deadlines for the information. Offer to send a visual – for example, *The Scotsman* has a daily listings which includes a photo of one of the events. Finally, the use of advertorial could be considered, possibly in conjunction with other museums, to publicise the museum's retail activities, for example.

If publicity is being sought from television or radio, it is worth remembering some of the specific needs of these media. Television is very visual and will require a lively, colourful event and a good talker. Radio will similarly need a good talker who can come out with some interesting anecdotes.

Events can be created especially for the media, and also in collaboration with the media. For the re-opening of the Edinburgh Museum of Childhood, the museum launched a competition in conjunction with the Edinburgh *Evening News* to identify a VIC (Very Important Child) to officiate at the opening ceremony. The media enthusiastically covered the event, capturing public interest in the re-opening (Coutts 1988).

Developing relationships with journalists, though, is the key to good media coverage. Regular contact is essential, not just when the museum has something to say. The Arts Council of Great Britain (1993) recommends that journalists should be cultivated by taking them for a drink or a meal, while a card thanking them for a favourable review can never go amiss. The museum wants to generate as much good publicity as it can, both to communicate to its potential target markets and to encourage word of mouth.

WORD OF MOUTH

In selling a service, a museum will want to build on word of mouth communication. Several writers, including Young (1981), have suggested that word of mouth communication is more important than advertising for services. This hypothesis is supported in a museum context by market research cited by DiMaggio (1985) and conducted by McLean (1992). Users talk to other potential users about their experiences, with personal recommendation being the preferred source of information about a museum. Grönroos (1990) has outlined a communications pattern illustrating the role of word of mouth referrals. An existing, or a new, visitor to the museum will have certain expectations. Once the decision to purchase has been made, the visitor will interact with the museum and discover the technical and functional quality of the service being supplied. As a result of the experiences that follow from these interactions and the judgements made about the quality of the museum's service, the visitor will or will not return. Positive or negative word of mouth communication will then influence the extent to which others use the museum. Negative experiences tend to have a greater impact than positive experiences. Negative word of mouth communication then, can significantly reduce the impact of other forms of communication, while positive word of mouth means that less communications are required.

Museums should try to capitalise on word of mouth. For example, by using testimonials of other satisfied users' experiences in leaflets. Promotional items such as sweatshirts and umbrellas can provide tangible clues implying 'club' membership. Developing relationships with visitors is also crucial, since a visitor who feels a sense of loyalty towards a museum, and a feeling of 'belonging', is more likely to discuss the museum with relatives and friends.

CONCLUSIONS

The promotional efforts of a museum tend to be regarded as the principal functions of marketing. However, they are only one aspect of the marketing activity of a museum: that of communicating to the public about the museum. Clearly, as each element of the promotions mix needs to be integrated, so does each of the marketing activities need to be integrated with the promotions. There is no point in publicising a price reduction two weeks after it is instigated, or advertising a special event after it has finished. Museums should adopt a holistic approach to their communication efforts, which means that they should be aware of all aspects of the museum's operations that impinge on the experience of the visitor. The marketing planning process should ensure that consideration is given to the whole communication effort.

8

Resource attraction

Most museums are non-profit-making institutions. In the past, they could normally rely on continuous funding from their funding bodies, usually central and local government in the UK, or also benefactors in the US. However, two significant changes have altered this 'dependency culture', as it has been called with some derision. First, the advent and phenomenal growth, particularly in the UK, of independent museums. Although to a large extent the independent museums receive some funding from municipal authorities and grant-giving bodies, this income is not sufficient for survival. Independent museums have to generate their own income. The second change has been the demise of automatic annual increases in funding for local authority and central government museums. The political and economic climate has changed, bringing in demands that museums become accountable, show 'value for money', and that they use market mechanisms to seek plural funding. In other words, museums can no longer rely on public subsidy for survival. The issue of income generation and resource attraction has come very much to the fore. There are, of course, fears that the pendulum may swing too far, and museums may be forced to 'commercialise' in order to generate funds. This may be the case already with a number of independent museums. However, museums were not originally established to make money, nor is their current *raison d'être* income generation: that can be left to commercial leisure organisations, or until the spectre of privatisation becomes a reality. 'Value' in museums is the value of the collection, manifested in its value to the public in terms of their experience. Value is not financially driven in museums but experience-driven.

There is a fatal flaw in commercialisation of museums. Unlike some other leisure organisations, museums are not self-supporting. Except in rare circumstances, they are incapable of making a profit. Despite this, museums are survivors; they are less likely to go bankrupt and be closed than other business organisations. Their permanence enables their policies to retain a sense of stability. But there are also coinciding problems. Morton, for example, has stated that,

> If there is no intention that public museums should compete directly with commercial organizations (and there are certainly not the resources to do that effectively) then an important problem for museum staff is to

fashion and maintain a clear identity for museums as different kinds of institutions from those in the commercial arena.

(Morton 1988: 137)

The answer is already implicit in museums. They are not commercial organisations. They exist 'for the public benefit' (Museums Association 1984), not to profit from the public. Such a motive is an indictment of their commercialisation. If resource attraction is carried out under the auspices of the museum's mission and goals, then there should be no need to compromise the museum. On the contrary, a museum that rejects its goals in favour of an unsympathetic commercialism will only reflect contradictions in its image. In the long term this will result in confusion amongst users and ultimately in fewer users. Resource attraction, therefore, must be grounded in the goals of the museum.

As in all non-profit activities, there are two principal means of attracting additional resources: income generation and development activities. Income generation encompasses all aspects of income that can be self-earned, including pricing strategies, catering, retailing, publications, special events, and conference and room hire. Development activities include all aspects of resource attraction from external sources, encompassing fundraising and sponsorship, Friends and members schemes, and attracting volunteers.

INCOME GENERATION

Pricing strategies

The key problem in services pricing which distinguishes it from the pricing of goods is the difficulty in assessing the cost of providing the service. The fixed costs, particularly staff salaries, can amount to a substantial proportion of the overall budget. The problem is exacerbated by the non-homogeneity of services, where a wide range of prices is attached to apparently similar services. A local government museum which makes no admission charge may be compared to a small independent museum which charges an entry fee. Equally, museums which do charge may be compared to other leisure activities in terms of price.

Pricing connects the product to the value placed on the product by the potential user. It enables the potential user to make comparisons among alternatives, particularly if they are disparate alternatives. However, monetary price is not the only 'price' that may be incurred. According to Fine (1981), there are other costs, related to the social price, which may need to be taken into consideration. Time is one cost, which is a precious commodity for many people. There may be disadvantages attached to the museum's location (place costs) or attached to the museum's physical characteristics (sensory costs). There may be feelings of discomfort, inferiority, or even social disapproval from others. Thus the benefits of the museum need to be traded off against these costs associated with the museum. The costs should also be recognised and minimised through other aspects of the marketing strategy. It has been suggested that non-monetary prices assume greater importance where the service is free, where there would be expected to be no barriers to access (Prottas 1981). Consequently, the direct monetary price may not be the significant cost.

Monetary price is not just a way of obtaining revenue, although this is the pivotal role it plays in the marketing mix. Pricing decisions can contribute to image-building in a service and can be significant in denoting the value of the museum to the potential user. Price can also be used for market segmentation purposes, to reach specific markets. Price can be a powerful statement which goes beyond the revenue that it generates.

In UK museums, in particular, there is still considerable debate on the efficacy and ethics of charging for what is a public service. In the pages of *Leisure Management* two respected museum directors sparred over museum charges. Patrick Roper, development director of the National Maritime Museum contends that,

> The argument that national museums should be free because they belong to the nation is a position so absurd that one wonders how the scholars and academics who have traditionally run these places ever arrived at it ... Many things belong to the nation – roads, for example – but while there is often a general contribution through taxes, the principle of some form of additional payment by those who use them is accepted.
>
> (Roper 1990: 36)

The opposite extreme is voiced by Julian Spalding, director of Glasgow Museums and Art Galleries:

> It is particularly mean for our society to charge for what it has inherited, especially as much of it, nearly all the great paintings for example, were given free to the nation by wealthy individuals for all to enjoy. All that was asked by these donors was that the nation looked after them.
>
> (Spalding 1990: 37–8)

Spalding further contends that museums that have introduced charges have often experienced a corresponding reduction in their number of visitors. For example, the London museums that introduced charges in the late 1980s saw a resulting 40 per cent drop in visitor figures. Numerous other statistics confirm this thesis: for example, attendance at the National Museums of Wales fell by 42 per cent following the introduction of compulsory admission charges in December 1988 (*Museums Journal*, April 1990); visitor numbers at Swansea's museums increased fourfold following the abolition of entrance fees (*Museums Journal*, November 1993); and the Museum of Childhood in Edinburgh earned more after charges were abolished, from income generated in the shop (Coutts 1988).

Recently, Bailey has responded to the debate by claiming that:

> The case against admission charges is based on philosophical arguments that relate to social equity, freedom of access and right to culture.

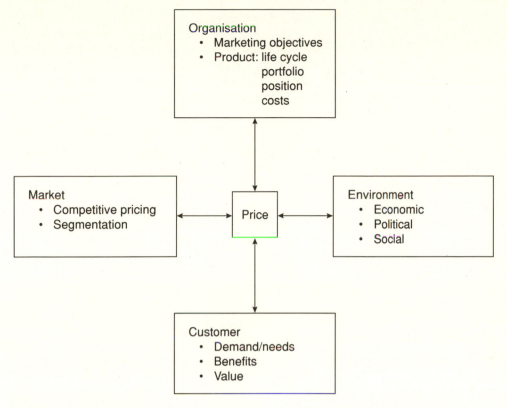

Figure 8.1 Pricing policy

Source: Adapted from T.J. Hannagan, *Marketing in the Public and Non-Profit Sector*, Macmillan Press Ltd, 1992

However, a free service largely used by affluent groups, but paid for by both poor and rich taxpayers, is hardly to be applauded for its social progress.

(Bailey 1995: 33)

Spalding could respond, quite legitimately, that his museums are used by a representative cross-section of the population of Glasgow, poor and wealthy alike. Whatever the arguments though, if a museum's funding is being cut, and attempts at persuading a local authority of the value of free admission have failed, then the reality of charging takes over. As Diggle claims though, 'Charging for admission can actually help a museum achieve larger attendance as well as larger revenues without an ethical downside' (Diggle 1995: 32). Perhaps the final word should be given to the UK Museums Association, which states:

Above all, it is essential that policy in relation to admission charges is formed in such a way that it does not discourage people from viewing the collections or from using the museum. The Association's code on admission charges states that 'central and local government have an

overriding responsibility to maintain the tradition of free access . . .';
and that if charges are levied the revenue must be reinvested in the
museum. The Code also maintains that the decision as to whether or
not to charge should be left up to individual museums, but that free
admission should be provided for the equivalent of at least one day a
week, and there should be reduced rates on all other days for children,
the elderly, the unemployed and disabled people.

(Museums Association 1991a: 13)

Many independent museums do not have the luxury of decision on this issue,
and in order to survive must charge for admission. There are various influences
at play on the ultimate decision to charge and the setting of prices. Pricing
policies are influenced by four factors:

- those under the control of the museum itself
- those that operate in the market in which the museum operates
- those influenced by users' needs
- those determined by the marketing environment.

Figure 8.1 illustrates these factors.

Organisation – marketing objectives

Prices should be determined by the marketing objectives. As one element of
the marketing mix, price should relate to all other aspects of the mix. The
price should also be consistent with the total marketing strategy for the
museum. The marketing objectives of a museum may, for example, emphasise the priority of access to minority groups – price decisions must reflect
this.

Organisation – product life cycle

The age of the product can sometimes impact on the level of pricing. A new
museum with little competition in the surrounding area may find that visitors
will bear a high price. However, as the museum is established and is increasingly
relying on repeat visits, and as other attractions open up in competition to
the museum, it may find it necessary to reduce the price to guarantee its visitor
levels.

Organisation – product portfolio

The price of a product can be influenced by the price of other products in
the museum's portfolio of products. Decisions need to be made on what
products to make a charge for, and at what level the charges should be set.
Bryant (1988: 22) has outlined examples where variable prices may be charged:

- admission charges
- discounts
- special discounts through the travel trade for organised outings and tours

- school parties and educational programmes
- admission to special events
- literature, merchandising, catering
- filming and TV facility fees
- copying of photos, plans, and documents for research
- hire of facilities
- loan of collection items
- consultancy or advice
- endorsement, use of the museum's good name or reputation
- reproduction or copyright fees for commercial use of collections material
- charges for seminars and meetings
- use of research and library facilities

To this list could be added:

- charges for identification of objects

Organisation – product positioning

Price denotes quality. Generally, high prices denote high quality; low prices poor quality. Due to the intangibility of services, many potential users will base their decision to purchase on the value that is perceived from the price. This may need to be taken into account if the price is to reflect the image of the museum. However, since visitors do not find free or low-priced admission to be unusual in a museum, the price–quality factor may not be so prevalent. Certainly 'The Gold of the Pharaohs' exhibition at the Edinburgh City Arts Centre did not suffer from withdrawal of visitors because they perceived the low admission charge to denote poor quality.

Organisation – product costs

Non-profit organisations often use a cost-plus process to arrive at a price. This is because it is easier to judge cost than demand. Thus a price can be arrived at by adding around 10 to 20 per cent to costs after subsidy has been deducted. However, 'The problem with a cost-orientated pricing policy is that price may be established independently of the rest of the marketing mix rather than as an intrinsic element of it' (Hannagan 1992: 133).

Market – competitive pricing

Pricing strategy depends on the type of market in which it is involved. In a competitive market, if a museum charges a higher price than its competitors it will lose users. If it reduces prices to below those of competitors it may face over-capacity in demand. A museum needs to be aware of the prices being charged by competitors. Here it is important to remember the concept of customary prices. On comparing alternatives, users consider price and value. The museum's price should bear a sensible relation to the prices of competitors in terms of the museum's product offering.

Market – segmentation

Given the nature of the museum experience, it will have a different value for each individual user. Ideally, then, each price should be an individual price, estimated on the value perceived by the user. This could cause some complications! Differential pricing can be used to target different groups of people. It is already widely practised in many museums, with different prices for senior citizens, the unemployed, students, groups, and for different times of the day or week. However, these patterns have tended to develop traditionally rather than as non-revenue goals of reaching certain market segments and forcing attendance time patterns to improve the museum experience for all visitors.

It may also be the case that concessionary pricing creates a 'second-class citizen', that it is felt to be a crude form of means testing. An alternative method of enabling take-up by those groups without stigmatising them, would be to vary prices according to the time of day or week, rather than discriminating among people. This can also help to alleviate the problem of overcrowding. Moreover, as Bailey comments,

> A charging policy that simply attempts to make affluent users pay more than 'needy' groups is particularly inappropriate where service take up is voluntary and where the service is subject to crowding. Concessionary visitors may be so stimulated to use the service that they create crowding and so drive away the affluent groups that generate most revenue.
>
> (Bailey 1995: 33)

Bailey suggests that a time dimension be incorporated into the charge structure. Concessions could be made available several days a week, with other days being retained for admittance to those who pay the full charge. He suggests weekdays for concessionary groups and weekends and evenings for full-charge days, for those who are employed. Obviously this would need to be well promoted to potential users.

A museum may also decide that local residents who pay local taxes should not be subject to a charge, but that tourists should be liable to an admission fee. Tullie House in Carlisle devised an identity card, which has a photograph of the individual, a serial number, and a name (Winterbotham 1992). Nearly a third of the population of the city of Carlisle has taken up the card, which has proved to be popular, giving the holders a certain cachet. It has also been useful for assessing market segments, since the museum retains the address of each card-holder. It is then possible to assess where the museum is popular, and where it may need to develop its target audience.

Customer

Ultimately the customers will decide if the price is set at the right level, through their power of withdrawal. The users' needs must be understood in relation to the nature of the experience. The users' costs can be monetary and non-monetary. Thus the costs perceived by the user will also include the time taken to travel to the museum. The ease of obtaining the service and the quality of it and the way it is perceived are all perceived benefits of the user. Price then, should reflect the perceived value of the museum to the user. A temporary exhibition of a well-known artist's paintings may have more value for the user, for example, and so a correspondingly higher price may be charged for admission.

Environment

Economic, political, and social factors will impact on the price a museum is able to charge. The price may be directly regulated by central or local government. For example, charges were introduced to the national museums in the UK as a response to the Commons Select Committee decision in 1990 which came out in favour of charging (*Leisure Management* 10(2) 1990). Political and social decisions may mean that price is governed and changed by external regulation, ultimately deterring the museum from following organisational, market, and customer influences in price-setting. Political and social decisions can override economic realities.

There may even be an attempt to fudge the distinction between a fixed price and a voluntary donation, such as the Victoria and Albert Museum's voluntary admission, although it is unlikely that many users will walk through the turnstile without paying and not feel some discomfort. Most museums, particularly if they do not charge, operate a donations box. These boxes need to be prominently positioned and incorporate an appealing request for funds. Visitors to the British Museum are even able to make donations by credit card. Fully automatic machines have been installed at strategic points in the museum which accept any of the usual credit cards. A small souvenir card is then issued as a small token of appreciation (*Museums Journal*, January 1991).

Various factors can impact on the pricing strategy of a museum. Decisions on other elements of the marketing mix itself may impact on price-setting. For example, promotional pricing may be used when a lower price is charged for a period in an attempt to stimulate demand. Another example is the Friends organisation for the Royal Academy in London, which has a subscription system that allows a price rebate on exhibitions. Lovelock and Weinberg (1988: 267) usefully sum up the various inputs to pricing decisions as follows:

1. costs associated with the product
2. availability of internal and external funds to subsidise operations
3. total capacity available
4. museum's need for up-front money
5. extent and nature of competition in any given situation
6. pricing policies of competitors
7. potential market size for a specific product offering, reflecting:
   - type of offering
   - location
   - scheduling

8   additional costs (beyond purchase price) incurred by users

9   price elasticity of potential users, reflecting:
- different market segments
- variations in product characteristics

10   purchasing behaviour of potential users
- How far in advance is purchase/use decision made?
- Preference for advance reservations, season tickets
- Preferred payment/reservation procedures
- payment made directly to originating museum versus payment through retail intermediary
- cash versus cheque or credit card

11   alternative products offered by the museum

12   changes in the external environment that may affect:
- users' ability or willingness to pay
- nature of competition
- size of market (and segments within market)
- museum's cost and financial situation
- ability of museum to determine preferred pricing policies without third-party 'interference'.

Each of these factors needs to be taken into account when making decisions on internally generated income.

If a museum is to achieve its mission, it needs the resources to do so. Revenue derived from admission can often be the key to survival for museums. A Policy Studies Institute survey of independent museums in the UK found that admission charges made up just under half of the museum's income (*Leisure Management* 10(2) 1990). A good understanding of the influences on pricing decisions and on pricing practice can be the key to financial solvency.

CATERING

Catering facilities have the dual impact of generating income and creating an atmosphere in a museum. Eating areas (and sometimes bars) can be a social focus, acting as a meeting place. They are a contrast to the subdued silent atmosphere of the museum, being a place to discuss what has been seen. At times they may also usurp the glories of the museum. The Scottish National Gallery of Modern Art in Edinburgh has a superb café which attracts customers for its use alone, without even glancing at the gallery itself. Some may throw up their hands in horror at this. But the gallery is being used as a community resource. Café patrons who may not otherwise enter its hallowed portals are crossing the gallery's threshold. A museum needs to entice these café users into the rest of the museum, not resent them.

Many museums do not run their own catering facilities, preferring, or being forced by legislation, to put the managing of the facilities out to tender. A museum has three choices: manage the facilities itself; pay a contractor a management fee, while taking a reduced share of the profits; or franchise the facilities, receiving only a percentage of the turnover. Large operations and small local operations can run the service on behalf of the museum, taking some of the risks out of the venture as well as the time that is required to organise and run it. On the other hand, they also take much of the profit, and the museum loses control over the service, particularly the quality, and its ultimate contribution to, and consistency with, the rest of the marketing efforts. A museum would need to seriously weigh up the pros and cons on who should run it.

Before deciding on establishing a catering facility, a number of considerations need to be taken into account. First, market research needs to establish if there is really demand among the museum's users for such a facility. Account would also need to be taken of the volume of users, at times of the day, days of the week, seasonal variations, and between popular and less popular exhibitions.

Location is also a crucial factor, particularly since many museums are in off-centre locations. Consideration needs to be given to the number of businesses in the locality which could generate custom at lunch-time; whether the street in which the museum is situated has sufficient passing trade; and how accessible and visible to the passer-by the location of the facility would be. The competition in the area also needs to be assessed. What are they offering? At what price? Is there another museum or arts venue that has a café acting as a social venue? Can an alternative be offered in terms of price, variety, and so on?

It would be advisable if going it alone to buy in professional help at the outset, particularly if creating licensed premises, and if safety considerations are to be taken into account. The ultimate decision to introduce a catering facility though, rests on the museum's organisational goals, and therefore its objectives for such a facility. Is the facility to be a significant contributor to the museum's net income? Is it to provide a service, a social and community focus, for users? Is it to attract more users and to develop relationships with current users? If the latter, then it can be used to produce special offers for direct marketing campaigns; mount special promotions to attract users; provide a welcoming aspect for users; offer additional services for Friends, members, sponsors, and outside users; provide spin-off publicity such as the special themed evenings that the Bede Monastery Museum in Jarrow runs.

The national museums in London have contracted out their catering facilities after being actively encouraged to do so by the Office of Arts and Libraries. They have consequently found an increase in the quality provided, where,

> eating ripe runny brie with Bath Oliver biscuits or sipping Earl Grey tea while seated in the wood-clad surrounds of the revamped BM [British Museum] cafeteria is a far cry from the dollop of industrial cheddar on a cream cracker or cup of stale tea on a formica table that it once provided.
>
> (Marsan 1993b: 31)

A catering facility can contribute to the overall experience of the museum, while at the same time being an important part of the identity of the organisation. According to Richards, 'the relevance of the catering to the visitor market needs and the quality of the catering can have a considerable effect upon visitor numbers, levels of visitor satisfaction and profit opportunities to the operator' (Richards 1992: 60). Ultimately though, it must integrate with the rest of the marketing mix if it is not only, hopefully, to provide additional income, but also play a significant part in the marketing strategy.

RETAILING

The museum shop has been transformed in recent years from a small sales-desk selling posters and cards to a large shop offering a variety of merchandise. Some of the national and larger museums now sell merchandise by mail, while others use direct mail sales. Although the main reason for the growth in retail efforts is economic, there are also other factors to consider. The shop and the goods sold in it can reinforce the image of the museum and keep its identity in the forefront of the public's mind, through for example, re-usable carrier bags. Specially produced items emblazoned with the museum's name can carry a subliminal message, while good retailing activity can occasionally attract the media's attention. Moreover,

> sales of products connected to an organization's history or collection contribute to its educational mission and allow it to reach a wider public. From the consumer standpoint, such products can add beauty or interest to the home environment and serve as pleasant souvenirs of a museum visit.
>
> (Lovelock and Weinberg 1988: 475)

Shopping is now a part of the day-out activity for many people, and museums have the opportunity to benefit from this.

In the US the sophistication of the museums' retail operations can be mesmerising. For example, the Smithsonian Institution in Washington DC has nine stores and a mail order catalogue. The most popular item sold is a freeze-dried ice cream, similar to those eaten by space shuttle passengers. The merchandise sold can vary as much as the museum, from high-quality original design work in the Scottish National Gallery of Modern Art to orreries in the Science Museum. It has been estimated that as many as 3,000 of the 8,000 museums in the US operated shops in 1991, generating revenues of $500 million (Harvey 1992).

However, as with catering, retail activities involve risk. In the private sector small retailer turnover is high, the development and running of a shop or mail order catalogue requiring considerable amounts of both money and time. Many museum shops may in fact run at a loss (Arts Council of Great Britain 1993). A museum would also need to consider whether to run the shop itself, or as with catering facilities, to contract out the running of the shop for a percentage of the turnover. It may even be possible to run the shop with volunteers, managed by a paid permanent member of staff.

As with catering facilities, the decision to have a shop should start with the museum's goals and should be compatible with the rest of the marketing effort. Market research, finding out what current users would want to buy from a shop, should establish the type of shop that would be appropriate. At this point it would be worth conducting a professional feasibility study to assess all the factors – environmental, marketing, and financial – that would need to be taken into account.

Decisions on location would then need to be made. Some museums such as the Museum of the Moving Image (MOMI) site their shop at the end of the visit where users must filter through before leaving. Others have the shop in the foyer entrance. Basically, the shop should be located where there is a maximum flow of users, keeping in mind visibility from outside, security, visitor flow, and access for the disabled. Again, at this stage professional advice on space planning and fitting out should be sought from an architect and a retailer.

Objectives for the retail operation should then be set, and where possible should be quantifiable in order to monitor performance. Again specialist advice will help here, but performance indicators should include actual income breakdowns; spend per visitor; profit margins and net contributions. A marketing strategy with its own marketing mix can then be devised for the shop.

The product range needs to be decided. Too often, museums opt for tacky, poor-quality souvenirs which do not reflect the image of the museum. Often the items are only tangentially related to the collection, while few museums offer products that differentiate them from other museums or souvenir shops, or seek to originate products (Butler 1993). Rather, it could be argued that museum stores need a higher ethical standard in terms of merchandise than other retail outlets, because of their social goals. According to Harvey, 'The museum shop has always been an extension of the museum – a way to extend the learning experience, to capture the enthusiasm of young collectors, and to allow visitors to bring home a souvenir of the experience' (Harvey 1992: 41).

The museum must decide if it is to commission items or even produce some of them itself, such as catalogues. Commissioned items can range from shopping bags with the museum's logo to mugs, posters, cards, stationery items, pens and pencils, and even higher-quality gifts such as scarves, bags, T-shirts, and jewellery. Items from the collection could be reproduced for sale or on cards and prints. The Toulouse Lautrec exhibition at the grand Palais in Paris provided a special tent, 'Supermarché Lautrec', in which visitors could purchase unusual souvenirs, such as a replica of the artist's cane complete with a secret phial which holds two glasses of wine (Richards 1992). The British Museum has a cast service where customers can order plaster-cast reproductions of the art treasures in the collection.

High quality, specialised and expensive items may not generate many sales, whereas mass-produced lines that are available elsewhere may sell well, but do not reflect the museum's mission. Such products may make money and may even promote the museum, but they are not necessarily educational. A balance needs to be achieved, but one that ensures the museum's mission is being promoted. A good understanding of the museum's users and their expectations of the shop would also need to be taken into account. The quality of the souvenirs should reflect the spending power and social aspirations of the market segments that it attracts. Some visitors may wish to buy a reminder of their visit, while others may wish to purchase a gift for others. If large numbers of children visit the museum, then inexpensive reminders of the trip and small gifts would be needed, kept within the budget of the schoolchild.

There are a number of ways in which the shop can be promoted. Include discounts to Friends and others in a mail-out from the mailing list. Use signs at, for example, special exhibition sales points, which remind visitors of the wide variety of items available for sale in the shop. Special promotions such as book signings and late night openings could be organised during special exhibitions. A museum may also decide to promote its shop before Christmas if it is likely to attract a relative amount of passing trade. In fact, all the promotional tools that are used for promotion of the museum can be harnessed for promoting the museum shop.

Mail order catalogue sales are a risky form of augmenting distribution, and should be left to larger museums, such as the national museums, which can afford the set-up and distribution costs that would be required. The items chosen for such catalogues should also reflect the museum's mission, perhaps even more so, because these catalogues will be reaching vast numbers of people who have never visited the museum before. Again, specialist help would be required in developing a gift catalogue. The Victoria and Albert Museum has encountered problems since the company that handled its Christmas catalogue in 1993 went into receivership. Consequently, several suppliers are declining to be involved in subsequent Christmas catalogues (*Museums Journal*, September 1994).

In some countries, museum shops are becoming an essential part of the revenue creation equation. In the US, for example, a number of museums have begun to open satellite shops in suburban malls. Museums are also beginning to recognise the potential in licensing products reproduced from their collection. The Smithsonian, for example, generally receives up to 10 per cent royalties on all net sales from the manufacturer. The advantage of licensing is that the museum not only benefits from selling the products in its own store, but that the items may be sold all over the country (Harvey 1992).

Finally, as the Arts Council of Great Britain advises,

> bear in mind . . . customer care and access. The success of your shop will depend largely on how much people enjoy shopping there. They will probably be able to get a lot of the things you sell elsewhere, but your

aim should be to create an environment that isn't duplicated anywhere else. This environment will ideally be one that both contributes to and gains from the other activities and experiences you are offering the visitors to your gallery.

(Arts Council of Great Britain 1993: 14)

In other words, market your shop as you would your museum!

PUBLICATIONS

Publishing very rarely makes money for museums, but with effective marketing it may be possible to make a small profit. Usually a museum will publish for reasons other than commercial ones. Research publications will document aspects of the museum collections, while catalogues for special exhibitions will be produced for educational purposes. Publications may also be produced to enhance the status of the museum, raising its profile. The same process as for any marketing effort needs to be pursued – decisions on the product, the target readership, distribution, price, and promotion. Does the product need to be a glossy detailed book, or will lists of the names of the paintings and a biography of the artists, for example, suffice? Is it to be targeted to all users, or only a segment of users, such as subject specialists and collectors? Will it be distributed merely through the museum, or also by specialist distributors? Establish a price which this target market will bear, but which will also give a realistic income. Finally, promote the publication; send press releases to the media and encourage reviewers; include details of it on mail-outs to the mailing list; inform the target groups through clubs and societies.

The Phoenix Art Museum collaborated with Henry N Abrams publishers of New York. Consequently, their initial outlay for a catalogue of nineteenth-century English painting was $3,000 plus the efforts of the staff, in contrast to $120,000 for a solo publishing venture. In return the museum had to guarantee that it would purchase between $20,000 and $30,000 worth of catalogues. Museums could also give consideration to videotapes in conjunction with, or as an alternative, to publications.

It is rare that publications can generate considerable income. Instead there are usually other reasons for their production. However, by using specialist advice and by drawing on the experience of other museums, it may be possible to develop a publications marketing strategy that will ultimately generate income for the museum.

SPECIAL EVENTS, CONFERENCES, AND ROOM HIRE

Special events for the museum's target audience, such as musical concerts, workshops, open days, gala days, demonstrations, and so on, have the potential to generate income as well as create publicity, and ultimately achieve some of the objectives of the museum. Conferences and room hire can also generate income. Businesses are constantly seeking new and unusual venues in which to hold a conference, entertain clients, or launch a product. Use of the museum for special events can also have its downside, as Glasgow Museums and Art Galleries found to their cost, when a painting was stolen during a function. Security, then, is a key consideration. There are also other issues that need to be taken into account, such as space available for hire; establishing the levels of service that can be offered; potential damage to the fabric and furniture; the problem of smoking; the relationship of the event to the ethos of the museum. What staffing implications will there be? Will catering and equipment be required? How soon before the event will the space be required for setting up?

When organising for room hire and conferences, decisions will need to be taken on whom to target: companies (possibly included as part of a sponsorship package); professional or voluntary associations (the UK Museums Association Annual Conference usually hosts a sherry party in a museum). Assess resources against the competition: what does the museum have to offer that is unique – a particular ambience; superior catering facilities? Make sure potential clients can learn about the facility. Use direct marketing for potential clients, enclosing descriptions of the facilities, pictures of the rooms, and a map of the location. Ensure the museum is listed in corporate tourism brochures, in the telephone book at the local Visitor and Conference Bureau. The Arts Council of Great Britain (1993) also recommends targeting other local conference facilities and hotels, offering 'spiller' arrangements for special events, such as a cocktail party in the museum. It can add an interesting dimension to an otherwise tedious conference schedule! Conference room hire can also be an aspect of relationship building with corporate sponsors, as a 1987 programme for an American Museums Association Conference about marketing the museum for social events, was called 'Some enchanted evening. Building better corporate relations through a facilities use program' (quoted in Shorland-Ball 1988: 151).

An unusual venue was proposed by the Bristol Industrial Museum for corporate hospitality during the 'International Festival of the Sea' in May 1996. If it had proceeded as planned, companies would have been offered the opportunity to entertain in glass-fronted hospitality marquees erected on the roof of the museum. The marquee would have given a grandstand view of the many hundreds of historical and traditional ships that filled the harbour for the festival.

DEVELOPMENT ACTIVITIES

Fundraising and sponsorship

Fundraising is a time-consuming and sometimes costly activity. It should also be a long-term strategy. As Dudley Hafner commented,

[fund] development means bringing the donors along, raising their sights in terms of how they can support you, giving them ownership in the outcome of your organization. That takes a long-term strategy rather than putting together an annual campaign to go out and collect money.

(Hafner, quoted in Drucker 1990: 67)

In other words, it is essential to develop long-term relationships with donors.

According to Lovelock and Weinberg (1988) there are a number of criteria to follow when developing a fundraising strategy. First recognise both the monetary and non-monetary needs of the organisation. Money is not the only resource a donor can give. Volunteered time through the expertise of an employee of the donor organisation can be very effective. This has been organised by the Association for Business Sponsorship of the Arts (ABSA) in the UK, where a corporate sponsor donates the services of an employee for a specified period of time, to give advice on a particular management aspect. Donors may also wish to give gifts-in-kind, such as computer equipment from a computer manufacturer, rather than financial assistance. Offer prospective donors alternative formats for donation, setting the museum's own priorities for the type of gift it requires.

Second, it is important to emphasise those sources that offer the best giving potential relative to the solicitation effort required. Solicitation takes time and effort and can be expensive. It is essential that the museum gets a good return on the resources invested. When making proposals to foundations, corporations, or government granting agencies, there is no guarantee of a successful financial outcome. As Lovelock and Weinberg recommend: 'as in many areas of marketing, gathering advance information about the marketplace for grants, gifts, or other types of donated resources will help a fund raiser to focus on the better prospects' (Lovelock and Weinberg 1988: 438). It is a common mistake of museums to underestimate the resources required not only in costs and staff time in raising money, but also in subsequently servicing a sponsor. It may be necessary to take a long-term view, budget for returns over the long term as well as short term, recognising that a fundraising campaign will take time to establish itself and succeed.

Third, avoid the risk of becoming over-reliant on a single source. If a major funder withdraws or reduces its funding, a museum could lose a substantial proportion of its revenue. Reliance on one donor can also mean loss of control. An independent museum that receives substantial grants from a local authority could find itself having to respond to local authority demands on its policy development and even exhibitions programme.

It is also important for a museum to develop clearly established fundraising and sponsorship priorities which fit its overall mission. Use the marketing strategy to make decisions on priorities. If the mission is to broaden the social range of museum users, priority would perhaps be given to opening a café, rather than purchasing an expensive artefact. Equally, decisions may need to be taken on excluding potential sponsors because their policies may be in conflict with the goals of the museum. It is also important that the sponsor's views do not lead to bias in the exhibition being sponsored. Porter (1988) cites the Nuclear Physics–Nuclear Power Gallery which opened at the Science Museum in 1982. The project was sponsored by the United Kingdom Atomic Energy Authority with smaller sums coming from the Central Electricity Generating Board and British Nuclear Fuels Limited. Without full consultation of the staff, a number of panels in the display were changed, with the end result that the exhibition 'fails to acknowledge adequately the controversial nature of its subject' (Porter 1988: 97). Sponsorship should be carefully handled with a distance being kept between the museum and the sponsor. Sponsorship should be mutually advantageous and should not place the museum in a position where the sponsor places undue influence on the museum. It may be expedient to avoid sponsorship from a business that has a particular interest in the subject matter.

Depending on resources, a museum can focus on a single approach or on a mix of approaches for attracting funds. There are a variety of fundraising techniques ranging from applications to grant-giving bodies, and lottery applications, to sponsorship and corporate gifts-in-kind, to a 'benefit' event and simple requests for donations from users.[1]

According to Lovelock and Weinberg (1988), planning for a fundraising effort requires the following strategy:

- application of funds
- identification of prospects
- benefits and costs for prospective donors
- identifying the competition
- identifying potential for giving
- selection of communication channels
- determination of appeals
- timing and location of solicitation
- appropriateness of reminders.

Define the 'product' of the fundraising effort. Usually donors prefer to give for a specific purpose. Many museums seek donations for one particular activity, such as a temporary exhibition. However, it could also be beneficial to have ongoing 'products', illustrations of 'giving opportunities' – what specific sums of money could be spent on. Compile a shopping list, such as benches in the galleries or new computing equipment, and suggest them to potential donors. Donors of small amounts of money, in particular, need to feel that their gift is not being swallowed up, but that it is useful in itself.

Sponsors may also want to know whom they are going to reach by supporting the museum. Keep up-to-date details on visitors, and from market research build up a basic socio-economic profile. Be ready to offer this information immediately. Equally the museum must identify target markets to solicit. Users on the mailing list are an obvious source of prospective donors. Enlist Friends to give names and addresses of possible donors. Maintain regular contact with previous donors.

Keep them up to date with the museum's activities to build up a relationship with them. Build a database of contacts drawn from existing marketing lists.

It is essential that the museum offers some kind of return for giving. Depending on the company, there are a number of reasons why it would sponsor a museum, including:

- publicising the company's brand name
- improving the general image of the company
- to impress and develop relationships with clients and influential people
- to develop good relations with the local community
- to attract and retain high-quality staff and encourage good public relations within the company.

Individual donors will benefit mainly from the satisfaction of having given to a worthy cause. Other donors may expect some other exchange, such as publicity, invitations to exhibition openings, and so on. For information on the requirements of sponsors, in particular, it is worth consulting publications that tackle sponsorship from the sponsoring organisation's viewpoint, such as *The Effective Use of Sponsorship* (Wragg 1994), which gives an essential insight into the requirements of businesses in deciding to sponsor.

As many museums have experienced, there are a lot of other organisations competing for a limited supply of gifts and grants. Moreover, sponsorship funding for the arts is becoming increasingly scarce. According to the Association for Business Sponsorship of the Arts (ABSA), sponsorship across museums and the visual arts in the UK fell 20 per cent in 1993 (*Museums Journal*, December 1994). Most companies, foundations, and government granting agencies have only a fixed amount of funds to donate. Requests for funds are often dealt with on a competitive basis. Ensure that the museum has submitted an explicit and well-reasoned strategy for use of the funds. The designers of the presentation should put themselves in the position of an outsider who needs to understand the organisation. In a competitive position only the most professional presentations, outlining the benefits and opportunities, will succeed in gaining access to resources.

It can be difficult to identify a donor's potential for giving. A request for a modest sum, where a generous sum may have been given, would only result in the donation of the smaller sum. Again, a shopping list of alternatives, giving their cost, leaving it to the donor to select the appropriate amount, can be an expedient option. Track from previous publicity on prospective donors' giving, the level of gift that has been given in the past. Assess the potential for repeat giving from previous donors.

The same principles for communication for other marketing programmes apply to fundraising. Although initial contact is usually by mail or telephone, try and develop personal contacts. Make contact with the person who has an influence on the funding decision and encourage them to develop a personal interest in the museum. Developing relationships can be an important aspect of building confidence and generating interest in the museum.

Deciding on the content of the solicitation message is quite a skilled technique. Remember that, as with all marketing, gift-giving involves an exchange. Therefore, as well as emphasising the museum's needs for funds, suggest reasons why the donor would want to give. Timing and location of solicitation can also be crucial, particularly where donors have limited amounts of money to give, or only meet on specific dates to make decisions on funding. Find out when these dates are, and remember that funds are often committed a year ahead, so ensure the museum's case is presented in good time.

If a prospect has responded to a previous appeal, it is worth making a renewed appeal. Repeat gifts are usually easier to obtain once a relationship is established. Past experience should act as guidance on reminders, while financial expediency should also indicate the efficiency of reminders.

Finally, set in place performance measures, such as the total funds raised relative to the target; fundraising expenses as a proportion of total funds received; percentage of prospects who actually gave; trends relative to previous campaigns.

Ironbridge Gorge Museum received financial and ideological support from the educational division of the petroleum company, BP, which resulted in the production of a teacher's handbook (West 1988). Becks Bier sponsored the Gilbert and George exhibition at the Hayward Gallery, to which it contributed £30,000. A special Gilbert and George label was designed, and six million bottles with the label were distributed. In return Becks Bier received wide press coverage and was able to associate the brand with the visitors to the gallery, who tend to be young and style-conscious (Gwyther 1988). The Rock and Roll Hall of Fame and Museum in Cleveland is benefiting from $5 million of investment from AT&T. The company is helping to design a high-technology wing, which will incorporate AT&T equipment, providing classrooms and homes with worldwide access to the museum's programming (Adams 1995).

The key to the planning of a fundraising programme is to build long-term relationships with all potential sponsors and donors. Maintain the relationship even when they are unlikely to give money, otherwise they will feel that their involvement is only about their financial contribution. As the Arts Council of Great Britain states:

> as a marketing person, you have a role to play as 'diplomat' for your gallery. Much of the most effective fundraising and sponsorship is done through personal contact. You need to be able to explain the gallery's work to anyone who comes in contact with the organisation.
>
> (Arts Council of Great Britain 1993: 10)

FRIENDS AND MEMBERS SCHEMES

The number of Friends in UK museums has doubled over the past ten years to 200,000. The Royal Academy in London has a Friends scheme with 70,000 members. Friends make up more than half of the gallery's one million visitors a year, while in 1994, the net income from Friends totalled £1.6 million, although administrative costs, including ten full-time staff, cut profit to just over £600,000. Perks of membership include a quarterly glossy magazine, free admission for the Friend plus one guest and up to four children, a special Friends' room with tea and coffee, and private viewings. At the other end of the scale, the Welsh Miners' Museum Society has twenty members (Heaton 1992).

Friends and Members schemes can be advantageous for a number of reasons, although most notably for their potential to generate income for the museum, both directly, and through Friends' contacts with, for example, potential sponsoring companies. The Friends of the Victoria and Albert Museum raised around £80,000 for the museum in 1991 (Heaton 1992). A Friends scheme can also assist in audience development, where for example, some arts organisations offer special schemes to attract children. Friends can also influence public attitudes to the museum, and ultimately broaden the base of support (ibid.).

However, 'some museums are beginning to question the role – and cost – of Friends schemes' (Cordrey 1995: 19). Friends organisations, originally set up to make money, often end up being subsidised by museums through the cost of free admissions, mailings, and staff time. The National Gallery, for example, considered setting up a Friends group because of the growing number of public enquiries. However, as the gallery already has free admission, it was difficult to see what 'added value' the gallery could offer Friends. Instead the gallery runs a patrons' scheme, where individuals are invited to make a donation of around £1,000, in return for which they receive regular gallery news and sneak previews of new acquisitions.

It is important to be clear about the aims of a Friends organisation before it is established. For example, the Glasgow Friends organisation, the Glasgow Art Galleries and Museums Association, has three main functions: contributing to the purchase of new items; supporting an in-house magazine; and organising a volunteer guide service. The Arts Council of Great Britain suggests that, when setting objectives for the scheme, it is, 'probably a fundamental mistake to try and mix differing objectives like audience development and income generation' (Arts Council of Great Britain 1993: 3). Income generation, for example, would target people with a high disposable income, which would be incompatible with the objective of audience development. It is also important that the scheme is located in the wider marketing strategy and fits with other priorities.

The scheme could be set up independently or under the auspices of the museum. It is preferable to run the membership scheme from within the museum, or at least the organisers should share a mutual understanding of the scheme's roles. When setting up a scheme, again it should be remembered that with all marketing activities there is an exchange relationship. There needs to be a clear policy in the relationship between fees charged and the benefits derived. Sophisticated schemes will offer different levels of payment with increased levels of benefit for those who pay more. It is also worth including an additional donation facility on any membership application form.

Examples of benefits might be: private viewings; special opening times – the Tate Gallery has a special time for Friends; lectures and events; chances to attend fundraising dinners or parties; benefits from other museums; financial discounts on, for example, admissions and items sold in the café and shop. The Friends of the National Motor Museum at Beaulieu receive free admission and between five and eight social events a year, including a chance to win a seat in the museum's car for the London to Brighton run each November.

It is essential that the scheme is costed realistically, including all marketing costs, for example: direct mail and database maintenance; promotional activities; staffing costs; publications and the cost of postage; income lost through discounts; and the cost of the special events. The Natural History Museum succeeded in offsetting some of the costs of establishing a Friends scheme, by attracting £250,000 sponsorship from Glaxo Holdings plc to launch the scheme. Members are offered free admission to the museum, special events, and a magazine (*Museums Journal*, November 1994).

Launching the scheme requires decisions on target segments – for example, an income-generation scheme could be targeted at high-income users. Current donor lists, mailing lists, and lists for other arts organisations should be used. Promote the scheme through direct mail shots, telephone sales, and personal contact, particularly when recruiting high-value members.

Membership schemes are not necessarily confined to individuals. Corporate membership schemes are becoming increasingly more popular in museums. The National Maritime Museum has launched a corporate membership scheme, where for an annual membership of £5,000 (£2,500 for associate membership), companies receive discounts on the hire of rooms for corporate entertainment, private views of exhibitions, and other benefits. In this way the museum hopes to develop relationships with business, and in particular, maritime companies (*Museums Journal*, November 1994).

ATTRACTING VOLUNTEERS

As well as being the lifeblood of many museums, providing a much-needed resource, 'volunteer involvement and volunteer enthusiasm have the potential to improve every aspect of museums, provide opportunities to pilot new projects and engender strong links between the museum and the community' (Renton in Office of Arts and Libraries 1991b). In fact, much of the impetus for establishing museums has come from groups of volunteers. Weardale Museum in the north east of England is the result of the energy and enthusiasm of a number of volunteers (mainly local retired people, who wish to preserve their own heritage), rather than have items removed to large museums such as Beamish.

In the UK there are around 30,000 volunteers (Hall, L. 1995), compared with 40,000 people officially employed in the museum sector (Klemm and Wilson 1993). For example, Peterborough Museum has five full-time curatorial staff, and relies on a regular group of five volunteers out of between 15 to 20. The Smithsonian Institution more than doubled their paid staff by employing volunteers, some 5,252 in 1989 (Office of Arts and Libraries 1991b).

All museums should have a volunteering policy that, first, is integrated into the marketing strategy and consequently reflects the museum's mission; second, includes the reason for volunteer involvement; and third, includes a code of practice in the relationship between the volunteer and museum (Hall, L. 1995). A publication dedicated to museum volunteers, *Volunteers in Museums and Heritage Attractions* (Office of Arts and Libraries 1991b), outlines a useful plan for managing volunteers.

First, the volunteer policy must be 'tailor-made', to target the right people and to train them adequately, to maximise their abilities. It should be an 'attractive package', as competition for volunteers becomes keener during the 1990s. Museums must also ensure a degree of reciprocity, in other words, volunteering involves an exchange relationship, the volunteers having their own agenda, but expecting some kind of return, in terms of satisfaction, respect for their contribution, and good working conditions. Consultation should also play a part in the policy, particularly if changes are to take place in the way volunteers are deployed. 'Core' functions should be identified, especially where volunteers work alongside paid staff, with clear distinctions being made between 'core' and support functions. Supervision of volunteers is required, ideally by a volunteers co-ordinator who can increase the visibility and acceptability of volunteers amongst paid staff. Communications between volunteers and between volunteers and paid staff is essential, through, for example, newsletters, joint meetings, and the provision of a coffee room. It must be remembered that resources are required to operate a volunteer programme, in terms of equipment and space, as well as financial resources for training, insurance cover, expenses, and administrative costs. A manual outlining procedures should be produced, giving details on recruitment, induction, training, and so on. Finally, the volunteer policy should be regularly reviewed. As the Office of Arts and Libraries document comments:

> Volunteers offer a museum flexibility and a chance to pilot new schemes at low cost. They can fund raise to provide new acquisitions, give their time to help disabled visitors, and bridge the gap between the museum and the community through informal contact and formal public relations activities.
>
> (Office of Arts and Libraries 1991b: 72)

The American Museum of Natural History used to have an ambivalent attitude to volunteers, preferring to recruit them for management and scientific programmes, but discouraging them from other forms of work, such as visitor services, information services, sales, and public affairs (Nicholson 1983). There was concern that volunteers would compete with salaried employees, while there was also concern for the effect on the museum's relations with the trade unions. There were uncertainties voiced too over the likely attitude of local government, which supports many of the museum's basic services, if positions were being filled by volunteers. There was an attitude that volunteers could not be relied on, that they would not be as committed as salaried workers. More fundamentally, though, there was a fear that using volunteers implied a loss of professionalism.

However, an evolutionary change in the museum's attitudes gradually nurtured support for the value of volunteers.

> Volunteerism was introduced in the American Museum in a gradual way, carefully identifying the areas and functions where it could work effectively, testing it and our ability to make it work, evaluating its effectiveness, and the changes it required of us.
>
> (Nicholson 1983: 245)

Nicholson then goes on to stress the importance of defining real job tasks for volunteers so that they have, 'a sense of belonging, a sense of contribution, of learning, of contributing in productive ways, more so probably than it is for salaried employees' (Nicholson 1983: 246).

Volunteers now make up 10 per cent of the American Museum's total salaried employment. Volunteers have enabled the museum to develop programmes which would otherwise have been beyond its resources. Volunteers' tasks now include servicing information desks, guiding school classes, conducting general guided tours, serving as hosts and hostesses for special functions, and managing a visitor survey programme.

The American Museum set a number of principles to guide them in volunteer management. First, never to replace an employee with a volunteer, or replace a volunteer with an employee; to provide support and supervision from salaried employees; to treat volunteers as employees in their own right, while at the same time applying the same level of accountability to volunteers as to employees; and to train volunteers to the same degree as employees are trained. Finally, Nicholson states that, 'volunteerism at the American Museum involves a relationship that is symbiotic' (Nicholson 1983: 253). This is important since volunteerism implies a mutual interdependence, a two-way exchange, which needs to be managed and integrated with as much care as any other aspect of the marketing mix.

Not all voluntary work involves everyday activities in the museum. It also includes members of the museum's board or trustees who provide leadership and direction. Trustees or board members are usually either appointed by local or central government, often including local authority councillors, or are recruited by the museum from the local community. It is important that the right calibre of trustees are recruited and that the board is run in such a way that it makes an effective contribution to the museum. A number of training courses are now being run for boards of management, and for senior managers in handling the board. It is essential that the director develops and nurtures good relationships with the board. Members of the board can contribute to the museum in three ways: through their personal characteristics, such as association with a special community, market segment or geographic area; through their personal skills in management and marketing; and through their personal contact with potential donors or organisations and individuals possessing needed expertise (Lovelock and Weinberg 1988). It is crucial if marketing is to succeed in a museum, that leadership and commitment should come from the top, not only from the director, but from the board and in particular the chief executive. Thus marketing success requires an understanding and commitment to market from the chief executive and board. According to John Harvey Jones,

> Boards need to set themselves very clear tasks in exactly the same way that individuals do. Every year we [the Board of ICI] spend some time setting out what we consider to be the twelve most important tasks that we, as a Board, should have worked towards during the year. We then take time out a year later to review what progress we have made, at the time when we are setting out next year's targets.
>
> (Harvey Jones 1988: 205–6)

Resource development, whether it be fundraising and sponsorship, Friends and members schemes, or attracting volunteers, is people development. As Drucker (1990) points out, when talking of donors or of volunteers,

> you are building a constituency. You're building understanding, you're building support. You're building satisfaction, human satisfaction in the process. That is the way to create the support base you need to do your job. But it's also the way you use your job to enrich the community and every participant. And it's based on clear mission, on extensive and detailed knowledge of the market, on making demands on both your volunteers and your donors, but also on feedback from your performance.
>
> (Drucker 1990: 74)

Moreover, any revenue-generating scheme must remember that, 'The fine line museums constantly tread is to do good, in the sense of community service, and do well, financially' (Harvey 1992: 62). Often this requires sensitivity and careful balancing.

9

Implementing the marketing effort

No museum is equally good at all things; nor does it have the resources, or inclination even, to provide everything that its users' may demand. A museum must assess its capabilities in terms of its strengths and weaknesses, and try to identify users that best match its strengths. There will always be compromise in matching users with the museum's resources, but it should try and build on its strengths and reduce its weaknesses.

Equally, no organisation works in a vacuum. Whether it be a business or a museum, it will have an environment that contains all existing and potential users and competitors. There will in fact, be many factors outside its control. Changes in the environment, such as new legislation or the current economic climate, will present opportunities and threats for any museum. It is possible to reduce the uncertainties of resources and environment by keeping informed about them. Moreover, by planning, it is possible to use that information to guide and manage the marketing activity. Figure 9.1 illustrates the role of information-gathering in the planning process.

Marketing information needs are derived from the process of marketing analysis and planning. Once the required information has been obtained, it is fed into the planning process and there informs the marketing activity. An aspect of the planning process is to set indicators for evaluation and control of the marketing activity. This information is then fed back into the next stage of analysis and planning.

Marketing planning enables museums to adopt organised procedures for their marketing approach. It gives the museum a long-term orientation, rather than a short-term response to crisis outlook, having a three- or five-year timescale, depending on the demands of funding bodies. From this long-term plan, a one-year tactical plan can be developed.

Planning is a time-consuming and difficult task for any manager. The process is complicated for a museum by its multiple goals, many of which are non-financial, and its responsibility to meet the needs of stakeholders as well as users. Although these additional complexities make the development of a marketing plan more difficult, they make the use of the plan more vital if

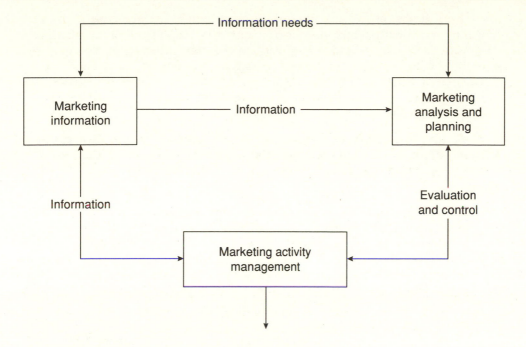

Figure 9.1 Information-gathering in the planning process

the museum is to manage its marketing efforts effectively (Lovelock and Weinberg 1988).

Since museums exist 'for the public benefit', marketing objectives must relate directly to how the museum is to develop that goal. Therefore, everyone in the organisation must be involved in the planning process and ultimately must be informed of, understand, and consciously implement the marketing plan. As museums develop business plans for funding purposes, marketing must be an integral consideration of the business planning process. In fact, developing a marketing plan is often the first step to devising a business plan.

Many museums do not have formal marketing plans, although increasingly, funding bodies are requiring proof of a business plan before considering applications for funding. Detractors of planning argue that the environment is too dynamic to plan, and that the museum needs to be versatile to respond to sudden change, and that it is not realistic to expect an already overworked staff to develop a plan. There are various reasons why museums do in fact need to plan. According to Malcolm McDonald (1989a), an organisation should develop marketing plans in order to cope with the increasing turbulence and complexity of the environment, the intense competitive pressures, and the increasing speed of technological change. It enables the organisation to help identify sources of competitive advantage; to force an organised and focused approach to marketing within the organisation, developing specificity in tasks and the basis of a control system; and to ensure consistent relationships both within and outside the organisation. Planning can help the organisation to attract funding – a well-argued case informed by an organised approach will be more successful. Finally, in terms of the organisation's employees, it helps to engender their support and commitment, because they are all working towards the same goals; their activities are co-ordinated and their actions related over time.

A marketing plan could be summarised as a systematic means of organising an analysis of a museum's market, the museum's position in that market, and a programme for future marketing activities. In order to be effective, though,

> Planning systems should be matched to the organization's individual style and capabilities. All planning systems, to be effective, require substantial involvement by key personnel. To generate meaningful involvement, the plan must be seen as an important part of the organization's decision process. Smaller organizations will tend to have plans of narrower scope and possibly less formality than those of larger organizations. The goal in every case is a pragmatic plan that specifies a course of action designed to produce concrete results.
>
> (Lovelock and Weinberg 1988: 105)

As with all marketing activities, successful planning depends on commitment from the board or trustees and the director of the museum. It is also important that the marketing plan fits into the total business planning system, since operations planning is integral to marketing planning. A museum is likely to have an overall marketing plan, and individual plans for specific products, such as a plan for each target market, a separate plan for the shop, or a plan for a temporary exhibition. These plans need to be distinctive but well co-ordinated to ensure that they are integrated into the overall marketing plan.

Employees and stakeholders must be involved in the planning process, and will require the resources and skills to implement it. In some situations this may require a rethink of the museum's organisational structure, which sometimes acts as a barrier to the successful implementation of a marketing plan. Effective planning requires effective communication to and between employees. Ultimately the plan will only succeed if it has the general support of the museum's personnel.

A number of approaches to marketing planning have been developed, some based on best practice case studies, while others are shrouded in academic obscurity. One approach that has proved resilient in practice, and clear and precise to follow, is the marketing planning framework developed by Malcolm McDonald in *Marketing Plans: How to Prepare Them, How to Use Them* (McDonald 1989a). This chapter largely follows this framework which, in turn, follows five major phases, each of which answers a question about the museum:

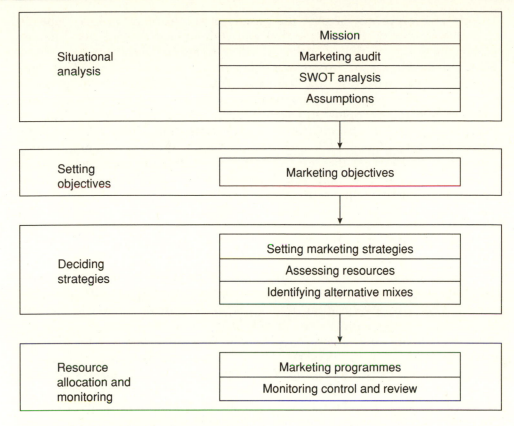

Figure 9.2 The marketing planning process

1   *Situational analysis*
    Where are we now and how did we get here?
2   *Setting objectives*
    Where do we want to go?
3   *Deciding the strategy*
    How will we get there?
4   *Assessing resources*
    What will it take to get there?
5   *Monitoring the plan*
    How will we know we are getting there?

Each of these phases is then broken down into ten major steps. These phases together with the associated steps are shown in Figure 9.2. A summary of a marketing plan for a sample museum is outlined at the end of the chapter.

The following description of a marketing plan is perhaps only an ideal for many museums, and realistically a number of factors will prohibit such a comprehensive process. Because the success of the planning process depends to a large extent on the co-operation and commitment of so many different players, it is almost inevitable that it will fall short of the description given here. Employee resistance to the marketing effort, lack of understanding from trustees of the marketing function, and lack of interest and co-operation from political funders, can all compound the difficulties and divert the immense task involved in developing an effective marketing plan. A degree of realism needs to be injected into what is a prescriptive outline. Those committed to developing a marketing plan need to use all the skills of communication, diplomacy, and tact, if they are to come anywhere near achieving what is outlined here. The following then is the process which museums should be aiming for in developing a marketing plan.

SITUATIONAL ANALYSIS

The situational analysis gathers information about the museum's internal and external environment. It should include a summary of the historical situation, the present condition, possible future trends, and an assessment of previous marketing efforts. There are four areas for consideration in the situational analysis. First, the museum's overall mission and goals. This is followed by an analysis of every aspect of the museum's marketing: an internal analysis of the organisation and product; the market; competitors; and the external environment. Consideration is then given to the strengths and weaknesses of the museum's resources, and the opportunities and threats in its environment. Finally, the implications of the audit are summarised, along with any assumptions made.

Mission

The first step then, is to develop an effective mission statement, which will strategically focus all of the museum's activities, not just its marketing. The mission statement states the purpose of the organisation as a whole, and should be the starting point of any management planning. Hence, the museum's operations and marketing will be working in unison, guided by the overall goal of the museum. The mission statement asks the question, 'What business are we in?', defined in terms of the underlying need the organisation is trying to serve. The mission statement should outline the overall scope of the museum. It should be followed by separate objectives that detail how the mission statement is to be achieved. Each objective should be broken down into a set of targets to which are attached a timescale and, ultimately, a cost. Payne defines a mission statement as

> an enduring statement of purpose that provides a clear vision of the organization's current and future business activities, in product, service and market terms, its values and beliefs, and its points of differentiation from competitors. A mission helps determine the relationships in each of

the key markets with which the organization interacts, and provides a sense of direction and purpose which leads to better independent decision-making at all levels of the organization.

(Payne 1993: 42)

The mission statement should describe what the museum wants to do in terms of its cultural and social policy and aspirations. It should also identify whom the museum is doing it for by identifying the user groups it wishes to attract. The mission statement should be drawn up by the directors and senior members of staff, and should then be endorsed by the board of trustees. It must be achievable with the museum's existing or potential resources; physical, human, and financial. It should be realistic and not be a dream statement! Measurement should be able to take place, with performance measures set for each objective in order to track progress of achievement. Once formulated it should be communicated to all employees and should form the baseline of all activities. A mission has true value when it is implemented into action. A prerequisite then is that employees must believe in it.

Marketing audit

The marketing audit is the information-gathering process that seeks all relevant data on the museum's own resources and its external environment. As a US West Coast Museum commented in the introduction to its audit,

> The purpose of this audit is not so much to find solutions to specific questions such as 'where should we distribute our flyers?' or 'what price should we charge for lectures?' but rather to examine and comment on the framework from which such questions are answered. The process of decision-making is germane to the success of 'museum marketing' as a whole and should be addressed before answering specific operational questions.
>
> (quoted in Lovelock and Weinberg 1988: 48)

It is useful to break the audit down into four parts to which attention can be focused:

- internal analysis
- market analysis
- competitor analysis
- environmental analysis.

Time and resource factors, where a comprehensive audit can take three months or more to compile, dictate that a marketing audit must be selective but comprehensive. Ultimately, the information amassed must be distilled to inform the future direction of the museum. Too little information will allow gaps in future planning, while too much information, if much of it is irrelevant, will only lengthen the time taken to develop a marketing plan.

185

Internal analysis

Although not conducted in this way in most marketing textbooks, it can be useful in the museum context to break the internal analysis down into four parts: an outline of policy; an assessment of resources; a consideration of the marketing resources; and an analysis of marketing activities centred around the elements of the marketing mix. The rationale for focusing on the marketing mix is that, first, the SWOT analysis appraisal of the strengths and weaknesses of the museum's resources is conducted in terms of the marketing mix, which means that it is an automatic continuation of the process, rather than reassessing the material already amassed. Second, the marketing strategy is ultimately decided in terms of the marketing mix, and so again it enables a focused continuation of the information-gathering process. The one drawback is that it is all too easy, once the information is gathered, and when deciding the strategy, to refer only to the internal analysis and the analysis of the strengths and weaknesses of the resources, while ignoring the other data and analyses collected. Therefore this approach is recommended with a caveat: the analysis of the museum's environment must not be neglected, but should be integrated with the resource analysis in the final strategic decisions. The following outlines some of the factors to be taken into account when undertaking an internal analysis. The lists are not exhaustive, and clearly the relevance of each aspect outlined will depend on the individual museum.

Purpose

It is worth outlining the history of the museum first, in order to assess the rationale for much of the museum's policy decisions and activities in the past. Much of this information will already have been obtained when deciding on the mission of the museum. The areas that need to be considered will include the following:

History

- date of foundation; history of formation
- brief history of museum, taking into account the history of the amassing of the collection
- legal status: trust/limited company/charity
- size and composition of board or management committee
- ownership.

Policy

- collection acquisitions and disposals
- exhibitions and special events programming policy: balance between different styles/periods/techniques; appeal to different market groups and tastes

- outreach and education work
- image and reputation: local and national
- commitment to quality.

Resources

The type of information required will include: physical resources; human resources; and financial resources.

Physical resources

- nature of collection: scope and value of collection; preservation facilities; environmental controls; security measures
- description of external appearance of building: prominence as local landmark; architecture and materials (if noteworthy); listed status
- location of building: proximity to rail and bus stations; incidence of passing trade; proximity to public car parks; direct access to thoroughfares; access for coaches; redevelopment plans for nearby sites
- description of interior of building: decor and colour schemes; state of repair; number of exhibition areas with their size; available space
- technological resources: computers; word-processing facilities.

Human resources

- number of employees: full- and part-time; curatorial staff; volunteers
- skills: management; professional; future potential; level of experience
- staff responsibilities: job titles; departmental structure
- services of external personnel: local authority; corporate sponsors
- work experience placements.

Financial resources

- major funding organisations and status of funding
- income for past five years: sources of income – earned; grants; sponsorship; donations; other.

Marketing resources

Consideration needs to be given to: the role of marketing in the museum and the resources available for the marketing function, which includes an assessment of the physical, human, and financial resources.

Role of marketing

- marketing philosophy: formalised strategy; personnel involved in determining philosophy

- role of marketing in museum: activities undertaken by marketing; resources devoted to marketing; interaction with other operational areas; inter-relation of marketing for users with stakeholders and other publics
- marketing personnel: seniority of marketing officer or member of staff responsible for marketing; numbers and levels of staff working on marketing problems.

Physical resources

- technological resources: computer systems; word processing; information systems for marketing information on target markets; database for mailing list; desk-top publishing; in-house printing; use of Internet.

Human resources

- marketing and marketing-related staff: outline responsibilities; level of experience; seniority in museum; degree of influence on marketing planning; voluntary help
- involvement of senior management and board/trustees in marketing decisions
- services of a local authority for marketing activities
- support of Friends
- advertising agency or market research agency.

Financial resources

- total marketing budget; decisions on budget; proportion of overall income
- marketing budget expenditure
- additional resources available for contingency

Marketing activities

The marketing activities are assessed in terms of the elements of the marketing mix: product; price; place; promotion; and people. The following factors will need to be included:

Product

The museum product can be examined in terms of the core product, namely (1) the museum building and (2) the exhibition; and the supplementary product, namely (3) the services offered.

1   *Museum building*
    - external appearance: banners; signage on building; appearance of entrance
    - internal appearance: ambience; state of repair; furnishings; layout; noise; temperature; air quality; lighting; signage

2   *Exhibition*
- collection: presentation and interpretation; use of technology, special interpretative facilities; turnaround of permanent collection
- temporary exhibitions: blockbusters; involvement of local community
- exhibit development research undertaken

3   *Services offered*
- facilities: information desk; cloakroom; bars; catering facilities; shop; opening hours; number of seats in galleries
- facilities for the disabled: wheelchair access; wheelchair seats; hearing loop; disabled lavatories; lift; braille signs
- educational services: workshops; lectures; resident artist; schools education
- special events
- service quality: complaints procedure

Price

The following factors need to be included in the consideration of price: (1) sales trends for past five years (if appropriate); (2) pricing policy; and (3) fundraising.

1   *Sales trends*
- income totals per exhibition: average size of audience; average ticket yield per exhibition
- types of sale: students; children; groups, etc.
- seasonal variations: per month or per quarter

2   *Pricing policy*
- procedures for establishing and reviewing pricing policy
- pricing procedure: demand oriented; competition oriented; cost oriented
- variations in price: by market segments; time of use; discounts for groups
- methods of payment: credit cards
- promotional pricing: incentives

3   *Fundraising*
- income generation: variety of services offered for which a charge is made; income from services offered; pricing policy for services offered
- resource development: target markets for fundraising efforts; benefits offered to potential donors; income from fundraising; current and past trends and future expectations
- Friends and volunteers: policy on Friends organisation; use of Friends in fundraising; corporate membership; policy on volunteers; deployment of volunteers.

Place

An assessment needs to be made of the time and place of the museum's service delivery.

- availability: opening hours; after-hours facilities (e.g. answering machine); seasonality
- access: location of museum; signage; public transport; car parking facilities; disabled access
- reception or information desk: opening hours
- computers: mailing list
- ticket agents
- outreach facilities.

Promotion

Promotion can be broken down into (1) promotional resources and (2) the various elements of promotional activity, together with an assessment of their effectiveness.

1 *Promotional resources*
   - promotional budget: decisions on budget; as a proportion of overall income; of earned income; according to needs; previous year plus inflation
   - promotion budget analysed by type of expenditure
   - additional resources available
   - desk-top publishing, in-house printing, photocopying facilities
   - advertising agency
   - promotional activities with other museums or organisations in marketing consortia
   - promotional objectives and relation of promotional activities to each other
   - systems for handling customer enquiries resulting from promotion
   - measure of effectiveness used
   - decisions on design of promotions for different target markets
2 *Promotional activities*
   - corporate identity: image; brand; use of logo; typeface, etc.
   - personal selling activities: lectures; fundraising; increasing use of services
   - promotional literature: print quantities by type of print, season, and exhibition; distribution methods and analysis of outlets
   - use and creativity of direct mail: use of database for target marketing; size and segmentation of mailing lists; retrieval systems and scope for personalisation; use of other direct marketing techniques, such as telephone sales
   - sales promotion: incentives; linked ticket schemes
   - advertising: advertising policies; use of paid advertising media

- public relations: effectiveness of media relations; effectiveness of press releases; development of Friends organisations; relations with stakeholders; relations with staff.

People

A number of factors need to be taken into account, including:

- staff morale and motivation
- arrangements for communications: briefing and consultation meetings
- advice and involvement from board members
- use of Friends and volunteers
- training and development: training budget; training policy.

Market analysis

The marketing audit is critically concerned with understanding in detail the markets with which the museum interacts. Since museums have a number of markets, and not just the user markets, consideration should be given to each market in turn. The following factors will need to be taken into account, investigating users, stakeholders, and other relevant publics.

Users

- *Description of the characteristics of current users*: a summary of findings of market research, in the form of a quantitative survey, and possibly qualitative focus groups, including trends over time and an outline of lifestyle and behavioural information, describing the users' perceived benefits and relating to lifestyle segmentation classifications. It is helpful to compare the demographic information with the demographic profile for the town/city/region to show whether the audience differs in certain respects from the population as a whole. An assessment can be made of the major growth opportunities.
- *Frequency of attendance*: aggregating the data to show proportions of users attending: every month or more often; every 2–3 months; 2–3 times a year; once a year; less often than once a year. These data are vital in order to assess the size of the museum's audience and how many of them are repeat attenders.
- *Type of party booking*: by school; club; society; employing organisation; and so on.
- *Analysis of potential audiences*: look at scope for development. The various analyses of existing and potential audiences should enable an assessment to be made of: particular gaps in the existing audience; of postcode districts that would benefit from more intense promotion; of opportunities in audience overlap. Opportunities to develop particular markets such as young people, organised parties should be identified.

- *Benefits offered to each market segment*: matching of products to segments.

Stakeholders and other publics

- description of stakeholders and other publics, such as Friends, volunteers, donors, professional organisations: relationship with these publics; their interactions with the museum
- benefits offered to each of these publics
- importance of each of these publics to the museum.

Competitor analysis

All museums have competitors, both direct and indirect. Competitors exist not only in the user market, but also in other markets, such as the fundraising market, or volunteer market. The significant current and potential competitors should be identified, and the more important of these should be studied in depth. The following factors should be taken into account:

- *Analysis of competition as perceived by users*: quantitative research programmes should include a question relating to respondents' visits to other museums or leisure venues in the region or nationally. If there is space, they should be asked to indicate their usage of other leisure activities, such as participating in sport, eating out, going to the cinema.
- *A description of all direct and indirect competitors, both current and potential*: their capacities; appropriate policy; market share; and apparent strengths and weaknesses
- *Competition in other markets*.

Environmental analysis

An assessment needs to be made of the external environment, both of the current situation and of possible changes. Consideration should be given to the following:

- the significant, relevant, short-term and long-term developments and trends in each of the museum's external environments: market; social; economic; political; legal; stakeholder; competition; technology
- the impact of these factors on the organisation and its target markets.

The marketing audit should be an ongoing activity. Records of attendance levels and financial records should be examined regularly. Evaluation of the effectiveness of promotional efforts should be conducted and consulted on a regular basis, and the measurement of performance should be constantly assessed. If a museum has not previously undertaken a full-scale marketing audit, it might be a good idea to hire a consultant to oversee it, particularly

Strengths	Weaknesses
Opportunities	Threats

Figure 9.3 Strengths, Weaknesses, Opportunities, and Threats (SWOT) analysis

since the audit should be impartial, and staff do tend to be biased in favour of the museum! The first time an audit is undertaken can be extremely time-consuming and often those responsible for undertaking it will find that many of the systems for monitoring performance and so on will not be in place. It is then a learning experience, and as each audit is undertaken, systems for amassing and detailing the required information will be created. The information retrieval should become an ongoing activity of the museum, with ideally a review or audit taking place annually. At first a lot of irrelevant information will be gathered, but as each successive audit is undertaken, the museum will become adept at seeking the appropriate information. Moreover as the museum learns about the process and sets information retrieval systems in place, the whole process should become considerably less time-consuming, and ultimately more informative.

SWOT analysis

Having gathered all the information in the marketing audit, the next stage is to evaluate the strengths and weaknesses of the museum's internal position compared with the opportunities and threats posed by the external environment. A SWOT is an acronym for the analysis of these internal Strengths and Weaknesses, and external Opportunities and Threats. It provides a simple method of synthesising the results of the marketing audit. Figure 9.3 shows a matrix framework for the SWOT analysis, showing how the internal strengths and weaknesses relate to external opportunities and threats.

The strengths and weaknesses can be assessed using the marketing mix structure and the analysis of the museum's policy and resources, while the opportunities and threats will be examined taking into account all the external environment issues, including the market and the competition. Often it will be found that what is considered a strength in one respect is a weakness in another. Considerable consultation is required with all staff members and stakeholders to acquire an accurate representation. It would not be possible to list every strength, weakness, opportunity, or threat, so some degree of selection will need to take place.

It is useful to rank the strengths and weaknesses according to the relative strength and the relative weakness and their importance to the museum. In this way they can be prioritised according to the impact they will have in achieving the marketing function. Decisions can then be made on which strengths to enhance and weaknesses to ameliorate. The opportunities and threats can also be ranked according to their probability of occurrence and their impact on the museum. The museum may not be in a position to maximise an opportunity or reduce a threat, but it should be able to anticipate change more accurately and be proactive rather than reactive.

Assumptions

The final stage of the situational analysis is to identify the key assumptions. Key assumptions are the estimates of future conditions that will impact on the marketing plan; in other words, those external factors over which the museum has no control, but can make an educated guess on the situation in the near future. Some examples might be educative legislation, local authority funding reductions, or an increase in competition with the opening of a new heritage centre.

Once identified, the implications of the key assumptions from the marketing plan should be derived. On implementation of the strategy, the monitoring and review process can review any changes, which may either confirm the key assumptions or else necessitate an alteration to them. Key assumptions may be critical and so need to form the subject of contingency plans.

SETTING MARKETING OBJECTIVES

A marketing objective is a precise statement that outlines what is to be accomplished by the museum's marketing activities. It specifies the results expected from the marketing efforts. Essentially, marketing objectives are about matching the products with the markets. Marketing objectives state what is to be achieved, when results are to be achieved, but not how the results are to be achieved (Quinn 1980).

According to Payne (1993), each marketing objective should be:

1   *Relevant*
    The marketing objective should be relevant in relation to the corporate mission and objectives
2   *Specific*
    It should focus on clear and identifiable goals.
3   *Measurable*
    The objective should be quantified.

4   *Time bound*
     It should have an achievement date attached to it.
5   *Challenging*
     Objectives should be realisable, but should stretch people in achieving
     them.
6   *Focused*
     Marketing objectives should focus on issues relating to both the markets
     and products, which the museum wishes to address.

The marketing objectives should cover the planning period of three or five
years. They derive from the mission statement of the museum, and may relate
to the following:

- development of the product
- development of the market
- development of income.

When considering future options, it is worth assessing current performance
and predicting whether the marketing objectives will be achievable, taking into
account current evidence. Too often marketing objectives become dream state-
ments and are far removed from hard reality. A useful technique for considering
the difference between existing performance and the target required as a result
of the process of objectives setting, is 'gap analysis'. Gap analysis identifies
the extent to which existing marketing strategies will be able to deliver the
desired level of performance required. The gap analysis shows the requirement
of the task to be achieved by measuring the gap between the marketing objectives and the present trend. It helps to stimulate the search for new marketing
strategies to achieve objectives and reduce the gap. This technique helps the
museum to introduce a degree of reality into the task of marketing objective
setting, although at the same time it should not preclude vision.

DECIDING STRATEGIES

Setting marketing strategies

Marketing strategies outline the broad plan of action to achieve marketing
objectives. The strategies are developed in relation to the positioning of the
museum and are determined within the structure of the marketing mix. Targets
will be set under each element, to which is attached a timescale and ultimately
a cost. Consideration should be given to the relationship of the strategy to
the marketing objectives. A marketing plan is set in place as much to help
the museum achieve its mission as to provide a framework within which
promotional activity can take place. The chosen strategy should, therefore, be
appropriate for the fulfilment of this mission.

The museum may find considerable overlap between its business strategy and
its marketing strategy. Perhaps the significant difference is that the marketing
strategy can guide the museum in its relationship with its markets and with

PRODUCT

		Existing	New
MARKET	**Existing**	Market penetration	New product development
	New	Market development	Diversification

Figure 9.4 Ansoff growth vector matrix

Source: Ansoff (1957)

its competitors, both of which must ultimately influence the museum's mission (Wind and Robertson 1983).

Positioning

The marketing audit will have yielded some indications concerning the desirability or otherwise of the museum altering its product benefits or the emphasis attached to them in approaching different market segments. Certain product benefits may need to be developed and others given less prominence. The museum should make these decisions before drafting a new strategy. It may be that once decisions have been made on positioning, the objectives will require to be amended accordingly.

There are three options when deciding on target markets: concentrate on a single segment with one product; offer one product to a number of segments; target a different product at each of a number of segments, possibly using niche marketing to target a very precise market segment. Decisions also need to be made on the range of products to be offered. Clearly, such decisions must be consistent with the resources and competence of the museum to achieve them.

When considering the future direction of the museum in terms of the relationship between products and markets, it can be useful to focus attention on the way in which the museum sees itself developing. The 'Ansoff growth vector matrix' developed by Ansoff (1957) is a simple matrix diagram outlining the possibilities for growth of any organisation. The Ansoff matrix helps a museum to define its overall strategic thrust or its vision for the future. Figure 9.4 summarises the alternative options open to the museum:

Market penetration

By using existing product offerings, the museum can build up market share in its existing market. It may involve some modification to the products, but

MARKET SEGMENTS

PRODUCTS	Children	Families	Tourists	Ethnic communities	Arts societies	Special needs
Blockbusters	*	*	*	*	*	*
Workshops	*	*		*		*
Lectures					*	
Open days	*	*				
Shop	*	*	*			
Café	*	*	*	*	*	*

Figure 9.5 Product–market fit matrix

is the least risky of the four options. It will rely heavily on promotion, though, to build on existing target markets.

Market development

While keeping the existing product range, the museum can attempt to attract new market segments. Although riskier than market penetration, it should be a strategy built on the strengths of the museum.

New product development

By using its knowledge of the existing market, the museum can develop new or related products for these markets. It is riskier than market development, but should be informed by an understanding of the museum's users.

Diversification

This is the most ambitious of the four options and requires a commitment to vision! Here new market segments are entered using new products.

Once the decision on the strategic vision of the museum has been reached, the next stage is to match the proposed target markets with the museum's current and proposed products. A useful tool for making decisions on target market and product matching is the product–market fit matrix, illustrated in Figure 9.5.

First, describe all the current and potential user market segments in terms of easily identifiable market sectors, and list them along the top of the matrix. Then identify all the products offered by the museum as well as proposed products, and list them down the side of the matrix. The idea is to produce a product–market fit table which matches the market sectors with the products

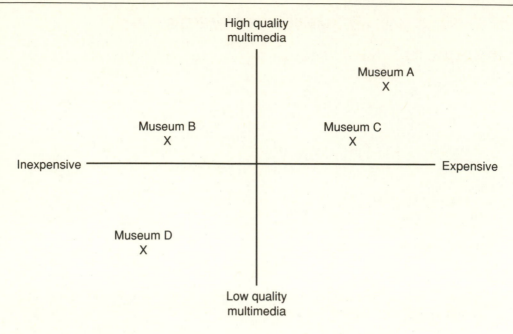

Figure 9.6 Perceptual map

they use or potentially might use. This enables the current user profile for each product element to be analysed.

Positioning brings together the market analysis, the internal analysis of the museum's resources, and the competitive analysis. Positioning forms the framework on which the marketing strategy is developed. It enables the museum to differentiate itself in terms of the image in the user's mind. It is important to position the value of the product in the minds of the target market. To do this, Kotler (1991) recommends that distinguishing characteristics are selected which satisfy the following criteria:

1   *Importance*
    The difference is highly valued to a sufficiently large market.
2   *Distinctiveness*
    The difference is distinctly superior to other offerings that are available.
3   *Communicability*
    It is possible to communicate the difference in a simple and strong way.
4   *Superiority*
    The difference is not easily copied by competitors.
5   *Affordability*
    The target customer will be able and willing to pay for the difference. The distinguishing characteristic(s) will be perceived as sufficiently valuable to compensate for any additional cost.
6   *Profitability*
    The organisation will achieve additional profits as a result of introducing the difference.

The positioning process involves identifying the most important attributes of the museum's products. It is then possible to locate these attributes on a perceptual map. A two-dimensional perceptual map can be used, which identifies competitors' services in relation to the selected attributes. Separate positioning maps can be drawn for each market segment. A five- or seven-point rating scale is constructed using bipolar adjectives that apply to the product benefits. The product benefits will have been derived from focus group research or survey research. Once these have been determined, survey research can then request respondents to evaluate the relative similarity of different competitors services on the rating scale. These can then be plotted on the perceptual map. Figure 9.6 illustrates a positioning map for a museum, Museum A, and its competitors where the benefits deemed to be important by the museum's visitors were price and the use of multimedia in the museum. Museum A attained a high score on its use of multimedia but was considered to be expensive.

A decision then needs to be taken if the position is distinct enough to differentiate the museum's product from its competitors and whether it should reposition itself. It may be that an opportunity is identified, a position which is not met by competitors' products. Positioning allows the museum to determine what its current position is, what it could be, and what actions are needed to attain it. As Payne comments, 'positioning involves giving the target market segment the reason for buying your services and thus underpins the whole marketing strategy' (Payne 1993: 120).

Assessing resources

Most marketing strategies will assume some level of growth, either in audience or income or both. This will have implications for the deployment of the museum's resources, whether they be physical, financial, or human. The implications will need to be costed in terms of each of the resources, for example, purchase of computer equipment, costings for sponsorship requests, or staff training needs. The demands on resources will then need to be compared with the target of additional income.

If the strategy requires a major reinvestment of resources, the strategic targets may have been set at too high a level. This exercise emphasises realism, although it does not pay to be too cautious, as organisations also need to innovate (Drucker 1954). It may be that the marketing objectives need to be reassessed to accommodate the realities of the resource situation.

Identify alternative mixes

Before the strategy is finalised, it is expedient to consider alternative mixes to determine if an alternative strategy might be more effective at achieving the marketing objectives. The alternative mixes can be assessed using both analysis and trial and error, in order to decide on the best use of available resources. Ultimately a decision needs to be made on the most effective marketing mix, which can then be implemented as marketing programmes.

While going through this process it is worth considering the development of contingency plans. A museum cannot anticipate every eventuality, but the impact of different sets of assumptions on the environmental opportunities and threats should be assessed, and where appropriate a broad contingency plan should be developed. These contingency plans can then be put into operation if certain situations arise.

RESOURCE ALLOCATION AND MONITORING

The final stage of the marketing strategy is to develop marketing programmes and put in place evaluation controls.

Marketing programmes

The overall three- or five-year strategic marketing plan should be developed in terms of the five elements of the marketing mix. These then need to be detailed as programmes for implementation in one-year operational plans. These operational plans allocate activities so that every member of staff knows what their responsibilities are. The plans also allocate the physical and financial resources available.

Marketing programmes are similar to marketing objectives and strategies in that they should do the following:

- have an established timetable and be able to be carried out within a defined period of time
- identify the resources needed to carry them out
- provide for monitoring and control of performance.

The programmes should be detailed and cover the various activities required, such as budgets, resource allocations, and staff responsibilities. It is essential that they are co-ordinated in their implementation since they are not individual components but an integrated whole.

Monitoring the plan

According to McCann and her colleagues,

> no marketing plan is a tablet of stone. Many different kinds of circumstance will entail alterations to objectives and targets; certain promotional tactics may not work or will become inappropriate within the context

of the [museum] programme. Some targets will not be reached; others will be surpassed.

(McCann *et al.* 1993: 44)

The marketing plan should be monitored, controlled, and reviewed in order to ensure that the short-term strategies are consistently achieving the long-term marketing objectives and mission of the museum (Guiltinan and Paul 1988). If performance does not match objectives, corrective action can be taken. Short-term control systems can plot results against objectives on a regular basis. The control systems will have been set in place along with the targets in order to measure performance. Continual records will be kept, while market research and promotions monitoring will also need to be assessed. Strategic control systems are more long term and require the appraisal of the plans on an annual, or preferably twice-yearly basis to assess critically whether the plans are in line with the museum's capabilities and its environment. The outcome may be a redefinition of the marketing objectives and even of the museum's mission. Although strategies are set on a three- or five-year basis, the planning process is an ongoing review, which will require constant monitoring and control.

The planning process provides a framework within which a museum should be better fitted to achieve its objectives. It is an approach that orders priorities and maximises the use of the museum's resources. The whole process should involve the widest consultation, since everyone involved in the museum bears some responsibility for ensuring its successful implementation. Ultimately, though, as McCann and her colleagues comment,

> conducting a marketing audit and developing a marketing plan can only be successful if the [museum] itself fully recognizes the value of the process and is prepared to undertake some possibly radical re-thinking of its purpose and how it will fulfil the role for which it was created.

(McCann *et al.* 1993: 46)

As a caveat, though, McDonald (1989b) has identified a number of problems which create barriers to the development and implementation of marketing planning. These include:

- confusion between tactics and strategy
- isolating the marketing function from operations
- confusion between the marketing function and the marketing concept
- organisational barriers, which in the case of museums includes the political context, and the influence of stakeholders
- lack of in-depth analysis
- confusion between process and output
- lack of knowledge and skills
- lack of a systematic approach to marketing planning
- failure to prioritise objectives
- hostile corporate cultures.

Several of these barriers relate to the need for a more marketing-oriented culture in service organisations. According to Payne (1993), there are two issues critical to successfully implementing marketing in a service firm: first, the development of a comprehensive and integrated marketing plan; and second, the development of a marketing-oriented and customer-focused attitude throughout the service organisation. The final chapter will consider the creation of a marketing-oriented culture in a museum.

Writing a report

Finally the marketing plan should be formalised as a written document. The shape that the document takes depends on the requirements of the museum, although it may contain the following sections:

- executive summary
- marketing audit summary
- SWOT analysis
- marketing objectives
- marketing strategy
- action programmes.

As an illustration of the structure, the following is a brief summary of a marketing plan devised for a fictitious natural history museum.

FICTIONAL CASE STUDY
MARKETING PLAN FOR CURRIE NATURAL
HISTORY MUSEUM

Currie Museum is a natural history museum with mainly regional specimens and a small ethnography collection. It has a shop, toilets, and a drinks dispenser. The museum is situated in the town centre, but is isolated from the shopping area by major roads. It is open all year, seven days a week, charging an admission with concessions.

The museum receives funding from the municipal authority, Currie Council, the annual block grant covering maintenance costs and the staffing salary cost. Income from admissions and from the shop are retained by the museum to cover all other costs incurred. The museum spends just under 4 per cent of its self-generated budget on promotions.

The museum has been operating a policy of staging temporary 'blockbuster' exhibitions for a period of up to two years. This policy has augmented the visitor figures to 100,000 visitors per annum.

At present there is no effective marketing programme at the museum, although it has developed a business plan for its local area museum council.

Mission

Currie Museum's mission has been defined as follows:

> 'Through conservation, research, and exhibition, to enable the public to appreciate the wonders of the natural world.'

The mission is not specific about its public, and does not consider what is now the corporate identity, which is to project an image of a museum that is conscious of conservation issues. It may need to be reappraised as a consequence of the marketing planning exercise.

The overall objectives to be achieved have been set as follows:

1   To collect and conserve natural history specimens, especially those of regional and national significance.
2   To enable the public to learn about natural history.
3   To increase repeat visits from local people.
4   To widen the visitor profile to include under-represented groups from the local area.
5   To provide research facilities for the study of natural history.
6   To inform the public of conservation issues to the extent where they actively put them into practice.
7   To increase the earning potential of visitor services.
8   To develop income from corporate donors and grant-giving bodies.
9   To maintain local government funding support.

These overall objectives were then broken down into goals, which were quantified for performance measurement purposes.

Marketing audit

Internal analysis

Purpose

History

The museum was founded in 1862 by Currie Natural History Society. The collection was amassed by various members and was housed in a building donated to the Society by a wealthy benefactor in 1868. Until 1880, admission was strictly limited to Society members and friends, but after that date, the general public were admitted free of charge. After the First World War, the Society was in a state of financial crisis, and so negotiations were held with Currie Council to take over the collection and building.

The museum is now under municipal authority control, and is accountable to its management committee, whose composition is evenly split between councillors and local people. The chair of the committee is a councillor appointed by Currie Council.

Policy

The museum has until recently had no formal acquisition and disposals strategy, but has now devised a basic policy. In recent years the display of the museum's permanent collection has taken second place to the blockbuster exhibitions, which are seen as the lifeblood of the museum. The blockbusters have been chosen for their appeal to a wide audience and little effort has been made to appeal to different market groups apart from school groups. Equally, education work is confined to school parties, while there is little attempt at outreach beyond the occasional lecture to women's institute groups, and so on.

The museum is well known in the area, the only other museum in Currie being a small art gallery. However, it does not have a reputation beyond the Currie area. Although the museum is keen to offer a quality service to its visitors, no attempt has really been made to assess the visitors' views of quality, or to assess the museum's own operations in terms of the quality that it provides.

Resources

Physical

The collection of natural history artefacts is largely of local origin, with a national dimension. A significant proportion of the collection is not on display, but is kept in storage. There are two curators who work on documentation and research of the collection, although they have little time to undertake any active preservation work. There is also a small ethnographical collection, which does not really complement the theme of the museum. In the past the museum has not invested in environmental controls, while security is largely confined to use of attendants.

The building is a rather awesome nineteenth-century structure. It has been separated from the town's shops by a main road. There is a small car park, although there is ample free parking in Currie town centre. The interior of the building is suffering from age, with peeling and yellowing paintwork. It has two floors, the large gallery in the ground floor being used for blockbuster exhibitions, while the less popular displays, such as the ethnographic display, are on the first floor.

The two administrative staff have access to word-processing and database facilities while the museum has recently installed software for market research purposes. There is a computer in the foyer for visitor use, which locates the galleries and objects in the museum, using question and answer techniques. A crowd usually gathers around the computer which has proved very popular.

Human

The museum has ten full-time staff: a director, an assistant director, two curators, two administrators, two shop assistants, and two attendants. There are eight part-time staff, two technicians, attendants, and ancillary staff. At present there are two volunteers, both working with the museum's curators. The director and assistant director have qualifications in Museums Studies, while the two curators both have university qualifications in their specialist subjects. The director does not attend training courses, although the assistant director has attended a few training courses run by Currie Council on management skills. Otherwise there is little assistance from Currie Council, although it does have a marketing department. The museum appointed a consultant to undertake their first visitor survey three years ago, and have subsequently repeated the survey on an annual basis.

Financial

Currie Council is committed to funding the museum, although funding has not increased in real terms for the past two years. The museum has received a small number of grants from the area museum council and from other sources. It has not been very successful in attracting sponsorship and receives few other donations.

Marketing resources

Role of marketing

This is the first time the museum has formally developed a strategy. The assistant director has been delegated the task, but is strongly supported by the director and the chair of the management committee. The impetus came from Currie Council, which demanded that the museum draw up a marketing plan. In the past, marketing has been regarded as merely promotions, but the assistant director is keen to develop the role of marketing and integrate it with other operations. Much of the role of the assistant director has in fact been in marketing activities.

Physical resources

The museum has two computers for administrative use, which includes a database and market research software. The museum usually uses Currie Council's printing facilities, which are of a high standard.

Human resources

The assistant director has assumed much of the responsibilities for marketing, but is keen to appoint a marketing assistant. In the past the museum has received help from marketing students who are attending Currie College. The management committee have in the past taken little interest in marketing, but is increasingly demanding that the museum become more marketing-oriented. The museum has not used the local authority's marketing department in the past, although the assistant director is receiving assistance from them in drawing up the plan.

Financial resources

The expenditure on promotional activities in the past has accounted for around 4 per cent of the museum's self-generated income.

Marketing activities

Product

The museum has softened the frontage of the building with banners, and has a sign which is clearly visible from the adjacent main road. The foyer is unwelcoming, the tickets for admission being sold from a booth. The whole museum has a dilapidated air, and appears dark and dingy, and smells musty. The exception is the gallery, which houses the blockbuster exhibition, which is bright and lively. There are no signs in the interior, apart from a notice locating the toilets.

The displays tend to be very traditional, laid out in chronological order. There are some exceptions where multimedia have been introduced, and two displays which focus on the issues relating to conservation. Temporary exhibitions focus very much on the blockbusters, with little use of the reserve collections, and certainly no involvement of the local community in display production. Special events are occasionally arranged, usually focusing on the blockbuster exhibition, although there have been behind-the-scenes open days.

Surveys have shown that only 20 per cent of visitors are aware of the museum's conservation stance. Most visitors are fairly satisfied with the facilities offered by the museum, although research has shown that there is considerable demand for a café. The museum was awarded a grant to create facilities for wheelchair users, both access and toilet facilities. There is no access though to the upper floor, and no other disabled groups are catered for. There is a shop with a fairly large stock of books and small souvenirs targeted at groups of schoolchildren. There are toilets and a drinks dispenser with benches beside it, and there are few seats in the galleries. There is no complaints procedure, although there is a suggestions box in the foyer.

The museum is keen to attract school parties, and the director personally welcomes the groups, and has developed some school packs in conjunction with local teachers. A lecture series is run in the winter season, although it is not particularly well attended. Researchers are always welcomed, and are encouraged to join the staff at tea breaks and so on.

Price

The museum charges for admission, with half-price concessions, while there is also a family ticket. Schools groups gain free admittance.

The museum has received small grant awards from various bodies and has attracted a few donations from local companies. It has a donations box in the foyer. There is no Friends organisation, although there are often volunteers undertaking research in the museum.

Place

The museum is open from 10 am to 5.30 pm Monday to Saturday, and from 2 pm to 5 pm on Sundays. The museum has good public transport links, and although its car park is small, there is plenty of parking space locally. There are a number of signposts directing the visitor to the museum.

Promotion

The promotional budget amounts to 4 per cent of total earned income. Most of that budget is spent on leaflets, which market research has proved to be effective. The leaflets are produced with the assistance of Currie Council. They are distributed in local outlets, such as libraries and doctors' surgeries. The museum is also included in local tourism leaflets.

The museum recently developed a corporate identity with the help of a professional designer in the local authority. It now has a logo and distinctive typeface. The museum has in the past advertised on buses, but found from research that this was fairly ineffective. The museum relies on the goodwill of the local newspaper for publicity.

People

Staff meetings are conducted monthly, with all professional staff and representatives from attendants and ancillary staff involved. There is a small training budget, although most training is paid for and undertaken by the local authority. All attendants have been on customer care courses. Some members of the management committee are business people, and have often given freely of their advice. The museum has good relations with Currie Council, and at the present has a very committed management committee chair.

Market analysis

Users

The museum has been conducting surveys of visitors for the past three years, and has a clear idea of the profile of users. One-third of users are members of school parties, while children represent one-third of non-school visits. Few older people are attracted. The majority of visitors live in the local area, tend to come in family groups, and are repeat attenders. The museum also attracts a reasonable proportion of visitors for research purposes.

Stakeholders and other publics

Currie Council has been very supportive of the museum. The local tourist board has included the museum in its publicity and actively promotes the museum, although the town of Currie is not a tourist destination. Volunteers have been a constant source of help on the curatorial side, although less so in other areas.

Competitor analysis

The only other museum in the area is a small art gallery. However, Currie has a large leisure centre which has sports facilities and a theatre. Survey findings indicated that the vast majority of the museum's visitors attended the leisure centre both for sport and the theatre.

There are few specialist gift shops in Currie, and certainly none selling the range of goods on offer in the museum shop.

Environmental analysis

The museum is aware of recent education legislation which impacts on its services to schools. The economic situation also suggests that funding from Currie Council is likely to be reduced in the long term. The population of Currie is increasing as new homes are built, predominantly for families. The leisure centre is expanding, with a studio theatre being built.

It is assumed that the museum will continue to receive funding from its local authority. However, if this is substantially reduced, it is recognised that a contingency marketing plan will need to be put into place, which places more emphasis on fundraising activities.

SWOT analysis
See Figure 9.7

MARKETING OBJECTIVES

1   To increase the use of the permanent collection in quiet periods between blockbuster exhibitions so that 10 per cent of the reserve collection is exhibited per annum by year 3.
2   To develop the image of conservation, so that an additional 10 per cent of visitors are aware of the museum's image in each of the next three years.
3   To develop a commitment to quality in the museum, by setting in place a quality strategy by year 2.
4   To programme refurbishment of the museum over the next three years by year 1.
5   To investigate the feasibility of a café by year 1.
6   To encourage local groups to participate in the development of a new display by year 3.
7   To increase frequency of visits by 5 per cent per annum over the next three years.
8   To establish a Friends organisation by year 1.

STRENGTHS	WEAKNESSES
• Unique museum in area • Disabled facilities • Repeat visits from families • Liaison with school groups • Conducts market research • Enthusiastic staff • Keen volunteers • Income from shop • Leaflets successful • Good relations with local media	• Diversity of collection • Lack of turnaround of permanent collection • Lack of facilities for hard of hearing and the partially sighted • Little outreach work • Failure to integrate market research findings into operations • Lack of interior signage • Lack of marketing skills • No Friends organisation • Unwelcoming foyer • Dilapidated decor • Over-reliance on local authority income • Lack of awareness of non-visitors
OPPORTUNITIES	THREATS
• Conservation a global issue • More families moving into area • Computer technology for promotion purposes	• Leisure centre expanding • Local authority increasing funding commitments to leisure centre • Sponsorship being reduced in museums in general

Figure 9.7 SWOT analysis for Currie Museum

9   To introduce new programmes for families and children by year 2.
10   To increase income development by 15 per cent per annum over the next three years.
11   To develop the shop to increase earning potential by 5 per cent per annum over the next three years.
12   To increase awareness of the museum in the local community by 10 per cent per annum over the next three years.
13   To increase the promotional budget to 6 per cent by year 3.

The museum is conscious that a number of issues arising in the SWOT analysis have not been dealt with in the marketing plan for the next three years. Alternative mixes have been developed to incorporate these issues, and will be used as contingency plans if circumstances change.

Marketing strategy

Positioning

It is clear from the analysis and from developing perceptual maps that the museum should continue to target local people, families, and school parties. To meet the needs of these groups, Currie Museum needs to emphasise the benefits already on offer and augment its product to create additional product benefits. The resource implications should be dealt with by the increased funding expected from fundraising, while many of the incentives will be self-financing. Two major initiatives will be started with little cost implications: the involvement of the local community in developing displays, and the introduction of new programmes for families and children. The initiative that will take substantial resources is the café, but at this stage, a feasibility study will investigate the resource implications and demand for such a facility.

Product

The corporate identity of the museum needs to be reinforced throughout the museum, not only in its promotional literature but also in its whole image. Consequently, the displays will need to be redesigned to incorporate the conservation message. Multimedia can be effective at getting the message across – a number of computers in the foyer could double up both to orient the visitor and to emphasise the conservation message.

While redesigning the displays, local groups can be involved, starting with a group for the disabled to capitalise on and make them aware of the excellent facilities on offer for the disabled. Local groups can also be involved in temporary exhibitions using the reserve collections. Blockbuster exhibitions should be interspersed with these temporary exhibitions, to vary the product and to encourage more repeat visits.

A quality strategy will include the need for a blueprint of the museum's interactions with its visitors, and a customer complaints procedure. The foyer should be made more welcoming – the computers will help, but the ticket booth needs to be replaced with a desk which can double up as an information desk.

The stock in the shop should be reappraised and enlarged – market research and a review of local shops and any gaps in merchandise will be required. A study will also need to be conducted into the feasibility of a café, both in terms of demand and resources.

New programmes should be introduced for families and children. Workshops can also double-up for school use. Demand for workshops and events can be assessed using the museum's market research.

Price

The museum should establish a Friends organisation, to assist with fundraising and to help as volunteers, for example, for events and workshops.

Companies, especially those that are conscious of their environmental image, should be approached for sponsorship funding. Local employers in Currie should be targeted and personally approached.

Relationships with Currie Council are important and must be maintained. However, using the market research and the marketing planning as a base for applications, the museum should be targeting more grant-giving organisations, and should be looking towards government grant funding for the café, if the go-ahead is given by the feasibility study.

Place

The museum's transport links are good, as is signposting. The building though is rather awesome. Tubs of plants at the entrance and a brightly lit foyer will make it more welcoming.

Promotion

The museum needs to raise awareness and increase use of the museum by local people. Research data should be used to target prospective visitors accurately with a mail-out. An incentive can be offered, such as a coupon for a 15 per cent reduction in the shop. A mailing list should be set up to include workshop participants, and Friends, possibly developing it for mail-outs of promotional literature. The mailing list should be used for openings for temporary exhibitions. The shop should be publicised, with press advertising at Christmas – a good time to increase sales income.

The museum should approach Currie's new leisure centre to ascertain if it can place a display in the centre. This would have the effect not only of raising awareness, but also of starting to build links with the museum's main competitor, in the hope that in the future they can co-operate.

The promotions budget needs to be increased, while in the long term consideration should be given to the appointment of a marketing assistant, who can co-ordinate the promotional activities. Negotiations with Currie Council for additional funding for this post will need to be instigated. Although the museum has good relations with the local press, the museum should develop its contacts with local radio and television.

People

The museum should make more use of the expertise available in Currie Council. This may also help it to build closer links with the municipal authority. It should also make take-up of Currie Council's training programmes a priority. The assistant director, in particular, who is responsible for marketing, should be sent on a marketing course.

The museum has good relations with its management committee, but should also use its expertise to better advantage. The museum should develop the annual report that it submits to Currie Council to include its achievements, and a sample of press cuttings, and so on. In time, this could be developed as a newsletter.

Good relations need to be maintained with the staff. It is also important that the director and assistant director thoroughly communicate the marketing plan to the staff, and amend activities so that marketing is better integrated with the other operations activities.

Once a Friends organisation has been established, the museum can use this as a source of volunteers to assist with special events and workshops which can be labour-intensive.

Sample marketing action plan and monitoring system – year 1

Product

1   Assess the potential of the reserve collection for temporary exhibitions – by September.
2   Develop the displays to incorporate the conservation message – ongoing.
3   Remove the ticket booth in the foyer and replace with a desk – by July.

4 Investigate purchase of computer technology for use in the foyer, for orientation and to emphasise the message on conservation – by February – in place by September.

5 In consultation with staff, draw up a blueprint of the customer and museum service interaction – by August.

6 Set up a customer complaints procedure and communicate to staff – by March.

7 Instigate feasibility study for café – by February.

8 Use research to investigate demand for different types of events and workshops for families and children – by May. Arrange programme of workshops for year 2 – by October.

9 Using market research investigate demand for goods in the shop – by May.

The strategy will be broken down into action programmes for each of the elements of the marketing mix for each year of its implementation, with a time period for each initiative. The targets will be monitored for achievement. It has also been agreed that the museum will make weekly checks on ticket sales and shop income; hold monthly feedback sessions with attendants concerning visitor concerns and reactions; and hold biennial sessions to discuss the progress of the plan.

10

Future developments for marketing the museum

Rapid change is now inevitable for museums, as the pace of development in society speeds up. Museums must not only respond to these changes, but anticipate them, if they are to remain relevant to society. This final chapter considers how museums can attempt to nurture a marketing orientation that will cushion the blows of change, and assist them in capitalising on change rather then being buffeted by its onslaught. Creating a marketing orientation is a long, slow process for any organisation, and will be equally so in museums. Some may aspire to a marketing orientation, but few will attain it. Nevertheless, it is a goal to which all museums should be aiming.

Consideration is given in this chapter to the issues and challenges that are likely to impact on museums in the future. Some suggestions are then made for future research into museums marketing, research which is essential if museums are to be informed, and ultimately be in a strong position to anticipate and respond to change.

ORGANISING FOR A MARKETING ORIENTATION

For strategic marketing planning to have any value for the museum, the strategies adopted must be effectively implemented. As Bonoma has commented, 'marketing is long on strategy, but short on recommendations for how to get the job done once strategic directions have been chosen' (Bonoma 1984: 6–7).

In the past, museums have survived and grown and still been inept at marketing effectiveness. This has been possible because other competitors have also been ineffective in their marketing. Effectiveness requires a marketing orientation throughout the museum, not just amongst those who have responsibility for marketing. Marketing cannot be an add-on function (Drucker 1973). Instead it is an orientation that pervades the whole museum and impacts on every area of organisational practice. There is a distinct difference between marketing activities and marketing process. Marketing activities consist of promotions, marketing research, and so on, and are principally the responsibility of the marketing department or marketing officer. Marketing process involves the whole museum, processes effectively maintaining the match between the

215

museum's products and the museum's publics. Such processes are the responsibility of all the different functions in the museum. Achieving a marketing orientation requires the establishment of processes rather than activities.

A museum can assess the effectiveness of its marketing by undertaking a marketing effectiveness audit, as originally devised by Kotler (1977) for companies that are manufacturing products. Adapted to museums, that audit will include the following:

1 *Customer philosophy*
   To what extent does the museum director and management committee acknowledge the importance of the needs and wants of its users and other publics in shaping the museum's plan and activities?
2 *Integrated marketing organisation*
   To what extent is the museum capable of undertaking analyses of its markets; its competitors; and planning, implementation, and control?
3 *Adequate marketing information*
   Is the information extracted of sufficient kind and quality to conduct an effective marketing programme?
4 *Strategic orientation*
   Does the museum have vision when creating marketing strategies and long-term plans, and to what extent have these proved successful in the past?
5 *Operational efficiency*
   Are the museum's marketing plans implemented cost-effectively, and are the results monitored and modified effectively?

The audit gives the museum an insight into the perceived level of marketing effectiveness in the museum. It can identify the shortfalls and assist in developing a programme to improve the museum's marketing orientation. It can take three to six years to develop a marketing orientation, for as Payne remarks, 'The development of a marketing orientation where it has not previously existed will require a major change in attitudes and a fundamental shift in shared values' (Payne 1993: 243).

The principal condition required for a marketing orientation is good communications (Bonoma 1984). Much of the marketing task is to influence others, and to gain the support of every member of staff. Equally, communication skills are also required to interact with the external public: not only users, stakeholders, and other publics, but also market research agencies, the media, advertising agencies, and so on. Much negative criticism of marketing will need to be overcome, and the trust of its detractors gained. Ethical concerns need to be anticipated and responded to.

Good communications presupposes strong leadership, which is committed to developing a marketing orientation. The museum director must be convinced of the value of marketing and insist that it underpins the museum's values. The director must become a champion for marketing. Responsibility for the marketing activities must be a senior management function, and although perhaps the activities may come under the jurisdiction of a separate marketing department, the marketing processes are the responsibility of every member of staff in the museum. This can be summarised as follows:

> It is often thought that the appointment of a marketing officer means that marketing is being done. This is simply not the case. What is needed is for marketing to be embraced as a management function by the Board and senior management.
>
> (Arts Council of Great Britain 1991: 6)

A number of methods can be adopted to achieve a marketing orientation within a museum (adapted from Palmer 1994):

- Appoint senior management who have an understanding and commitment to marketing.
- Train non-marketing managers and staff to empathise with the expectations of users.
- Use outside consultants who can apply their previous experience of developing a marketing culture.
- Formalize the marketing planning process so that managers use the structured approach to collecting information and formulating a marketing plan. In fact, the use of information has been identified as a source of marketing orientation (Kohli and Jaworski 1990).

Organisational cultural factors can hinder the adoption of a marketing orientation (Jelinek *et al.* 1983). In some museums the culture is one of inertia, of a negative response to change, and a reactive attitude. However, the marketing process is designed to enable marketing-led strategic change within an organisation (Piercy 1990). Museums have the additional difficulty of coping with the diversity of their marketing tasks. With multiple goals to achieve and the needs of multiple publics to satisfy, the marketing task is more complicated. Therefore all the more reason to develop a marketing orientation to simplify the tasks and remove ambiguity over the expectations of marketing.

The size of the museum does not preclude a marketing orientation. The smaller the museum, theoretically the easier the adjustment, although often the slow decision-making processes in a democratically run museum can hinder the smooth transition. A larger museum has a cohort of staff as well as stakeholders, who all need to make the investment in marketing. There is no room for complacency. To serve the purpose of the museum, marketing needs to be at the hub of the purpose. Marketing does not offer a quick-fix solution; it is a way of thinking, a conviction that museums are for people.

THE FUTURE FOR MUSEUM MARKETING

Priorities and values have developed quite significantly in museums in recent years. There are also those who voice concern at the changes. It is worth quoting Peter Jenkinson at length, since he succinctly voices the concerns of many in museums:

The museum democratisation project that has been gaining momentum over the last half century, particularly at local and regional levels, has now run into trouble in the face of a regime that believes that its responsible citizens should be avid consumers of culture, but not necessarily active participants in the creation and transformation of culture.

There is widespread anxiety about what the future holds and widespread frustration that we now appear to be going in reverse, having worked so hard to begin to open up museums to diverse audiences, to forward policies of cultural equity, to break down barriers, to experiment with new methods of presentation, interpretation and education, to encourage a critical curatorship and a spirit of enquiry, and to support living artists, not just dead ones. We appear to be moving away from the ideal of access for all, to a new environment where access to museums and galleries is dependent upon the ability to pay; where the establishment of programmes is based either on cynical, spurious or snobbish assumptions about what would be popular, or on the sponsorship that might be available; where only quantity counts and not quality; where publicly subsidised museums that do not attract large audiences are seen as an unacceptable and unaffordable self-indulgence; and where notions of democratisation are considered distinctly quaint. We are witnessing the re-erection of the economic, social and intellectual barriers that so many of us have struggled to clear away and, potentially, a relocation of the ownership of museums, returning them to the influence of the rich and powerful who have always controlled 'Culture'.

(Jenkinson 1993: 22)

Jenkinson then finishes his article by emphasising that 'access, quality and cultural diversity are the key issues as we move towards the next century' (ibid.: 23). These three issues have been the key issues throughout this discussion on marketing. Developing access, quality of service, and recognising the diversity of groups within society, are all the cornerstones of museum marketing. It is within the power of museums to construct culture, using people as critics and creators. It is within the power of museums to develop relationships with people, to collaborate and form partnerships to generate new ideas and new museum meanings. It is through marketing that museums can harness that power and ensure that the anxieties voiced by Jenkinson are redundant. As Lovelock and Weinberg comment:

Marketing provides the link or bridge between the organization and its environment. Marketing helps an institution to move away from bureaucratic inertia and move toward responsiveness to and anticipation of changing needs. As such, it helps an organization to fulfil its mission by keeping the institution relevant in a dynamic environment.

(Lovelock and Weinberg 1988: 429)

It is worth returning to the fundamentals of museum marketing at this stage to reflect on its future. At its most basic marketing is about an exchange. So what is the future of this exchange relationship? What benefits will the museum have to offer? Writing about American museums, although equally relevant for any museum, Nowlen suggests that, 'New majorities have appeared in major metropolitan areas and they are not European. Many have a different view of the material world, of the value of objects wrested from their context and of the idea of collecting itself' (Nowlen 1995: 25). These minority groups are rarely represented on the museum's management committees let alone the museum staff. Although many museums are attempting to enable these minorities to participate in the museum by recognising their historic role in the community, this participation is not equal, and tends to be a 'them' and 'us' situation.

Increasingly, the director's role is shaped towards fundraising and the requirement to take a keen interest in financial performance (Nowlen 1995). It can be argued that museums are now better managed, with great improvements in public service. At the same time museums are more widely held as educational institutions, with the number and quality of educational programmes expanding. Too often though the response to change in the museum environment is reaction rather than a fundamental shift in the museum's structure to reflect these new roles.

The values that museums offer in return are wide ranging. First they offer financial benefits in the guise of their economic impact in tourism spend. Compared to other tourist attractions, though, such as theme parks and casinos, which have significantly more substantial tourism benefits, the economic argument begins to pale.

Museums also offer in return an educational role. However, as the American Association of Museums' report, *Excellence and Equity* (1992) asserts, in order to fulfil this role, museums must reflect the cultural diversity of their local community and ensure that the interpretive process accounts for this variety of cultures. Moreover, decision-making in the museum should reflect a much wider involvement of the community, of people outside the museum. As Jenkinson asserts:

> We have to be able to accommodate the competing claims for history and provide a space for controversy, for the sorting out of disputes, in the very public forum of the museum. We have to become fully conscious of our own role as museum professionals in the process of cultural production and prepare for the surrender of all, or some, of our power, in the project of creating socially useful museums.
>
> (Jenkinson 1989: 151)

Nowlen puts forward a further benefit offered by museums, which,

> begins with the notion that what we know as museums are simply the largest and most public expression of a common, private and deep human need: to find meaning, to take comfort in, and to celebrate, moments of beauty, discovery, truth and happiness.
>
> (Nowlen 1995: 28)

Museums are intimately related to the needs expressed by every human being.

To respond to these needs the museum must consider the various issues which were considered in Chapter 1:

- Are museums about objects or experience?
- Does history exist and how does the museum respond to the reinterpretations of history?
- Is authenticity about objects or interpretation, or ultimately experience?
- Is there such a thing as reality, or are we surrounded by hyperreality?
- Is the divide between elitism and populism being eroded as many postmodernists assert?
- Can museums transcend self-definition that maintains transcendent categories and ethnocentric visions?
- Or do museums have a new identity, 'as places where meaning-making is imaginatively but responsibly managed' (Nowlen 1995: 29)?

These are ongoing debates which cannot be answered easily, if at all. They are, though, fundamental to an understanding of the relationship between the public and the museum. In order to serve society, museums must reflect that society (ICOM 1975). These debates are also inextricably linked to the environmental factors that impact on the museum. It is worth reflecting on future developments in the museum's environment.

In terms of demographics, Middleton (1990) summed up the changes as: more children and family groups; the growing importance of older people; a more affluent society, which is more educated and sophisticated; and growth prospects from tourism markets. More fundamentally, the attitudes of the public are changing. As Davies (1994a) suggests, museums should focus on segmenting children, day-trippers and local visitors. He warns that demand may only grow very slowly, a view confirmed in the UK by the British Tourist Authority's figures for 1994 (*Sightseeing in the UK* 1994), which indicate that museum visits increased by only 1 per cent.

Competition is on the increase between museums and other leisure attractions. Many museums, particularly municipal museums, are facing severe financial cutbacks and lack of support. This, though, can present museums with the opportunity to develop new practices and new partnerships (Hooper-Greenhill 1994). A quality and customer service culture can only benefit museums as well as their users. Attention to the needs and wants of users will be paramount in this new culture, yet will fulfil the museum's overall purpose. The preservation and conservation of material culture is itself a public service.

With the postmodern condition of de-differentiation, the tendency is towards globalisation and the breaking down of established hierarchies. Museums can play a significant role in reducing the high–low cultural divide (*Charter for the Arts in Scotland* 1993). They can also be enablers for asserting identity, be it national, regional or local. New majorities, such as African-Americans, are now the norm in many metropolitan areas of the US. With the development of supranational companies and supranational organisations

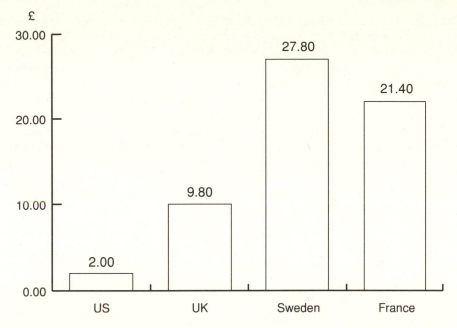

Figure 10.1 Public expenditure on the arts (pounds sterling per head of population)

Source: Data from A. Feist and R. Hutchison, *Cultural Trends 1990*: 5, Policy Studies Institute, 1990

such as the European Union, micro-nationalism or regional identities are strengthened, such as the Basques in Spain and the Scots and Welsh in the UK. There is a growing need for 'roots', for a sense of identity, which can be manifested in museums. The controversy over the Lewis Chessmen (loaned back to the Scottish island of Lewis for an exhibition in 1995 by the British Museum) is a case in point. The permanent 'repatriation' of these chess pieces is being sought by local Lewis people, who feel a sense of 'ownership' for their past.

Increasing awareness of environmental issues is also a fundamental concern of museums, which themselves have a 'green' consciousness. Preservation and conservation underpin these values, and offer museums the opportunity to promote their crucial role in society. Heritage is no longer merely the detritus of bygone ages, it is a manifestation of our current cultural condition.

The most significant threats to museums come from central and local government. The current political climate is one of short-term vision and lack of forward consensus. Museums may increasingly enhance their income through income generation and income development. However, few museums can survive without public subsidy or wealthy benefactors. Public expenditure varies widely throughout First World countries. Figure 10.1 illustrates central and local government expenditure on the arts per head in a number of countries, as outlined by Feist and Hutchison (1990).

221

These figures do not reveal indirect funding, but what they do reveal is the attitude of government to the provision of public service. Kevin Walsh (1992) contends that many governments are denying the public their democratic access to educative facilities. He demands that decision-making for cultural institutions should be made at the local level. This would require a structural change in the museum, one though that confirms the trend towards increased participation. Perhaps a fundamental shift is required; one that recognises the inalienable right of the public to museums. Partnership is the key here, partnership between the museum and its community. Partnership should also develop along the lines of integration, of both historical and ecological conservation. For example, archaeological sites should not be treated in isolation from their landscapes (Walsh, Kevin 1992). In Denmark, ancient monuments, wildlife, and landscape are protected by one law, the Conservation of Nature Act.

Technology may well be the factor that will offer museums the greatest opportunity to develop their social role. Scottish museums are leading the way in opening up their museums to everyone, regardless of any access issues. SCRAN, an initiative led by the Scottish Museums Council, has been awarded £7.5 million in the UK government's lottery. Through SCRAN up to 1.6 million documents and more than 100,000 image and sound files from Scotland's museums and art galleries are to be linked into a computer database. The director of the Scottish Museums Council was quoted as saying that, 'It will mean that everyone will have the same level of access to the wealth of culture preserved in Scotland's museums collections regardless of age, ability or status, and certainly regardless of where they live' (*The Scotsman*, 31 October 1995). Increasingly, diverse new products are tied to interactivity and virtually instant response time, such as interactive electronic games and educational CD-Roms. Computer technology is the future: it must also be the future of museums.

Museums are in flux, with new approaches emerging all the time. Museums must do more than just respond; they must anticipate. Museums cannot do this alone though, and this is where the future of marketing in museums demands a macro orientation to marketing. It is no longer enough to develop a marketing orientation in the individual museum – the task is much greater if the museum is to act truly for the public benefit. Inter-museum collaboration is the way forward, not only at the local level but also at the national and even international level. Museums need to work less in isolation, forming links with other leisure attractions, and developing stronger bonds with stakeholders.

In the UK the initiative can start with a more holistic approach guided by the Museums and Galleries Commission and Area Museum Councils. A national strategy for market research is required (Yorke and Jones 1984; McLean 1995), which collects and compares market research. The initiative and leadership need to be shown by these organisations.

FUTURE RESEARCH

Marketing implementation is based on a sound understanding of the museum's resources and environment. In order to develop an effective marketing plan, a museum needs sufficient information to keep abreast of changes in its resources and environment. To date, though, little significant research has been undertaken into many of the issues and challenges that concern museums in their marketing effort. The following are some suggestions for redressing this imbalance:

1   *Current practice of marketing in museums*
    Too little is known or shared within the museum community on successes and failures in marketing practice in museums. Studies need to be instigated into the state of marketing in museums, investigating current practice, and the degree of sophistication of marketing techniques used.

2   *Marketing tools*
    Each of the marketing tools as outlined in this book needs to be further tested in the museum situation. Some of the areas which were highlighted for further consideration in this book include the following, although there will be more issues that will also require closer examination.
    - Which are the most appropriate segmentation variables for museums?
    - What are the needs of tourists compared to the needs of the local community?
    - How useful are the concepts of branding and corporate identity for the individual museum?
    - How does the collection relate to society in marketing terms?
    - How can museums best develop partnerships and cooperate with other museums and leisure attractions?
    - What are the best methods in the museum context of dealing with stakeholders; developing income; communicating to the public?
    - How can museums attempt to measure 'experience'?
    - How does the portfolio of products offered by the museum create experience?
    - What means can be used to convert staff and other relevant publics to marketing?

3   *New marketing thinking*
    Museums need to be at the forefront of new marketing thinking. Clearly, relationship marketing and service quality, two new recent departures for discussion, are particularly relevant to museums. Each of these theories needs to be considered in more depth in the museum situation, their application assessed, and their relevance tested.

4   *Issues of museology*
    A number of issues concerned with the museum and its role in society need to be addressed if the goals that marketing sets out to achieve are to be clear and focused. A consensus needs to be found on how museums can educate a public.
    - How can education and entertainment be balanced?

- What is the relationship between a museum and society, and between its collection and society?
- What role does the museum play in contemporary society?
- What relevance does a museum have in the postmodern condition?

5   *The museum in postmodern society*
An appreciation of the museum in postmodern society is required. Marketers must look to other academic disciplines to assess the condition of contemporary society. Without this understanding, museum marketing will be left behind, developing strategies for a society that no longer exists. Social and cultural contexts need to be examined both from a museum and a marketing perspective.

CONCLUSION

Ultimately, it is the museum's vision that concerns marketing, its vision of its role in society and for society. The collection, the building, the staff, stakeholders, and public, all act as catalysts at the moment of encounter. In this the marketing and organisational machinery falls away and the individual takes possession of aspects of the collection in a manner that transcends literal ownership. The museum has the capacity to fulfil the individual. Marketing can enable this fulfilment.

Appendix 1
Sample questionnaire for self-completion

THE COMPUTER MUSEUM

The Computer Museum is anxious to keep improving its facilities and services for visitors. To help us we would appreciate a few minutes of your time to answer the following questions. Please circle your response unless otherwise stated.

1   **Have you been to the Computer Museum before?**

    Yes   1

    No   2

    If YES, how many times have you visited the museum in the last 12 months, including today's visit?

    Once   1   5–9 times   3

    2–4 times   2   10+ times   4

2   **How did you FIRST hear of this museum?**

    Poster   1

    Leaflet   2

    Advert/article in magazine/newspaper   3

    From friends/relatives   4

    Known from school/college visits   5

    Tourist information   6

    Saw it when passing by   7

    Other   8

3   **Are you visiting this museum by yourself or with someone?**

By myself   1

With my family   2

With friends/business associates   3

With an organised group   4

4   **How did you travel here today?**

| Car | 1 | Coach | 3 | Foot | 5 |
| Bus | 2 | Train | 4 | Other | 6 |

5   **Did you have any difficulty finding the museum?**

Yes   1

No   2

6   **How long have you spent in the museum today?**

10–20 minutes	1	1–2 hours	4
20–40 minutes	2	More than 2 hours	5
40–60 minutes	3		

7   **Which of the following areas of the museum have you visited today?**

The special temporary exhibition   1

The Computer Software Exhibition   2

The Computer Hardware Exhibition   3

The café   4

The shop   5

8   **What facilities are not included in the museum which you would use?**

Baby-changing facilities	1	
Audio-visual presentation	2	
Guide book	3	
Other	4	Please specify . . . .

9   How would you rate the following in the museum?

(Please indicate on a scale of 5 to 1, 5 being very satisfactory, 1 being very unsatisfactory.)

Presentation of exhibits	5	4	3	2	1
Signposting in the museum	5	4	3	2	1
The café	5	4	3	2	1
The shop	5	4	3	2	1

10   Do you find the present opening times convenient?

Yes   1

No   2

11   Which aspect of the museum did you find enjoyable or particularly interesting?

. . . .

. . . .

12   How likely are you to visit this museum again?

Very likely   5

Likely   4

Unlikely   3

Very unlikely   2

Don't know   1

13   Do you have any suggestions for improvement? . . . .

. . . .

FINALLY A FEW DETAILS ABOUT YOURSELF

14   Are you . . .

Male   1

Female   2

15   To which age group do you belong?

Under 16	1	25–34	4	55–64	7
16–18	2	35–44	5	65+	8
19–24	3	45–54	6		

16   Please state your occupation, being as specific as possible. If you are a
HOUSEWIFE, RETIRED or UNEMPLOYED please state your previous
occupation.

. . . .

Many thanks for completing this questionnaire.

Notes

INTRODUCTION

1 A number of heritage centres that do not possess permanent collections refer to themselves as museums.
2 Throughout this book 'museum' is taken to include 'art gallery'.
3 Refer to *The Art Newspaper*, issues May 1991, February 1992, and May 1992, which feature the case of the Barnes Foundation. Barnes's will stipulated the maintenance of limited access to the museum by the public, banned all social events on the premises, and forbade the selling of any works of art.

1 THE MUSEUM CONTEXT

1 Note the reverence for the god-like 'Collection' in the 1920s.
2 The Museums and Galleries Commission was created by the UK government in 1981. It assumed a number of executive functions from its predecessor, the Standing Commission on Museums and Galleries, established in 1931. Since 1987 the Museums and Galleries Commission has achieved grant-in-aid status. It also acts as an advisory body to the museum community.

The first Area Museum Councils were established in 1959 and 1961, and by 1966 the whole of mainland Britain was covered. They are not statutory bodies, but are the result of voluntary agreements by representatives of museums and the organisations that run them. Since 1964 the UK government has provided the Area Museum Councils with sums of money which must be matched locally. They also act as advisory bodies to their local museum community.
3 The registration scheme has been in place in the UK since 1988. Museums that meet minimum standards as laid out by the Museums and Galleries Commission are entitled to be registered as a 'museum'. The main advantage of being recognised under the registration scheme is that the museum automatically becomes eligible for grant-aid and subsidised services from the Museums and Galleries Commission and the Area Museum Councils. It also presents museums with the opportunity to raise their profile through publicising their registered status and to foster confidence with other stakeholders such as the tourist boards.
4 With reference to a lecture on the new Sainsbury Wing at the National Gallery, given by Michael Wilson, designer, at Newcastle Polytechnic, Newcastle-upon-Tyne, on 14 November 1991, in which he described the techniques pursued for designing the gallery, from which it was apparent that the curatorial input was paramount.

2 THE MARKETING CONTEXT

1 The debate was played out in a series of articles on 'Scholarship in Museums' in *RSA Journal*, February 1991, particularly, N. Cossons, 'Scholarship and the Public', pp. 184–91, and N. MacGregor, 'Scholarship or Self-indulgence?', pp. 191–4.
2 See K. Marx, 'Capital: A critique of political economy, Volume 1', for an explanation of the concept of 'surplus value'.

3 THE MUSEUM'S ENVIRONMENT

1 For example, in the UK, the Policy Studies Institute publishes regular studies of cultural trends in their *Cultural Trends* publications, while the Henley Centre for Forecasting publishes a quarterly report, *Leisure Futures*. The tourist boards also keep up-to-date records on developments in the tourism market, while more local information is available from area tourist boards. *Sightseeing in the UK: Tourist Intelligence Quarterly* is also produced annually by the British Tourist Authority and the English Tourist Board. Other publications, such as Middleton's *New Visions for Independent Museums* (1990), and the extremely useful analysis of the market potential for museums in the UK, *By Popular Demand*, compiled by Davies (1994a), are invaluable, since they attempt to extrapolate the implications of the trends specifically for museums.

4 MUSEUMS AND THE PUBLIC

1 In the UK, the Museums and Galleries Commission appointed a disability adviser in 1989 and has published a *Disability Resource Directory for Museums* (1993), which gives valuable advice, as does their *Guidelines on Disability for Museums and Galleries* (1991). The Museums and Galleries Disability Association (MAGDA), founded in 1986 to provide a focus for work on provision for people with disabilities, has produced a set of notes on design for disability (Forrester *et al.* 1988), while the ADAPT fund, administered by the Carnegie UK Trust, offers assistance with the adaptation of buildings.

5 THE MUSEUM'S MARKETS

1 In the UK, the JICNARS system divides people into social categories A (upper middle class), B (middle class), C1 (lower middle class), C2 (skilled working class), D (working class), and E (those at lowest subsistence level). Another system which is commonly used is ACORN, which uses census data and postcodes to define different types of postal addresses according to the types of dwelling and the social status of those likely to be living in them. The ACORN system, published by CACI Information Services, is grouped from A to J, under such categories as agricultural areas, modern family housing with higher incomes, and older housing of intermediate status. The Arts Council of England uses the Target Group Index (TGI) to include questions on the arts. The TGI offers both ABCDE and ACORN information on users of art galleries, which can also offer an extremely useful starting point for museums.

7 COMMUNICATING THE MUSEUM PRODUCT

1 In the UK, for example, *British Rate and Data* is published monthly and is usually available at most public libraries. The *UK Media Directory* gives readership figures, but does not include costs.

8 RESOURCE ATTRACTION

1 In the UK, for example, some grants are available from the Museums Association, which manages the Beecroft Bequest, Daphne Bullard Trust, and Kathy Callow Trust Benevolent Fund. The Museums and Galleries Commission Improvement Fund is matched by funding from the Wolfson Foundation, while the Museums and Galleries Commission Purchase Grant Funds covers the arts with the MGC–V&A arts fund, and industry and science with the Preservation and Industrial Material (PRISM) fund. Other assistance towards purchase includes the National Heritage Memorial Fund, the National Arts Collections Fund and the National Fund for Acquisitions (Scotland). An alternative is Acceptance in Lieu, or the more recent Foundation for Sports and the Arts (a fund run by pools companies), and the National Lottery. The Heritage Lottery Fund awards have included £250,000 towards two permanent exhibitions at Catalyst: The Museum of the Chemical Industry, and £419,000 to the Dundee Heritage Trust to establish the Verdant Works Jute Museum (*Museums Journal*, June 1995).

As a reference for potential donors in the UK, *The Arts Funding Guide* (Doulton 1992) provides useful information on over 200 companies and 180 trusts that give money to the arts. It gives a clear outline of the funding possibilities for the arts, including museums. It also gives guidelines on how to solve funding problems, and gives examples of previous funding received from arts organisations.

References

Adam, T. R. (1939) *The Museum and Popular Culture*, Arlington, VA: American Association for Adult Education.

Adams, G. and Boatright, J. (1986) 'The Selling of the Museum', *Museum News* 64, 4: 16–21.

Adams, G. D. (1995) 'Cultural Tourism: The arrival of the intelligent traveller', *Museum News*, November–December: 32–7.

Addison, E. (1986) 'Is Marketing a Threat ... Or is it the greatest challenge that museums have ever faced?', *Muse*, Summer: 28–31.

—— (1993) 'Museum Marketing: A tool for survival', *Muse* XI, 2: 2–4.

Adorno, T. and Horkheimer, M. (1979) *Dialectic of Enlightenment*, trans. J. Cumming, London: Verso.

Ambrose, T. (1987) *New Museums: A start-up guide*, Edinburgh: Scottish Museums Council and HMSO.

American Association of Museums (1984) *Museums for a New Century*, Washington DC: American Association of Museums.

—— (1992) *Excellence and Equity: Education and the public dimension of museums*, Washington DC: American Association of Museums.

Ames, M. M. (1986) *Museums, The Public and Anthropology: A study in the anthropology of anthropology*, Vancouver and Delhi: University of British Columbia Press and Concept Publishing Company.

—— (1992) *Cannibal Tours and Glass Boxes: The anthropology of museums*, Vancouver: UBC Press.

Ames, P. J. (1988) 'A Challenge to Modern Museum Management: Meshing mission and market', *International Journal of Museum Management and Curatorship* 7, 2: 151–7.

—— (1989) 'Marketing in Museums: Means or master of the mission?', *Curator* 32, 1: 5–15.

—— (1990) 'Breaking New Ground: Measuring museums' merits', *International Journal of Museum Management and Curatorship* 9, 2: 137–47.

—— (1993) 'Effective Education for Everyone', *Museums Journal* 93, 5: 29–31.

Andreasen, A. R. (1982) 'Nonprofits: Check your attention to customers', *Harvard Business Review*, May–June: 105–10.

Ansoff, I. (1957) 'Strategies for Diversification', *Harvard Business Review*, September–October: 113–24.

Armistead, C. G. (1988) *Operations Management in Service Industries in the Public Sector*, West Sussex: Wiley.

Arts Council of Great Britain (1991) *Marketing the Arts: National Strategy discussion document*, London: Arts Council of Great Britain.

—— (1992) *Very Spaghetti: The potential of interactive multimedia in art galleries*, London: Arts Council of Great Britain.

—— (1993) *Marketing the Visual Arts*, London: Arts Council of Great Britain.

Ashley, R. (1989) 'Visitor Activity Management: A new approach to marketing for non-profit institutions', National Historic Parks and Sites Service. Presented at the Royal Ontario Museum, November.

Audit Commission (1991) *The Road to Wigan Pier?: Managing local authority museums and art galleries*, London: The Audit Commission for Local Authorities and the National Health Service in England and Wales.

Bailey, S. (1995) 'Feeling the Squeeze', *Museums Journal 95*, 4: 33.

Baker, M. J. (1987) 'One More Time – What is Marketing?' in M. J. Baker (ed.) *The Marketing Book*, London: Heinemann.

Baker, M. J. and Hart, S. J. (1989) *Marketing and Competitive Success*, Hemel Hempstead: Philip Allan.

Baker, N. (1991) 'Communicating the Character', *Museums Journal 91*, 3: 23–5.

Banks, J. A. (1957) 'The Group Discussion as an Interview Technique', *Sociological Review 5*, 1: 75–84.

Bartels, R. (1974) 'The Identity Crisis in Marketing', *Journal of Marketing 38*: 73–6.

Bateson, J. E. G. (1989) *Managing Services Marketing*, Orlandon, Fl.: Dryden.

Baudrillard, J. (1983) *Simulations*, New York: Semiotext(e).

Bazin, G. (1967) *The Museum Age*, Brussels: Desoer S. A. Publishers.

Beard, M. and Henderson, J. (1992) 'Deconstructing or Demolition: The chicken', *Museums Journal 92*, 12: 20.

Berry, L. L. and Parasuraman, A. (1991) *Marketing Services: Competing through quality*, New York: The Free Press.

Birney, B. (1986) 'A comparative study of children's perceptions and knowledge of wildlife and conservation as they relate to field trip experience at the Los Angeles County Museum of Natural History and the Los Angeles Zoo', unpublished PhD thesis, University of California at Los Angeles.

Bitner, M. J., Booms, B. H., and Tetreault, M. S. (1990) 'The Service Encounter: Diagnosing favorable and unfavorable incidents', *Journal of Marketing 54*, January: 71–84.

Bogaart, N. C. R. (1978) 'Reality in Motion: Audio-visuals as a means of transmitting information in museums', in G. Morley (ed.) *Visualization of Theoretical Concepts in Anthropology in Museums of Ethnography*, New Delhi: National Museum of Natural History.

Bonniface, P. and Fowler, P. J. (1993) *Heritage and Tourism in 'the Global Village'*, London: Routledge.

Bonoma, T. V. (1984) *Managing Marketing*, New York: The Free Press.

Booms, B. H. and Bitner, M. J. (1981) 'Marketing Strategies and Organisation Structures for Service Firms', in J. Donnelly and W. R. George (eds) *Marketing of Services*, Chicago: American Marketing Association.

Boorstin, D. (1964) *The Image: A guide to pseudo-events in America*, New York: Harper.

Booth, B. (1995) 'Webbed Feat Further the Cause of Science', *Museums Journal*, 95, 8: 24.

Borden, N. H. (1965) 'The Concept of the Marketing Mix', in G. Schwartz (ed.) *Science in Marketing*, Ontario: J. Wiley and Sons.

Borg, A. (1984) 'Outstations and their Management', in N. Cossons (ed.) *The*

Management of Change in Museums, proceedings of a seminar held at the National Maritime Museum, Greenwich, London, on 22 November.

Bourdieu, P. (1984) *Distinction*, London: Routledge & Kegan Paul.

Bowen, J. (1995) 'Collection of Collections', *Museums Journal 95*, 8: 24–5.

Boyne, R. and Rattansi, A. (1990) 'The Theory and Politics of Postmodernism: By way of an introduction', in R. Boyne and A. Rattansi (eds) *Postmodernism and Society*, Basingstoke: Macmillan.

Bradford, H. (1991) 'A New Framework for Museum Marketing', in G. Kavanagh (ed.) *The Museums Profession: Internal and external relations*, Leicester: Leicester University Press.

Brady, J. and Davis, I. (1993) 'Marketing's Mid-life Crisis', *McKinsey Quarterly* 2: 17–28.

Brawne, M. (1965) *The New Museum*, New York: Frederick A. Praeger.

Brown, S. (1995) *Postmodern Marketing*, London: Routledge.

Bryant, J. (1988) *The Principles of Marketing: A guide for museums*, West Sussex: Association of Independent Museums Guideline No. 16.

Burgess, R. G. (1982) 'Multiple Strategies in Field Research', in R. G. Burgess (ed.) *Field Research: A sourcebook and field manual*, London: George Allen & Unwin.

Butler, P. (1993) 'The Way Ahead for Museum Retailing', *Museum Development*, May: 21–4.

Cameron, D. F. (1971) 'The Museum, a Temple or the Forum', *Curator* 14, 1: 11–24.

Carlzon, J. (1987) *Moments of Truth*, Cambridge, MA: Ballinger.

Carmen, J. M. and Langeard, E. (1980) 'Growth Strategies of Service Firms', *Strategic Management Journal* 1, January–March: 7–22.

Carnegie, E. (1994) 'Natural Creation', *Museums Journal* 94, 9: 32–3.

Carrington, L. (1995) 'Power to the People', *Museums Journal* 95, 11: 21–4.

Chandler, M. (1954) 'An Evaluation of the Group Interview', *Human Organization* 13, 2: 26–8.

Charter for the Arts in Scotland (1993), Edinburgh: HMSO.

Cheek, N. H., Field, D. R., and Burdge, R. (1976) *Leisure and Recreation Places*, Ann Arbor, MI: Ann Arbor Science Publications.

Christopher, M., Payne, A., and Ballantyne, D. (1991) *Relationship Marketing: Bringing quality, customer service, and marketing together*, Oxford: Butterworth Heinemann.

Claxton, J. D., Fry, J. N., and Portis, B. (1974) 'A Taxonomy of Prepurchase Information Gathering Patterns', *Journal of Consumer Research*, December: 35–42.

Cohen, E. (ed.) (1979) 'Sociology of Tourism', *Annals of Tourism Research* 9, 1.

Conybeare, C. (1991) *Museum Visitor Surveys: A practical guide*, Taunton: Area Museum Council for the South West.

Cordrey, T. (1995) 'What Are Friends For?', *Museums Journal* 95, 10: 19–20.

Cossons, N. (1991) 'Scholarship or Self-indulgence?', *RSA Journal* CXXXIX, 5415: 184–91.

Costa, J. A. and Bamossy, G. J. (1995) 'Culture and the Marketing of Culture: The museum retail context', in J. A. Costa and G. J. Bamossy (eds) *Marketing in a Multicultural World: Ethnicity, nationalism, and cultural identity*, Thousand Oaks, California: Sage.

Coutts, H. (1988) 'A Tale of Three Projects', *Museums Journal* 88, 3: 132–4.

—— (1989) 'The Midas Touch: The economic impact of "Gold of the Pharaohs"', *Museums Journal* 89, 6: 25–7.

Cowell, D. W. (1984) *The Marketing of Services*, Oxford: Butterworth Heinemann.

—— (1994) 'Marketing of Services', in M. J. Baker (ed.) *The Marketing Book*, 3rd edition, Oxford: Butterworth Heinemann.

Crosby, P. B. (1984) *Quality Without Tears*, New York: New American Library.

Crowther, P. (1990) 'Postmodernism in the Visual Arts: A question of ends?', in R. Boyne and A. Rattansi (eds) *Postmodernism and Society*, Basingstoke: Macmillan.

Czeipel, J. A., Solomon, M. R., and Suprenant, C. F. (1985) *The Service Encounter*, Lexington, Mass.: Lexington Books.

Davies, M. (1990) 'Admission Charges Report "Totally Misconceived"', *Museums Journal* 90, 2: 8.

Davies, S. (1993) 'Victorian Values in Victorian Buildings? The Museums Profession in Crisis', proceedings of a conference on 'Professionalism and Management in Britain', University of Stirling, 26–28 August.

—— (1994a) *By Popular Demand: A strategic analysis of the marketing potential for museums and art galleries in the UK*, London: Museums and Galleries Commission.

—— (1994b) 'Back to Basics: II', *Museums Journal* 94, 9: 20–2.

Davis, D. L., Guiltinan, J. P., and Jones, W. H. (1979) 'Service Characteristics, Consumer Search and the Classification of Retail Services', *Journal of Retailing* 55, 3: 3–23.

Derrida, J. (1981) *Positions*, Chicago: University of Chicago Press.

Diai, R. (1994) 'Marketing and the UK Heritage Industry: The museum as a case study', unpublished MBA dissertation, University of Leeds.

Dibb, S. and Simkin, L. (1993) 'Strategy and Tactics: Marketing leisure facilities', *Service Industries Journal* 13, 3: 110–24.

Dibb, S., Simkin, L., Pride, W. M., and Ferrell, O. C. (1991) *Marketing: Concepts and strategies*, European edition, Boston: Houghton Mifflin Company.

Dickinson, R. A., Herbst, A., and O'Shaughnessy, J. (1986) 'Marketing Concept and Customer Orientation', *European Journal of Marketing* 20, 10: 18–23.

Diggle, K. (1984) *Guide to Arts Marketing*, London: Rhinegold.

—— (1995) 'Charging Ahead', *Museums Journal* 95, 4: 32–3.

DiMaggio, P. J. (1985) 'When the "Profit" is Quality: Cultural institutions in the marketplace', *Museum News* 63, 5: 28–35.

Doulton, A.-M. (1992) *The Arts Funding Guide*, London: Directory of Social Change.

Drucker, P. (1954) *The Practice of Management*, Oxford: Butterworth Heinemann.

—— (1973) *Management: Tasks, responsibilities and practices*, New York: Harper & Row.

—— (1990) *Managing the Non-Profit Organization*, Oxford: Butterworth Heinemann.

Duchesne, R., Fabry, P., and Hardy, R. (1988) 'Developing an Effective Marketing Function', *GMPSM Newsletter Supplement*.

Duncan, D. J. (1978) 'Leisure Types: Factor analyses of leisure profiles', *Journal of Leisure Research* 10: 113–25.

Durrans, B. (1988) 'The Future of the Other: Changing cultures on display in ethnographic museums', in R. Lumley (ed.) *The Museum Time-Machine: Putting cultures on display*, London: Comedia and Routledge.

Dwyer, F. R., Schurr, P. H., and Oh, S. (1987) 'Developing Buyer–Seller Relationships', *Journal of Marketing* 51, April: 11–27.

Eckstein, J. (ed.) (1993) *Cultural Trends Issue 19*, London: Policy Studies Institute.

Edwards, N. (1995) 'Sleuths in Sauchiehall Street', *Museums Journal 95*, 11: 22.

Elliott, R., Eccles, S., and Hodgson, M. (1993) 'Re-coding Gender Representations: Women, cleaning products and advertising's "new man"', *International Journal of Research in Marketing 10*, 3: 311–24.

Falconer, H. (1995) 'More Than Just a Job', *Museums Journal 95*, 9: 21–3.

Falk, J. H. and Dierking, L. D. (1992) *The Museum Experience*, Washington DC: Whalesback Books.

Featherstone, M. (1988) 'In Pursuit of the Postmodern: An introduction', in M. Featherstone (ed.) *Postmodernism*, London: Sage.

Feifer, M. (1985) *Going Places*, London: Macmillan.

Feist, A. and Hutchison, R. (eds) (1990) *Cultural Trends 1990: 5*, London: Policy Studies Institute.

Fewster, C. (1992) 'Sound Advice', *Museums Journal 92*, 5: 20–1.

Fine, S. H. (1981) *The Marketing of Ideas and Social Issues*, New York: Praier.

Firat, A. F. (1991) 'Postmodern Culture, Marketing, and the Consumer', in T. L. Childers *et al.* (eds) *Marketing Theory and Applications, Volume 2*, Chicago: American Marketing Association.

Firat, A. F. and Venkatesh, A. (1993) 'Postmodernity: The age of marketing', *International Journal of Research in Marketing 10*, 3: 227–49.

Firat, A. F., Dholakia, N., and Venkatesh, A. (1995) 'Marketing in a Postmodern World', *European Journal of Marketing 29*, 1: 40–56.

Fish, S. (1989) *Doing What Comes Naturally*, Durham, NC: Duke University Press.

Fleming, D. (1991) 'Immaculate Collections, Speculative Conceptions', *International Journal of Museum Management and Curatorship 10*, 3: 263–72.

Flipo, J. P. (1988) 'On the Intangibility of Services', *Service Industries Journal 8*, 3: 286–98.

Forrester, W., Thorpe, S., and Kirby, W. (1988) *Disability Design Museums*, London: Museums and Galleries Disability Association and GDIM.

Foxall, G. R. (1984) 'Marketing's Domain', *European Journal of Marketing 18*, 1: 25–40.

Frank, R. and Wind, Y. (1972) *Market Segmentation*, Englewood Cliffs, NJ: Prentice-Hall.

Fronville, C. L. (1985) 'Marketing for Museums: For-profit techniques in a non-profit world', *Curator 28*, 3: 169–82.

George, W. R. and Berry, L. L. (1981) 'Guidelines for Advertising of Services', *Business Horizons*, July–August: 52–6.

George, W. R. and Kelly, J. P. (1983) 'The Promotion and Selling of Services', *Business*, July–September: 14–20.

Goldshlag Cooks, R. (1994) 'Treating Disease', *Museums Journal 94*, 9: 29–31.

Govoni, N., Galpes, R., and Galpes, M. (1986) *Promotional Management*, Englewood Cliffs, NJ: Prentice-Hall.

Graburn, N. H. H. (1977) 'The Museum and the Visitor Experience', 'The Visitor and the Museum', proceedings of the 72nd Annual Conference of the American Association of Museums, Seattle, WA.

Griggs, S. A. (1992) *Evaluating Museum Displays*, Committee of Area Museum Councils Museum Factsheet, Cirencester: Committee of Area Museum Councils.

Grönroos, C. (1982) *Strategic Management and Marketing in the Service Sector*, Research Report 8, Helsingfors: Swedish School of Economics and Business Administration.

—— (1984) *Strategic Management and Marketing in the Service Sector*, Bromley, Kent: Chartwell-Bratt.

—— (1990) *Service Management and Marketing: Managing the moments of truth in service competition*, Lexington, Mass.: Lexington Books.

Guédon, M.-F. (1983) 'A Case of Mistaken Identity: The education of a naïve museum ethnologist', in F. Manning (ed.) *Consciousness and Inquiry: Ethnology and Canadian realities*, Ottawa: National Museums of Canada.

Guiltinan, J. P. and Paul, G. W. (1988) *Marketing Management: Strategies and programs*, 3rd edition, New York: McGraw-Hill.

Gummesson, E. (1991) 'Marketing-Orientation Revisited: The crucial role of the part-time marketer', *European Journal of Marketing* 25, 2: 60–75.

Gwyther, M. (1988) 'State of the Art in PR', *Business*, February: 44.

Haley, R. I. (1968) 'Benefit Segmentation: A decision-oriented research tool', *Journal of Marketing* July: 30–5.

Hall, L. (1995) 'All For Love', *Museums Journal* 95, 10: 25–8.

Hall, M. (1987) *On Display: A design grammar for museums*, London: Lund Humphries.

Halpin, M. M. (1978) 'Review of "The 12,000 Year Gap: Archaeology in British Columbia" and "First Peoples: Indian cultures in British Columbia" at the British Columbia Provincial Museum', *Gazette*, Canadian Museums Association 11, 1: 40–8.

Hannagan, T. J. (1992) *Marketing in the Public and Non-Profit Sector*, Basingstoke, Hampshire: Macmillan Press Ltd.

Harvey, A. L. (1992) 'Money Changers in the Temple?', *Museum News*, November–December: 38–43.

Harvey Jones, J. (1988) *Making It Happen: Reflections on Leadership*, London: Collins.

Heaton, D. (1992) *Museums among Friends: The wider museum community*, London: HMSO.

Hemmings, S. (1992) 'Chinese Homes', *Journal of Education in Museums* 13: 33–4.

Henley Centre (1989) 'The Discerning Consumer', *Leisure Management* 9, 5: 34–6.

Hewison, R. (1987) *The Heritage Industry: Britain in a Climate of Decline*, London: Methuen.

Hiemstra, R. (1981) 'The State of the Art', in Z. Collins (ed.) *Museums, Adults and the Humanities*, Washington, DC: American Association of Museums.

Hodge, R. and d'Souza, W. (1979) 'The Museum as a Communicator: A semiotic analysis of the Western Australian Museum Aboriginal Gallery, Perth', *Museum* 31, 4: 251–67.

Hoffins, S. (1992) *Multimedia and the Interactive Display in Museums, Exhibitions and Libraries*, Libraries and information research report, Wetherby, W. Yorks.: British Library.

Holman, R. H. and Wilson, R. D. (1982) 'Temporal Equilibrium as a Basis for Retail Shopping Behaviour', *Journal of Retailing* 58, 1: 58–81.

Hood, M. G. (1983) 'Staying Away: Why people choose not to visit museums', *Museum News* 61, 4: 50–7.

Hooper-Greenhill, E. (1994) *Museums and their Visitors*, London: Routledge.

Horne, D. (1984) *The Great Museum*, London: Pluto.

Houston, F. S. and Gassenheimer, J. B. (1987) 'Marketing and Exchange', *Journal of Marketing* 50, April: 81–7.

Hudson, K. (1975) *A Social History of Museums*, London: Macmillan.

—— (1977) *Museums for the 1980s: A survey of world trends*, London: Macmillan.

Huie, J. (1985) 'Understanding the New Breed of Consumer', in J. Gattorna (ed.) *Insights in Strategic Retail Management*, Bradford: MCB.

ICOM (1974, 1987) Definition of a 'Museum'. Incorporated in the Statutes of the International Council of Museums and adopted at the 11th General Assembly of ICOM in Copenhagen in 1974.

—— (1975) *The Museum and the Modern World*, Paris: ICOM.

Jameson, F. (1985) 'Postmodernism and Consumer Society', in H. Foster (ed.) *Postmodern Culture*, London: Pluto.

Janna, H. (1981) *The Role of Cultural Aims in Social and Economic Development*, Strasbourg: Council of Europe.

Jelinek, M., Smirich, L., and Hirsch, P. (1983) 'Introduction: A code of many colours', *Administrative Science Quarterly* 28: 337.

Jenkinson, P. (1989) 'Material Culture, People's History and Populism: Where do we go from here?', in S. Pearce (ed.) *Museum Studies in Material Culture*, Leicester: Leicester University Press.

—— (1993) 'Museum Futures', *Museums Journal* 93, 7: 22–3.

Johnson, S. (1755) *A Dictionary of the English Language*, London: W. Strahan, for J. and P. Knapton.

Jones, D. (1992) 'Dealing with the Past', *Museums Journal* 92, 1: 24–7.

Jones, D. G. B. and Monieson, D. D. (1990) 'Early Development of the Philosophy of Marketing Thought', *Journal of Marketing* 54, January: 102–13.

Jordanova, L. (1989) 'Objects of Knowledge: A historical perspective on museums', in P. Vergo (ed.) *The New Museology*, London: Reaktion Books.

Kelly, R. F. (1991) 'The Enemy Within . . . Marketing in the Arts', proceedings of the First International Conference on Arts Management, University of British Columbia, August.

Key, A. F. (1973) *Beyond Four Walls: The origin and development of Canadian museums*, Toronto: McClelland & Stewart.

King, S. (1991) 'Brand Building in the 1990s', *Journal of Marketing Management* 7: 6.

Kirby, S. (1988) 'Policy and Politics: Charges, sponsorship and bias', in R. Lumley (ed.) *The Museum Time-Machine: Putting cultures on display*, London: Comedia and Routledge.

Klein, M. and Lewis, R. C. (1985) 'Personal Constructs Theory: A foundation for deriving tangible surrogates in services marketing', in M. Bloch, G. D. Upah, and V. A. Zeithaml (eds) *Services Marketing in a Changing Environment*, Proceedings series, Chicago: American Marketing Association.

Klemm, M. and Wilson, N. (1993) *An Analysis of the Workforce in the Museums, Galleries and Heritage Sector in the UK*, Bradford: Museums Training Institute.

Kohli, A. K. and Jaworski, B. J. (1990) 'Market Orientation: The construct, research propositions and management implications', *Journal of Marketing* 54, April: 1–18.

Kotler, P. (1967) *Marketing Management: Analysis, planning, implementation and control*, Englewood Cliffs, NJ: Prentice-Hall.

—— (1972) 'A Generic Concept of Marketing', *Journal of Marketing* 36, April: 46–54.

—— (1973) 'Atmospherics as a Competitive Tool', *Journal of Retailing*, Winter: 48–64.

—— (1977) 'From Sales Obssession to Marketing Effectiveness', *Harvard Business Review*, November–December: 67–75.

—— (1991) *Marketing Management: Analysis, planning, implementation and control*, Englewood Cliffs, NJ: Prentice-Hall.

Kotler, P. and Andreasen, A. R. (1987) *Strategic Marketing for Nonprofit Organizations*, 3rd edition, Englewood Cliffs, NJ: Prentice-Hall.

Kotler, P. and Levy, S. J. (1969) 'Broadening the Concept of Marketing', *Journal of Marketing* 33, January: 10–15.

Lambuth, L. (1995) 'AMIE Awards', *Museum News*, September–October: 28.

Laufer, R. and Paradeise, C. (1990) *Marketing Democracy: Public opinion and media formation in democratic societies*, New Brunswick: Transaction Publishers.

Lavidge, R. J. and Steiner, G. A. (1961) 'A Model for Predictive Measurements of Advertising Effectiveness', *Journal of Marketing* 25, October: 61–5.

Leishman, M. (1993) 'Image and Self Image', *Museums Journal* 93, 6: 30–2.

Lewis, P. (1988) 'Marketing to the Local Community', *Museums Journal* 88, 3: 147–9.

—— (1991) 'The Role of Marketing: Its fundamental planning function: devising a strategy', in T. Ambrose and S. Runyard (eds) *Forward Planning*, London: Museums and Galleries Commission and Routledge.

Linenthal, E. T. (1995) *Preserving Memory: The struggle to create America's Holocaust Museum*, New York: Viking Penguin.

Lockett, C. (1991) 'Ten Years of Exhibit Evaluation at the Royal Ontario Museum (1980–1990)', *ILVS Review: a Journal of Visitor Behaviour* 2, 1: 19–47.

Lord, R., Dexter Lord, G., and Nicks, J. H. (1989) *The Cost of Collecting: Collection management in UK museums*, London: HMSO.

Lorente, P. (1995) 'The City's Beating Art', *Museums Journal* 95, 10: 29–30.

Lovelock, C. H. (1984) *Services Marketing*, Englewood Cliffs, NJ: Prentice-Hall.

—— (1992) 'Seeking Synergy in Service Operations: Seven things marketers need to know about service operations', *European Management Journal* 10, 1: 22–9.

Lovelock, C. H. and Weinberg, C. B. (1988) *Public and Nonprofit Marketing*, 2nd edition, The Scientific Press Series, Danvers, Mass: Boyd & Fraser.

Lowenthal, D. (1985) *The Past is a Foreign Country*, Cambridge: Cambridge University Press.

Lumley, R. (ed.) (1988) *The Museum Time-Machine: Putting cultures on display*, London: Comedia and Routledge.

McCann, Matthews, & Millman (1993) *Marketing Planning: An action guide*, London: Arts Council of Great Britain.

MacCannell, D. (1976) *The Tourist: A new theory of the leisure class*, London: Macmillan.

McCarthy, E. J. (1981) *Basic Marketing: A managerial approach*, Homewood, Ill.: Richard D. Irwin.

McCracken, G. (1990) 'Matching Material Cultures: Person–object relations inside and outside the ethnographic museum', in R. W. Belk (ed.) *Advances in Nonprofit Marketing*, Volume 3, Greenwich, Conn.: JAI Press.

McDonald, M. H. B. (1989a) *Marketing Plans: How to Prepare Them, How to Use Them*, 2nd edition, London: Heinemann.

—— (1989b) 'Ten Barriers to Marketing Planning', *Journal of Marketing Management* 5, 1: 1–18.

McDonald, M. and Dunbar, I. (1995) *Market Segmentation: A step-by-step approach to creating profitable market segments*, Basingstoke: Macmillan.

Macdonald, S. (1988) 'Dusting Down the V & A's Image', *Marketing Week* 4, November: 29.

MacDonald, S. (1992) 'Cultural Imagining among Museum Visitors', *Museum Management and Curatorship* 12: 367–80.

McGinnis, R. (1994) 'The Disabling Society', *Museums Journal* 94, 6: 27–33.

McGoldrick, P. J. (1990) *Retail Marketing*, Maidenhead, Berks: McGraw-Hill.

MacGregor, N. (1991) 'Scholarship and the Public', *RSA Journal* CXXXIX, 5415: 191–4.

McLean, F. (née Matheson, F.) (1992) 'Museum Policy and Marketing Strategies', unpublished PhD thesis, Newcastle-upon-Tyne Polytechnic.

McLean, F. (1993) 'Marketing in Museums: A contextual analysis', *Museum Management and Curatorship* 12, 1: 11–27.

—— (1994) 'Services Marketing: The case of museums', *The Service Industries Journal* 14, 2: 190–203.

—— (1995) 'A Marketing Revolution in Museums?', *Journal of Marketing Management* 11: 601–16.

McManus, P. M. (1991) 'Making Sense of Exhibits', in G. Kavanagh (ed.) *Museum Languages: Objects and texts*, Leicester: Leicester University Press.

Marsan, G. A. (1993a) 'Measure the Ecstasy', *Museums Journal* 93, 7: 27–8.

—— (1993b) 'Market Values', *Museums Journal* 93, 12: 31–3.

Marx, K. (1976) *Capital: A critique of political economy, Volume 1*, Harmondsworth: Penguin.

Maslow, A. H. (1970) *Motivation and Personality*, 2nd edition, New York: Harper & Row.

Mayo, E. P. (1992) 'Exhibiting Politics', *Museum News*, September–October: 50–1.

Mennell, S. (1976) *Cultural Policy in Towns*, Strasbourg: Council of Europe.

Mergolis, J. (1988) 'The Idea of an Art Museum', in L. Aagard-Mogensen (ed.) *The Idea of the Museum: Philosophical, artistic and political questions*, Queenston, Ontario: The Edwin Mellen Press.

Merriman, N. (1989) 'Museum Visiting as a Cultural Phenomenon', in P. Vergo (ed.) *The New Museology*, London: Reaktion Books.

—— (1991) *Beyond the Glass Case: The past, the heritage and the public in Britain*, Leicester: Leicester University Press.

—— (1995) 'Exploding the Immigration Myths', *Museums Journal* 95, 11: 23.

Middleton, V. T. C. (1985) 'Visitor Expectations of Museums' in Scottish Museums Council, *Museums Are for People*, Edinburgh: HMSO.

—— (1990) *New Visions for Independent Museums in the UK*, West Sussex: Association of Independent Museums.

Millard, J. (1992) 'Art History for All the Family', *Museums Journal* 92, 2: 32–4.

Mintz, A. (1994) 'That's Edutainment!', *Museum News*, November–December: 32–5.

Moore, K. (1993) 'Open House, Open Mind', *Museums Journal* 93, 3: 19.

Moore, K. and Tucker, D. (1994) 'Back to Basics', *Museums Journal* 94, 7: 22.

Moore, R. (1988) 'Research Surveys', *Museums Journal* 88, 3: 119–21.

Morris, B. (1990) 'Introduction', *Museums and Galleries Commission Annual Report 1989–90*, London: Museums and Galleries Commission.

Morton, A. (1988) 'Tomorrow's Yesterdays: Science museums and the future', in R. Lumley (ed.) *The Museum Time-Machine: Putting cultures on display*, London: Comedia and Routledge.

Mudie, P. and Cottam, A. (1993) *The Management and Marketing of Services*, Oxford: Butterworth Heinemann.

Munley, M. E. (1986) 'Asking the Right Questions: Evaluation and the museum mission', *Museum News* 64, 3: 18–23.

Murdin, L. (1991) 'Possible Industrial Action at Natural History Museum', *Museums Journal* 91, 6: 10.

Murray, D. (1904) *Museums: Their history and their use*, Edinburgh: James MacLehose & Sons.

Museums and Galleries Commission (1988) *Guidelines for a Registration Scheme for Museums in the United Kingdom*, London: Museums and Galleries Commission.

—— (1991) *Local Authorities and Museums*, London: Museums and Galleries Commission.

—— (1992) *Management Development and Marketing in Museums*, London: Museums and Galleries Commission.

—— (1993) *Disability Resource Directory for Museums*, London: Museums and Galleries Commission.

Museums Association (1984) Definition of a 'Museum'. Agreed at the Annual General Meeting. See Museums Association, *Code of Practice for Museums Authorities*, London: Museums Association.

—— (1991a) *Annual Report 1990–91*, London: Museums Association.

—— (1991b) *National Strategy*, London: Museums Association.

—— (1991c) *Museums Year Book 1991–2*, London: Rhinegold.

—— (1993) *Annual Report 1992–3*, London: Museums Association.

—— (1994) *Museums Briefing: Equal Opportunities*, London: Museums Association.

—— (1995a) *Codes of Ethics*, London: Museums Association.

—— (1995b) *Museums Briefing: Museums and the Schools Curriculum*, London: Museums Association.

—— (1995c) *Museums Briefing: Advocacy for Museums*, London: Museums Association.

Museums Journal (1994) 'Quality Control', *Museums Journal* 94, 1: 22–5.

Myerscough, J. (1988) *The Economic Importance of the Arts in Britain*, London: Policy Studies Institute.

National Audit Office (1993) *Quality of Service in 5 National Museums*, London: HMSO.

Nevett, T. and Nevett, L. (1987) 'The Origins of Marketing: Evidence from Classical and early Hellenistic Greece', in T. Nevett and S. C. Hollander (eds) *Marketing in Three Eras*, Lansing: Michigan State University.

Nicholson, T. D. (1983) 'Volunteer Employment at the American Museum of Natural History', *Curator* 26, 3: 241–53.

Noble, J. V. (1995) 'Controversial Exhibitions and Censorship', *Curator* 38, 2: 75–7.

Nowlen, P. (1995) 'A View from the Top', *Museums Journal* 95, 6: 25–9.

Office of Arts and Libraries (1991a) *Report on the Development of Performance Indicators for the National Museums and Galleries*, London: HMSO.

—— (1991b) *Volunteers in Museums and Heritage Organisations: Policy, planning and management*, London: HMSO.

O'Neill, M. (1990) 'Springburn: A community and its museum', in F. Baker and J. Thomas (eds) *Writing the Past in the Present*, Lampeter: St David's College.

—— (1991) 'After the Artefact: Internal and external relations in museums', in G. Kavanagh (ed.) *The Museums Profession: Internal and external relations*, Leicester: Leicester University Press.

—— (1995) 'Exploring the Meaning of Life: The St Mungo Museum of Religious Life and Art', *Museum International* 47, 1: 50–3.

Orna, E. (1994) 'In the Know', *Museums Journal* 94, 11: 24–7.

Palmer, A. (1994) *Principles of Services Marketing*, Maidenhead, Berks: McGraw-Hill.

Payne, A. (1993) *The Essence of Services Marketing*, Hemel Hempstead, Herts: Prentice-Hall.

Pearson, A. (1989) 'Museum Education and Disability', in E. Hooper-Greenhill (ed.) *Initiatives in Museum Education*, Leicester: Department of Museum Studies, University of Leicester.

Pearson, N. M. (1982) *The State and the Visual Arts: A discussion of state intervention in the visual arts in Britain, 1760–1981*, Milton Keynes: The Open University Press.

Peters, T. J. and Waterman, R. H. (1982) *In Search of Excellence: Lessons from America's best run companies*, New York: Harper & Row.

Phillips, C. (1983) 'The Museum Director as Manager', *History News*, March: 10–11.

Phillips, D. (1992) 'Deconstruction or Demolition: Or the egg?', *Museums Journal* 92, 12: 20–1.

Piercy, N. (1990) 'Marketing Concepts and Actions: Implementing marketing-led strategic change', *European Journal of Marketing* 24, 2: 24–39.

Porter, G. (1988) 'Putting Your House in Order: Representations of women and domestic life', in R. Lumley (ed.) *The Museum Time-Machine: Putting cultures on display*, London: Comedia and Routledge.

Price, J. (1993) 'Museums Go Live', *Museums Journal* 93, 6: 18–19.

Prottas, J. M. (1981) 'The Cost of Free Services: Organization impediments of access to public services', *Public Administration Review*, September–October: 526–34.

Quinn, J. B. (1980) *Strategies for Change: Logical incrementalism*, Homewood, Ill.: Richard D. Irwin.

Radley, A. (1991) 'Boredom, Fascination and Mortality: Reflections upon the experience of museum visiting', in G. Kavanagh (ed.) *Museum Languages*, Leicester: Leicester University Press.

Rathmell, J. M. (1966) 'What is Meant by Services?', *Journal of Marketing* 30, October: 32–6.

—— (1974) *Marketing in the Service Sector*, Cambridge, Mass.: Winthrop.

Regan, W. J. (1963) 'The Service Revolution', *Journal of Marketing* 47, July: 57–62.

Richards, B. (1992) *How to Market Tourist Attractions, Festivals and Special Events: A practical guide to maximising visitor attendance*, Harlow, Essex: Longman.

Robinson, A. and Toobey, M. (1989) 'Reflections to the Future', *Museums Journal* 89, 10: 27–9.

Robinson, K. (1983) *Museums – Lessons from the USA*, London: British Tourist Authority.

Robson, S. (1989) 'Group Discussions', in S. Robson and A. Foster (eds) *Qualitative Research in Action*, London: Edward Arnold.

Roper, P. (1990) 'The Great Debate: Museum Charges', *Leisure Management* 10, 3: 36–9.

Rosenau, P. M. (1992) *Post-modernism and the Social Sciences: Insight, inroads and intrusions*, Princeton, NJ: Princeton University Press.

Royal Commission on National Museums and Galleries (1929) *Final Report, Part II*, London: Royal Commission on National Museums and Galleries.

Runyard, S. (1994) *The Museum Marketing Handbook*, London: Museums and Galleries Commission and HMSO.

Runyard, S. and Anderson, B. (1992) 'MGC News', *Museums Journal* 92, 6: 39.

Ryan, C. (1991) *Recreational Tourism: A social science perspective*, London: Routledge.

Samuel, R. (1994) *Theatres of Memory*, London: Verso.

Sasser, W. E. (1976) 'Match Supply and Demand in Service Industries', *Harvard Business Review*, November–December: 133–40.

Sasser, W. E., Olsen, R. P., and Wyckoff, D. D. (1978) *Management of Service Operations*, Needham Heights, MA: Allyn & Bacon.

Scottish Tourism Co-ordinating Group (1991) *Tourism and the Arts in Scotland*, Edinburgh: Scottish Tourist Board.

Seagram, B. C., Patten, L. H., and Lockett, C. W. (1993) 'Audience Research and Exhibit Development: A framework', *Museum Management and Curatorship* 12, 1: 29–41.

Seaman, B. (1995) 'No Management Fad', *Museums Journal* 95, 9: 28.

Sekers, D. (1984) 'Independence Stimulates', in N. Cossons (ed.) *The Management of Change in Museums*, proceedings of a seminar held at the National Maritime Museum, Greenwich, London, on 22 November.

Shanks, M. and Tilley, C. (1987) *Reconstructing Archaeology*, Cambridge: Cambridge University Press.

Sherman, D. J. (1989) *Worthy Monuments: Art museums and the politics of culture in nineteenth century France*, Cambridge, Mass.: Harvard University Press.

Shorland-Ball, R. (1988) 'Marketing the Museum for Social Events and Activities', *Museums Journal* 88, 3: 150–1.

Shostack, G. L. (1977) 'Breaking Free from Product Marketing', *Journal of Marketing* 41, 2: 73–80.

—— (1984) 'Designing Services that Deliver', *Harvard Business Review*, January–February: 133–9.

—— (1985) 'Planning the Service Encounter', in J. A. Czeipel, M. R. Solomon, and C. F. Suprenant (eds) *The Service Encounter*, Lexington, Mass.: Lexington Books.

—— (1987) 'Service Positioning through Structural Change', *Journal of Marketing* 51, January: 34–43.

Sightseeing in the UK (1992), London: English Tourist Board.

—— (1994), London: English Tourist Board.

Simpson, J. A. (1976) *Towards Cultural Democracy*, Strasbourg: Council of Europe.

Smith, A. (1991) *What Are the Arts for?: National arts and media strategy discussion document*, London: Arts Council of Great Britain.

Smith, C. S. (1989) 'Museums, Artefacts, and Meanings', in P. Vergo (ed.) *The New Museology*, London: Reaktion Books.

Sorensen, C. (1989) 'Theme Parks and Time Machines' in P. Vergo (ed.) *The New Museology*, London: Reaktion Books.

Spalding, J. (1990) 'The Great Debate: Museum Charges', *Leisure Management* 10, 3: 37–9.

—— (1991) 'Is There Life in Museums?', in G. Kavanagh (ed.) *The Museums Profession: Internal and external relations*, Leicester: Leicester University Press.

Squires, D. P. (1969) 'Schizophrenia: The plight of the natural history curator', *Museum News* 48, 2: 463–77.

Stevenson, A. and Bryden, M. (1991) 'The National Museums of Scotland's 1990 Discovery Room: An evaluation', *Museum Management and Curatorship* 10: 24–36.

Stone, M. (1990) *Leisure Services Marketing*, Surrey: Croner.

Susie Fisher Group (1990) *Bringing History and the Arts to a New Audience: Qualitative research for the London Borough of Croydon*, London: Susie Fisher Group.

Teather, J. L. (1983) 'Museology and its Traditions: The British experience', unpublished Ph.D. thesis, University of Leicester.

Thomas, D. R. E. (1978) 'Strategy is Different in Service Businesses', *Harvard Business Review* 56, 4: 158–65.

Touche Ross (1989) 'Museum Funding and Services – The Visitor's Perspective', report of a survey carried out by Touche Ross Management Consultants.

Trevelyan, V. (ed.) (1991) *'Dingy Place with Different Kinds of Bits': An attitudes survey of London museums amongst non-visitors*, London: London Museums Service.

Urry, J. (1990) *The Tourist Gaze: Leisure and travel in contemporary societies*, London: Sage.

Van der Vliet, V. (1979) 'Marketing Museums: Problems and strategies', *SAMAB* 15, 5: 172–80.

Venkatesh, A. (1989) 'Modernity and Postmodernity: A synthesis or antithesis?', in T. Childers (ed.) *Proceedings of the 1989 AMA Winter Educators' Conference*, Chicago: American Marketing Association.

Venkatesh, A., Sherry, J. F., and Firat, A. F. (1993) 'Postmodernism and the Marketing Imaginary', *International Journal of Research in Marketing* 10, 3: 215–23.

Vergo, P. (ed.) (1989) *The New Museology*, London: Reaktion Books.

Vos, R. (1975) 'Bulletin Van Het Rijksmuseum', *Jaargang* 2.

Walsh, Kevin (1992) *The Representation of the Past: Museums and heritage in the post-modern world*, London: Routledge.

Walsh, Kieron (1995) *Public Services and Market Mechanisms: Competition, contracting and the new public management*, Basingstoke: Macmillan.

Weil, S. (1990) *Rethinking the Museum: And other meditations*, Washington, DC: Smithsonian Institution Press.

—— (1991) 'Review', *Museum News*, July–August: 63.

—— (1995) *A Cabinet of Curiosities: Inquiries into museums and their prospects*, Washington, DC: Smithsonian Institution Press.

Weisen, M. (1991) 'Museums and the Visually Handicapped', in Fondation de France and ICOM, *Museums without Barriers*, London: Routledge.

West, B. (1988) 'The Making of the English Working Past: A critical view of the Ironbridge Gorge Museum' in R. Lumley (ed.) *The Museum Time-Machine: Putting cultures on display*, London: Comedia and Routledge.

Willmott, H. C. (1984) 'Images and Ideals of Managerial Work: A critical examination of conceptual and empirical accounts', *Journal of Management Studies*, Winter: 48–64.

Wilson, G. (1991) 'Planning for Visitors', in S. Pearce (ed.) *Museums and the Community*, London: The Athlone Press.

Wilson, M. and McDonald, M. (1994) 'Marketing at the Crossroads – A Comment', *Marketing Intelligence and Planning* 12, 1: 42–5.

Wind, Y. and Robertson, T. S. (1983) 'Marketing Strategy: New directions for theory and research', *Journal of Marketing*, Spring: 12.

Winterbotham, N. (1992) 'Counting the Tullie Tally', *Museums Journal* 92, 4: 19.

Wittlin, A. S. (1949) *The Museum: Its history and its tasks in education*, London: Routledge & Kegan Paul.

Wittreich, W. J. (1966) 'How to Buy/Sell Professional Services', *Harvard Business Review* 44, March–April: 127–36.

Woods, R. (ed.) (1994) *Leisure Futures, 2*, London: Henley Centre for Forecasting.

Wragg, D. (1994) *The Effective Use of Sponsorship*, London: Kogan Page.

Wright, P. (1985) *On Living in an Old Country*, London: Verso.

—— (1989) 'The Quality of Visitors' Experiences in Art Museums' in P. Vergo (ed.) *The New Museology*, London: Reaktion Books.

—— (1990) 'Eyes on Stalks', *Arts Management* 9: 13.

Yorke, D. D. and Jones, R. R. (1984) 'Marketing and Museums', *European Journal of Marketing* 18, 2: 90–9.

Young, R. (1981) 'The Advertising of Consumer Services and the Hierarchy of Effects', in J. Donnelly and W. George (eds) *Marketing of Services*, Chicago: American Marketing Association.

Zeithaml, V. A. (1981) 'How Consumer Evaluation Processes Differ between Goods and Services', in J. H. Donnelly and W. R. George (eds) *Marketing of Services*, Chicago: American Marketing Association.

Zeithaml, V. A., Parasuraman, A., and Berry, L. L. (1990) *Delivering Quality Service: Balancing Customer Perceptions and Expectations*, New York: The Free Press.

Index

246